African Literature

A critical view

DAVID COOK

Professor of English, University of Ilorin, Nigeria;
formerly Professor of Literature, Makerere University, Uganda

African Literature

A critical view

88

LONGMAN

LONGMAN GROUP LIMITED
LONDON
Associated companies, branches and representatives throughout the world

© Longman Group Ltd 1977

First published 1977

ISBN 0 582 64210.8 (cased)

ISBN 0 582 64211.6 (paper)

Printed in Great Britain by
Western Printing Services Ltd, Bristol

Contents

Contents

Acknowledgements

We are grateful to the following for permission to reproduce copyright material:

Rex Collings Limited for the poem Anomistic Spells XI' by Wole Soyinka from *Poems of Black Africa*, ed. by Wole Soyinka; East African Publishing House for extracts from *Prostitute* by Okello Oculi, first and fifth stanzas from poem commencing 'Once When Birds Of Season' by K. A. Kassam from *Drum Beat* ed. by Lennard Okola, and part of the poem *Song of Lawino* by Okot p'Bitek; Heinemann Educational Books Limited for extracts from *Dying In The Sun* by P. Palangyo and extracts from *The Black Hermit*, also *The River Between* by Ngugi wa Thiong'o, the poem 'The Spear With a Hard Point' by Okot p'Bitek from *Horn Of My Love* and the poems 'Waiting For A Bus' by Amin Kassam, 'To The Living' by Richard Ntiru, 'The Street' by Jared Angira, 'I Love You My Gentle One' by Ralph Bitamazire all from *Poems From East Africa*, eds. David Cook and David Rubadiri; Heinemann Educational Books Limited and Humanities Press, Inc., N.J., for extracts from *A Grain Of Wheat* by Ngugi wa Thiong'o; Heinemann Educational Books Limited and Farrar, Straus & Giroux, Inc., for part of a poem from *A Simple Lust* by Dennis Brutus; Wm. Heinemann Limited for extracts from *No Longer At Ease* and *Things Fall Apart* by Chinua Achebe; William Heinemann Limited and author's agents for extracts from *A Man Of The People* by Chinua Achebe; Hutchinson Publishing Group Limited and author's agents for extracts from *Jagua Nana* by Cyprian Ekwensi; Granada Publishing Limited (publisher MacGibbon and Kee Ltd.) and Grove Press, Inc., N.Y., for extracts from *The Wretched Of The Earth* by Frantz Fanon © 1963 by Présence Africaine and *Black Skin, White Masks* by Frantz Fanon; Longman Group Limited for the poem 'Streamside Exchange' by

John Pepper Clark from his book *A Reed In The Tide* and extracts from *Home and Exile* by Lewis Nkosi; author's agents and New Directions Publishing Corporation for an extract from 'The Argentine Winter and Tradition' transl. by James E. Irby from *Labyrinths* by Jorge Luis Borges, copyright © 1962 by New Directions Publishing Corp., reprinted by permission of the publishers; Oxford University Press for extracts from *Three Short Plays* by Wole Soyinka, published by Oxford University Press (1963), reprinted by permission of the publishers; Martin Secker and Warburg Limited and Random House, Inc., for extracts from *Facing Mount Kenya* by Jomo Kenyatta.

Introduction

THIS collection of essays is arranged in a deliberate pattern; but neverthe-less each chapter can be regarded as a separate critical enterprise which may be of interest in its own right to anyone who is following up the reading of a particular work or the consideration of a particular genre of African writing.

The keynote of the whole study is struck by the first four chapters of Part II, each of which discusses a major example of African fiction in some detail, according to the general principles of traditional literary criticism. Similar criteria are used to consider works which are more controversial either because their achievement is uneven or because they do not fall with-in conventional literary categories. These particular studies are preceded by a section in which I have developed certain ideas about two major genres of African anglophone literature which for a number of years have occupied a central place in my own thinking.

A surprisingly high proportion of what has been published so far on African writing, even on a well-known author like Chinua Achebe, com-prises the indefatigable retelling of the plots, with some generalised, synop-tic commentary. Fortunately there are notable exceptions: a few penetrating articles, more often in leading journals than in books, really come to grips with their subjects by using critical precision in detailed argument. These form the kernel of the constructive literary analysis which now urgently needs to be extended if we are to achieve a significant body of serious criti-cism of African writing, as opposed to a collection of mere crammers and check-lists.

In assembling in this book some of my own critical opinions, I have constantly borne in mind – though I do not claim to have lived up to – Wole Soyinka's view of the contemporary critic's responsibilities:[1]

Criticism is so important because . . . a critic's job is not merely to review an existing piece of work but also to create an atmosphere of appreciation, of tolerance; to cultivate an experimental attitude not only in writers but in the audience.

In the last two chapters of Part II, instead of re-examining works which are already becoming established as modern masterpieces or classics, I have chosen to discuss representative novels from two other groupings: *Dying in the Sun* by Peter Palangyo, and *Jagua Nana* by Cyprian Ekwensi.

The first of these is an example of flawed and limited work which nevertheless possesses real quality and makes a unique contribution to the literature of our time. It is of the utmost importance that we should be able and ready to recognise literary excellence even if it is only fitfully sustained or is seriously blemished. It is likely that more writing of distinction in books will be found which are erratic in performance than in those of unflawed excellence or unquestionable genius; and so readers should be encouraged to appreciate what is of value in such works without over-estimating them as a whole.

An interesting literary situation prevails in Africa where the average newspaper critic and his readers assume virtually all published novels to have a similar critical status. In the West a large percentage of published fiction is contemptuously regarded as 'pulp' literature and is hardly ever discussed at critical level. I do not regard this as very healthy and I would prefer to encourage the more inclusive critical assumptions so prevalent in Africa.

Yet this situation also creates its own problems. There are works which, while violating many literary and aesthetic principles, achieve just the same a certain fire, dynamism and insight which make them worthy of rereading and discussion. It is not helpful to confuse our standards by putting this kind of writing on a par with works of more distinctive value; at the same time it is undiscriminating to dismiss such books superciliously. I have therefore tried to carry out a critical winnowing process upon one such novel, wishing to imply that there are others with similarly conflicting qualities which could likewise be usefully analysed. In such a case the reviewer must *believe* in the value of the inconsistent work, otherwise there is little point in trying to separate the metal from its ore; and here commentators vary radically in their perceptions. I have chosen a book which seems to me to justify this task of critical discrimination: Cyprian Ekwensi's *Jagua Nana*.

All forms of the written word contribute to a major force of persuasion. All writings which argue important issues, reach a large public, and possess the literary qualities that are likely to make them more than merely ephemeral, not only deserve, but invite and demand, critical analysis. The means by which a thoughtful public is convinced one way or another on crucial questions is of very real significance to a country or to a continent. In Part III I have therefore attempted criticism of works of non-fiction which have had, or should have had, a major impact on thinking about certain aspects of African experience. This section is introduced by an appraisal of a work which falls squarely between the established literary categories embraced in Parts I and II, and the non-fiction considered in my final chapters. *Prostitute* aptly demonstrates my contention that it is difficult, and in many respects pointless, to draw any sharp division between creative writing and rhetorical persuasion.

In deciding which prose works to discuss in Part III, I again took into consideration the quality of the writing, as well as its social importance, and my own interest in the work; and also the need to select a variety of styles which might offer some glimpse of the range of possible approaches. Without seeking to encroach upon the sociologist's or the political scientist's prerogative of specialist analysis of the arguments, I have considered the relationship between content and style, and the validity and integrity of the reasoning as it is presented rhetorically.

For the most part I have attempted to argue closely from the texts of the works under discussion. Detailed references were inevitable but I wanted to reduce the cumbersome apparatus of annotation to a minimum. Where there are many consecutive quotations from the work which is central to a particular chapter, I have grouped four, five or six page references together under a single footnote: for quotations which are indented and immediately strike the eye in glancing over the printed page I have merely listed the page numbers, but I have added the first words of quotations which are embedded in the text and may be harder to locate, unless they have been singled out by the footnote number.

I also give on page xiii for easy reference a list of abbreviations employed in the annotation for the names of works and publishers frequently referred to. Whenever there is an African Writers Series edition of a volume, references are to that edition.

It is pleasant to be able to thank some of the many friends who have helped and encouraged me in this project. Above all I am indebted to Richara Ntiru, poet, critic and member of a publishing team, and Hugh Dinwiddy, for long of Makerere and now, among other things, a freelance lecturer on African literature in England; they each gave much time and minute attention to constructive criticism of early drafts of the manuscript. Among others who have spurred me on and have made specific contributions by detailed suggestions at particular points are John Butler, Andrew Amateshe, Colin Sherwood, Dicky Wamala, Mathew Buyu, Timothy Wangusa, Frank Mugisha and Bing Taylor. I could not have completed work on this book without help in typing from Valentine Okoth, and in proof-reading from Willie Kabali-Musoke.

NOTE

1   Wole Soyinka in a recorded interview with Lewis Nkosi in Lagos, August 1962, *African Writers Talking*, ed. Dennis Duerden and Cosmo Pieterse, H.E.B., 1972

Abbreviations

A.W.S.:	African Writers Series (followed by serial number)
B.S.W.M.:	Frantz Fanon, *Peau Noire, Masques Blancs*, Editions du Seuil, Paris, 1952, trans by Charles Lam Markmann as *Black Skin White Masks*, Paladin, London, 1970
C.P.	Wole Soyinka, *Collected Plays*, O.U.P., London, vol. I, 1973; vol. II, 1974
D.B.:	*Drum Beat*, ed. Lennard Okola, E.A.P.H., 1967
D.I.T.S.:	Peter Palangyo, *Dying in the Sun*, H.E.B., 1968; A.W.S. 53
E.A.P.H.:	East African Publishing House, Nairobi
F.M.K.:	Jomo Kenyatta, *Facing Mount Kenya: the Tribal Life of the Gikuyus* Secker and Warburg, London, 1938
G.O.W.:	Ngugi wa Thiong'o (James Ngugi), *A Grain of Wheat*, Heinemann, London 1967; H.E.B., A.W.S. 36
H. & E.:	Lewis Nkosi, *Home and Exile*, Longman, London, 1965
H.E.B.:	Heinemann Educational Books, London
J.C.L.:	*The Journal of Commonwealth Literature*
J.N.:	Cyprian Ekwensi, *Jagua Nana*, Hutchinson, London, 1961; H.E.B., A.W.S. 146
Mod. Poetry:	*Modern Poetry from Africa*, ed. Gerald Moore and Ulli Beier, Penguin, London, 1963
N.L.A.E.:	Chinua Achebe, *No Longer at Ease*, Heinemann, London, 1960; H.E.B., A.W.S. 3
O.U.P.:	Oxford University Press
Poems E.A.:	*Poems from East Africa*, ed. David Cook and David Rubadiri, H.E.B., A.W.S. 96, 1971

Pros.:	Okello Oculi, *Prostitute*, E.A.P.H., 1968
R.B.:	Ngugi wa Thiong'o (James Ngugi), *The River Between*, Heinemann, London, 1965; H.E.B., A.W.S. 17
Seven A.W.:	Gerald Moore, *Seven African Writers*, O.U.P., London, 1962
T.F.A.:	Chinua Achebe, *Things Fall Apart*, Heinemann, London, 1958; H.E.B., A.W.S. 1
T.P.:	Wole Soyinka, *Three Plays*, Mbari, Ibanda, 1963
W.A. Verse:	*West African Verse*, ed. Donatus Ibe Nwoga, Longman, London, 1967
W.O.T.E.:	Frantz Fanon, *Les Damnés de la Terre*, Maspéro, Paris, 1961; translated as *The Wretched of the Earth* by Constance Farrington, MacGibbon & Kee, London, 1965; references are to the Penguin edition

PART I

Broad Perspectives

CHAPTER I

The Solitary and the Submerged

A study in Western and African literary environments

Up till now, published discussion of African literature has included too little detailed critical examination of specific works. But, of course, comprehensive arguments and large ideas are needed also, to stir the mind and form the basis of constructive and purposeful analysis. By contemplating works in proper perspective we may at the same time avoid the pitfall of considering one kind of writing by criteria established in relation to another; and so we may be deterred from deciding in advance what we expect from a work and condemning it for failing to live up to these demands, although it was aspiring to something quite different. With such considerations in mind, I begin this collection of essays by formulating general arguments about two of the principal literary genres: the novel and poetry.

In thinking about African fiction and perceiving how fundamentally similar many of its points of departure are in human and spiritual terms to those of other literatures, I find myself returning to a possible major difference between the main movements of European and American literature over the past hundred years and more, and the writing in English and French now swelling from West, East and Central Africa. Nothing is more important than to understand the assumptions with which a writer begins. It is notoriously difficult to break away from the concepts which have been bred into us; and fatally easy for an alien critic to impose his own attitudes where they do not belong. Any group of writers must share a set of familiar ideas rooted in certain social norms. Most artists are in a very real sense revolutionaries; but few, if any, are truly anarchists. The committed artist lives by his vision of order, of design, of pattern. The socially conscious writer does not set to work in a vacuum, but urges his society from what it is towards what it might be.

While Africa is in a process of change more rapid than has been typical of other societies, nevertheless traditional African social patterns remain strong in their own right and exert a very significant influence upon developments which are taking place under modern international pressures. In traditional society the individual is seen first and foremost as part of a corporate whole, and his existence as part of the social pattern overwhelms any private life he might lead within the confines of his own consciousness. Such a life is relatively public: it is not easy to keep secrets nor is it thought desirable to do so. In such a situation, social conventions exert great authority. The communal good is all-important and any personal denial of group commitment appears to weaken the whole and is deplored. In a village there are few places where an essentially private existence can be pursued. Contribution to the life and welfare of the community is the greatest good; and hence individualism is seen as negative. The determined nonconformist either becomes an outcast or offers to fill one of the few roles in which some degree of personal eccentricity itself becomes a norm. 'An individualist,' says Kenyatta in *Facing Mount Kenya*,[1] 'is looked upon with suspicion and is given a nickname of *mwebongia*, one who works only for only himself and is likely to end up as a wizard. . . . In the Gikuyu community there is no really individual affair, for everything has a moral and social reference.' Divergence from typical behaviour is deliberately discouraged in the young, and for the majority becomes unthinkable in later life.

This is essentially a good life, embodying the virtues of neighbourliness, mutual concern and involvement, and providing a reasonably fair division of opportunity and reward. It requires no special pleading in a novel like *Things Fall Apart* to demonstrate that in most respects the village provides a coherent and desirable life-pattern for the majority, essentially humane and moral. One of its drawbacks is the lack of opportunity it offers to anyone driven by the need for individual expression or the desire for personal goals. A strong emotional passion not in keeping with tradition is an embarrassment to be suppressed or to be regretted – as is clearly shown in *The Concubine*.

The novel and the drama are forms most frequently concerned with individual achievement, individual behaviour, individual error, against a background of more generalised social activity. It is not surprising therefore that the key figures in African novels and plays are typically at variance with their societies, however closely wedded to them they may be in certain respects – for instance Okonkwo, Waiyaki or Ntanya. In the challenge that these protagonists offer to group behaviour, they are unrepresentative. While the issues they raise may be those unavoidably facing their societies, they themselves become atypical. It is normal to be a unit in the close-knit social pattern; so that to break the set design is abnormal.

The hero in Western fiction is also characteristically an individualist, and the situation may at first glance appear to be very similar; but the apparent similarity makes the actual difference all the clearer, since the protagonist in a typical nineteenth- or twentieth-century British, French or American novel has as a rule a quite different relationship to his society at large. A lone individualist in a work of African fiction is an exceptional figure. A lone individualist in a Western work of fiction is representative of the inescapable position in which all mankind, it would appear, finds itself.

In an age of relative social cohesion in England, John Donne confidently proclaimed (as might an African elder) that 'no man is an island'. By the middle of the nineteenth century few serious authors would have subscribed to such a belief. Each individual seemed, by then, to be perched in solitude on his own little outcrop of life, cut off from other castaways by a deep and dangerous sea. From now on, unaccommodated man is faced with a massive social machine, to which he no longer feels he has consented nor can in any real sense contribute. Conventions are in no way chosen or adopted by general agreement but are imposed by a system beyond the control of groups of individuals. This kind of social machine does not bring people together; but rather creates a rigid, impersonal framework which holds them apart.

Henry Fielding, who lived before the period I am mainly concerned with, was already protesting against arbitrary centres of power whose petty prerogatives could be challenged only by someone more powerful; but there is still in Fielding's works a sense that society primarily exists as something made up of its individual members. Particular people are violently satirised, but things have not altogether fallen apart. Dickens was fighting against an administrative system as close-knit as that in the all-too-recognisable dream-world of Kafka or the imminent myths of George Orwell, which are at the very centre of my thesis. Yet in Dickens there remains at least some feeling that mankind opposed to the machine is itself a corporate body, a feeling that exists still, perhaps, in many contemporary African cities.

But the social fabric was to stiffen and to exert, remorselessly, ever greater control, and this process was, by definition, to be reflected in the pages of the major writers of the time. They would see the all-powerful centralised organisation, best characterised in *1984*, not as a warm, protective human amalgam of people, but as a menacing and inhuman monster, against which every individual would be pitted and by which individuals would, at the same time, be segregated from each other. My own illustrations will only be able rather arbitrarily to sketch in this process, which is one of the complementary aspects of my debate. I have therefore strengthened my argument by selective reference to a more comprehensive survey, the introductory 'Social and Intellectual Background' by G. H. Bantock to the last volume of the Pelican Guide to English Literature entitled *The Modern Age*.[2]

The essay begins by quoting Henry James's response to a writer who had said that he wanted to do the best he could with his pen: 'There is one word – let me impress upon you – which you must inscribe upon your banner, and that word is loneliness.' Bantock suggests that 'two basic themes of modern literature have been those of "isolation" and "relationship" within what has been considered a decaying moral order', and points out that these motifs have been reflected in the artists' own negative relationship to their community. Darwin and Freud have exerted exceptionally strong influences upon men's minds during our period. We are reminded that Freud worked 'within the framework of nineteenth-century assumptions – deterministic materialistic, and rationalistic'; and that Freud is in the Darwinian tradition of seeing man as 'simply a part of nature' since he is a 'biological phenomenon, a prey to instinctual desires and their redirection in the face of "harsh" reality'. Bantock quotes Beatrice Webb on the intimate effects of the vicious class war at the turn of the century, which led the successful social climber to spurn the failed acquaintance:

> What was . . . demoralising . . . because it bred poisonous cynicism about human relations, was the making and breaking of personal friendships according to temporary and accidental circumstances in no way connected with personal merit: gracious appreciation and insistent intimacy being succeeded, when failure according to worldly standards occurred, by harsh criticism and cold avoidance.

H. G. Wells's rather pompous claim as to his own contribution to his society is recalled: 'We originative intellectual workers are reconditioning human life.' On this pronouncement Bantock comments, 'The mechanical, abstract basis of community relationship could hardly be more clearly illustrated'; and he at once turns to D. H. Lawrence for confirmation of the depersonalisation of human contacts:

Why do modern people almost invariably ignore the things that are actually present to them? . . . They certainly never live on the spot where they are. They inhabit abstract space, the desert void of politics, principles, right and wrong, and so forth. . . . Talking to them is like trying to have a human relationship with the letter x in algebra. ('Insouciance', 1928)

He outlines the modern psychological arguments for a mass approach to problems: 'Modern psychology stresses group dynamics rather than in-dividual behaviour, the total configuration rather than the isolate.' As Barbara Wootton puts it in her *Social Science and Social Pathology* (1959), 'the logical drive, in modern social science, away from notions of individual responsibility is very powerful'.

All this adds up to a computer-like system of social conventions and controls, restrictive beyond the furthest extremes of African social tradition. And, I suggest, the Western novelist's reaction is totally different from that of his African counterpart, since conformity is being achieved by altogether different means, based on different sanctions, with quite different implica-tions. Before pursuing this issue, let me conclude Bantock's analysis of the European situation, as he quotes de Tocqueville's fear that 'the human mind would be closely fettered to the general will of the greatest number', and states his own alarm at the debasing effects of the mass media such as tele-vision: 'night after night a selection of programmes of inane triviality sterilize the emotions and standardize the outlook and attitudes of millions of people'. The climax of this line of thought is voiced by another quotation, from Hannah Arendt's *The Human Condition* (1958):

as though individual life had actually been submerged in the over-all life process of the species and the only active decision still required of the individual were to let go, so to speak, to abandon his individuality, the still individually sensed pain and trouble of living, and acquiesce in a dazed, 'tranquilized', functional type of behavior. . . . It is quite conceivable that the modern age – which began with such an unprecedented and promising outburst of human activity – may end in the deadliest, most sterile passivity history has ever known.

Again, these tendencies are seen to have been diagnosed long before by D. H. Lawrence:

The girl who is going to fall in love knows all about it beforehand from books and the movies . . . she knows exactly how she feels when her lover or husband betrays her or when she betrays him: she knows precisely what it is to be a forsaken wife, an adoring mother, an erratic grandmother. All at the age of eighteen.

Bantock suggests in one of his last paragraphs that the development of the 'stream of consciousness' technique was one form of artistic opposition to the general tendency of the age: 'In a world of increasing socialization, standardization, and uniformity, the aim was to stress uniqueness, the purely personal in experience'.

Indeed the creative artist found himself almost as a matter of course opposed to the administrative mechanism which was destroying life as he wished it to be. As in the African situation, the individual – very often the protagonist of a novel – is in confrontation with 'society'. But there is an essential difference. Whereas for the modern African writer such an individual is exceptional, and the society he is opposing has, to say the least of it, very many desirable qualities; for the European writer over the past hundred years or so, the individual depicted is representative of all individuals, who cannot help but be tyrannised, each and every one, by the machine, which is seen as possessing no qualities in itself which one would fight for or wish to see retained if one had the option. The only possibilities for the protagonist are tragic defeat, as for Jude or Tess; or tragic assertion, as in *Victory* for Heyst; or a desperate bid against odds to sustain the human spirit and human contact, as for Dorothea in *Middlemarch*. But, quite to the contrary, a valid happy ending is available to the African protagonist by an appropriate reconciliation with society, as for Gikonyo in *A Grain of Wheat*, for Ntanya at the end of *Dying in the Sun*, or indeed for Jagua Nana. In *The River Between* Waiyaki has been overwhelmed by narrow-minded prejudice; but he has not been standing against society as a whole: he has rather been attempting to reconcile its two diverging sectors. While Okonkwo in his death is seen as being braver than his society, he is at the same time less wise than the majority in preferring an inevitably destructive confrontation to a possibly constructive evolution.

I have chosen Hardy and George Eliot to illustrate the position of the Western writer in relation to his or her characters both because they are major figures, and also because they stand at opposite extremes in their reactions to the given situation. The one is pessimistic while the other, to use her own term, is a 'meliorist'; but each starts from the same premise, that human awareness is in desperate conflict with an oppressive society which possesses no real moral standards, and that in this fight individuals are separate from each other. In Hardy's novels efforts to make human contact fail; in George Eliot's they are fitfully though optimistically successful through constant and demanding spiritual effort.

The causes of this universal alienation are well-known and specific. Industrialisation and urbanisation, dependent on the cash nexus, lead to a breakdown in the natural cycle close to the land, so that society becomes an abstract and artificial machine, geared to controlling all impulses which threaten vested interests, not to co-ordinating energies for the benefit of the community as a whole. The new bureaucracy is not associated with any communal growth from grassroots; the individual feels himself to be at the mercy of impersonal forces and is truly aware only of his own private existence. Thomas Hardy noted in his London diary:[3]

> The city appears not to see itself. Each individual is conscious of *himself*, but nobobdy is conscious of themselves collectively. . . . There is no consciousness of where anything comes from or goes to – only that it is present.

The result of this isolation is disillusionment and general scepticism. All confident shared belief in mystical elements in life is lost; and the vacuum is filled by an arid rationalism. The common fears and common faith that held groups together voluntarily and meaningfully have become private fears and cynicism, or frantic assertion of the self. 'Considering his position', Hardy says of Clare in *Tess of the D'Urbervilles*,[4]

> he became wonderfully free from the chronic melancholy which is taking hold of the civilised races with the decline of belief in a beneficent power.

This sad sense of separateness is assumed to be so generally recognisable by readers, that the writers concerned do not feel it necessary to state the case briefly, but embody it as a set of assumptions in the whole fabric of their work; but we can make some attempt to identify significant passages.

Hardy takes it as one of the bases of his stories that impersonal forces normally separate the right people from each other and bring together the wrong people, so that even the potential positives in life are thwarted:

> . . . why so often the course appropriates the finer thus, the wrong man the woman, the wrong woman the man, many thousand years of analytical philosophy have failed to explain to our sense of order.

He sees this confusion as a fundamental failure of what he calls 'the social machinery' and elsewhere 'the artificial system of things'. The scheme of life may be neat enough but life's 'ill-judged execution of the plan' puts all inevitably awry:

> In the ill-judged execution of the well-judged plan of things the call seldom produces the comer, the man to love rarely coincides with the hour for loving. Nature does not often say 'See!' to her poor creature at a time when seeing can lead to happy doing; or reply 'Here!' to a body's cry of 'Where?' till the hide-and-seek has become an irksome, outworn game. We may wonder whether at the acme and summit of the human progress these anachronisms will be corrected by a finer intuition, a closer interaction of the social machinery than that which now jolts us round and along; but such completeness is not to be prophesied, or even conceived as possible. Enough that in the present case, as in millions, it was not the two halves of a perfect whole that confronted each other; a missing counter-part wandered independently about the earth waiting in crass obtuseness till the late time came. Out of which maladroit delay sprang anxieties, disappointments, shocks, catastrophes, and passing-strange destinies.

Mankind aspires magnificently but hopelessly. Eustacia Vye muses in *The Return of the Native*,[5]

> But do I desire unreasonably much in wanting what is called life – music, poetry, passion, war, and all the beating and the pulsing that is going on in the great arteries of the world? That was the shape of my youthful dream; but I did not get it.

And it is the very attempt towards human communion which causes all other kinds of failure in failing itself. But we are not left to think that all these twistings and confusions are simply the doings of unaided Fate. We are led to understand that the whole way that society is organised aids and abets the negative forces in the universe:[6]

> Strange that his first aspiration – towards academical proficiency – had been checked by a woman, and that his second aspiration – towards apostleship – had also been checked by a woman. 'Is it,' he said, 'that the women are to blame; or is it the artificial system of things, under which the normal sex-impulses are turned into devilish domestic gins and springes to noose and hold back those who want to progress?'

And so Hardy talks of life as 'the plight of being alive'; since 'social machinery' is in league with the universe, which is man's natural enemy, real contact between human beings is impossible. The statement is dramatised, but is nevertheless seen in general terms, as applying to everyone:

And then he again uneasily saw, as he had latterly seen with more and more frequency, the scorn of Nature for man's finer emotions, and her lack of interest in his aspirations.

George Eliot, on the other hand, completely refuses to submit to this situation, though it is precisely this situation that she is fighting against. Her starting point is an awareness of isolation:[7] 'Tom, like every one of us, was imprisoned within the limits of his own nature;' and her characters compound this situation by substituting their own egoism for real contacts with their fellows:[8]

> there were no beginnings of intimacy between her and other girls... Mrs. Vulcany once remarked that Miss Harleth was too fond of the gentlemen; but we know that she was not in the least fond of them – she was only fond of their homage.

George Eliot is even less a source of general statements than Hardy. We must look into her choice of key characters and significant situations in order to grasp her chief lines of thought. Dorothea Casaubon is the most determined idealist and positivist in *Middlemarch* and yet all her attempts to establish a real relationship with the one person who should be closest to her of his own volition, her husband, fail utterly:[9]

> And just as clearly in the miserable light she saw her own and her husband's solitude – how they walked apart so that she was obliged to survey him.

George Eliot rejects pessimism, yet she sees how persistent and alert men and women must be to ensure that an uncertain opportunity for contact should be made to bear fruit by force of will and responsiveness in unpromising circumstances – (the italics are mine):

> There is no general doctrine which is not capable of eating out our morality *if* unchecked by the deep-seated habit of direct fellow-feeling with individual fellow-men.

The gloomy vision is lightened by a genuine alternative – always on condition that the right kind of effort is continually made, and not otherwise:[10]

> There is always this *possibility* of a word or look from a stranger to keep alive the sense of human brotherhood.

As soon as this effort is relaxed, the conventional framework of society withholds us from real contact, and substitutes 'external identity', a formalised set of surface appearances:[11]

> that force of outward symbols by which our active life is knit together
> so as to make an inexorable external identity for us, not to be shaken by
> our wavering consciousness.

She epitomises an alarming total loss of faith in human relationships in the experience of one of her protagonists, Romola, but, like Hardy, emphasises in the process that this is not an uncommon course of events – what Romola has endured is representative rather than unique:

> No one who has ever known what it is thus to lose faith in a fellow-man
> whom he has profoundly loved and reverenced, will lightly say that the
> shock can leave the faith in the Invisible Goodness unshaken. With the
> sinking of high human trust, the dignity of life sinks too; we cease to
> believe in our own better self, since that also is part of the common nature
> which is degraded in our thought; and all the finer impulses of the soul
> are dulled. Romola felt even the springs of her once active pity drying-up,
> and leaving her to barren egoistic complaining.

Where people who are unsuited to each other come together in George Eliot we are left in no doubt about the causes of these unfortunate relationships. At best the characters are isolated from each other by inexperience; but far more commonly by wilful, selfish lack of human sympathy. George Eliot sees egoism as the tragic force confirming the separation of one individual from another:

> He was at present too ill acquainted with disaster to enter into the pathos
> of a lot where everything is below the level of tragedy except the passionate egoism of the sufferer.

She certainly sees the possibility of making the perilous journey from one island to another; but the characters start off marooned, each one alone, surrounded by forces and circumstances within the social framework which are likely to discourage them from the arduous voyage. This is demonstrated as a general condition by the chapter in *The Mill on the Floss* entitled 'St Ogg's Passes Judgement', wherein is described a social morality which laces humanity up in formulas and tries to substitute a ready-made, patent method of passing sentence on non-conformists, for the more exacting arts of patience and sympathy:

Retribution may come from any voice: the hardest, cruelest, most im-
bruted urchin at the street-corner can inflict it: surely help and pity are
rarer things – more needful for the righteous to bestow;

and again,

All people of broad, strong sense have an instinctive repugnance to men
of maxims; because such people early discern that the mysterious complexity of our life is not to be embraced by maxims, and that to lace ourselves up in formulas of that sort is to repress all the divine promptings and
inspirations that spring from growing insight and sympathy. And the man
of maxims is the popular representative of the minds that are guided in
their moral judgment solely by general rules, thinking that these will lead
them to justice by a ready-made patent method, without the trouble of
exerting patience, discrimination, impartiality – without any care to
assure themselves whether they have the insight that comes from a hardly-
earned estimate of temptation, or from a life vivid and intense enough to
have created a wide fellow-feeling with all that is human.

We are not attempting, of course, to suggest that Western society of this
epoch was unique in exerting such pressures; it is the weight they carry and
the part they play in a particular pattern of actions and reactions with which
we are concerned.

Frustration had an equally wide range of reference in the novels of
Thomas Hardy and of George Eliot: a comprehensive dampening of the
spirit which can be paralleled in the work of many European contemporaries and successors, but in few of the present generation of African writers.
Clym, Jude, Felix Holt, Dorothea, Casaubon, Lydgate are all reaching out
uncertainly towards a greater good, demanding mutual understanding and
self-sacrifice. None of them finds their society at all amenable to such idealism. Jude is one prototype, Dorothea another. 'I never could do anything
that I liked. I have never carried out any plan yet,' cries the latter, although
all her schemes are selfless and apparently practical projects to better the lot of
the underprivileged, to revive the discouraged and bring lonely individuals
back into communion with their fellows.

My present purpose is not to look into George Eliot's analysis of possible
ways out of this impasse, but to observe that for all her optimism she,
like Hardy, finds herself ministering to a society which is spiritually more
like an infinitely scattered archipelago than a continent. As many of my
quotations inevitably spill over into areas which are common ground between Western and African novelists, I shall therefore redefine my precise

line of argument, which seeks to identify a difference in emphasis without exaggerating it. First I will widen my field of reference by representative but inevitably scanty allusions to some other writers, having earlier suggested the scope of these issues by employing G. H. Bantock's survey as a touchstone.

I would refer to the long hours we spend inside Bloom's lonely mind in *Ulysses*, and to the agonised splitting of hairs to delineate the exact anatomy of non-communication in Henry James.

Conrad, like George Eliot, believed that contact could be made, but only after we have perceived the gap between individuals and have struggled to bridge it. The 'secret sharer', the man aware of his essential links with humanity outside himself, is a recurrent figure in Conrad, the exceptional individual who is willing to take the leap towards communion. Lord Jim is the very type of the lonely soul. The island of *Victory* is an image of separateness. Heyst has dismissed all possibility of human contact:[12]

> The people in this part of the world went by appearances, and called us friends, as far as I can remember. Appearances – what more, what better can you ask for? In fact you can't have any better. You can't have anything else.

When reality invades the island Heyst comprehends the actuality of Lena at length only in tragic consummation.

D. H. Lawrence insists on the individual's dual and conflicting needs to be separate and to be in communion; but where this balance is not achieved – as it is only rarely in such relationships as that between Birkin and Ursula – the result is an utter and destructive division. E. M. Forster is possessed by this concern about the lack of contact. In *A Passage to India* it cannot even be conceived that the racial groups might come together:[13]

> 'Why can't we be friends now?' said the other, holding him affectionately. 'It's what I want. It's what you want.'
> But the horses didn't want it – they swerved apart; the earth didn't want it, sending up rocks through which riders must pass single file; the temple, the tank, the jail, the palace, the birds, the carrion, the Guest House, that came into view as they issued from the gap and saw Mau beneath: they didn't want it, they said in their hundred voices, 'No, not yet,' and the sky said, 'No, not there';

while Forster's Europeans are also irrevocably at odds with each other. In Graham Greene's *The Heart of the Matter*[14] the main character is truly in touch with only two other people – his servant, for whose death he blames himself, and the young girl, because of whom he eventually commits suicide. Query in *The Burnt-out Case* reaches an extreme of spiritual isolation.

T. S. Eliot's poetry up to 'The Wasteland' epitomises a society's utter loss of social cohesion at the level of real human feeling and understanding, a society wearily getting through the hours and days of its boredom, each man in his separate compartment.

So far, for the sake of coherence, I have restricted myself to writers working in England and Ireland. Dostoevsky investigates crime as the ultimate loneliness, *Crime and Punishment* is a deliberate experiment in exploring the lonely mind. Even more apt to the present discussion is *The Idiot*, in which ironically the prince is dubbed a fool because he has visions and aberrations about making human contacts. In considering *Anna Karenina*, the question is not so much whether particular actions would have been equally disapproved of by other societies, but why a major writer chooses an alienated figure as in some way representative or significant. The same might be asked of *Madame Bovary*. And the presentation of the very different situation in each of these novels can be tellingly contrasted with that in *Jagua Nana*, whose protagonist cannot be described as 'alienated' from her surroundings in any usual sense of the word. Camus's outsider became a type figure for a whole generation, a whole aspect of civilisation. Chekov, Ibsen, Ionesco, Arthur Miller, Samuel Beckett, Sartre, Faulkner, Richard Wright, James Baldwin – the list is endless.

Do African writers find themselves in a similar tradition of basic assumptions about relationships within society? Once again, the passages quoted from various authors can do no more than illustrate what I think is a significant difference of emphasis, which should be taken into account in any serious discussion of African fiction if it is not to be seen through false spectacles.

First I must define the limits of this difference more carefully. The author himself (in common with other creative artists) is likely in any society to find himself something of an outsider, so it is not here that the distinction lies. Similarly, a writer's key characters may tend to be exceptional figures within their surroundings, while being placed in circumstances which are both poignant and in some degree representative, so these factors do not define any difference between the two traditions. In the Western novel, however, it is the loneliness of the protagonists which makes them typical or representative, whereas in the African novel the aloneness of the hero makes him exceptional. The problem for the Western protagonist is how to approach more closely to other human beings; the problem for the leading character in an African novel is more likely to be how to assert an individual viewpoint without becoming a total outcast. The African society which rejects non-conformists is itself an amalgam of people who have come together in agreement to conform to certain norms for the sake of the general good. Western society is seen as a machine, all people as people being alien to it so that they have only their isolatedness in common. Thus a typical hero in modern Western fiction may well be regarded by the novelist as significantly representative by virtue of his alienation, and may be regarded as exceptional only in the way that he reacts to his isolation – perhaps tragically, perhaps equivocally; while this kind of separateness is part and parcel of the character's uniqueness in many an African work, or at least identifies him with an urbanised minority.

Whether or not the people in a book are conscious of their separateness or their solidarity is here beside the point. In the one case the writer sees his society as permanently fragmented, and takes one or more fragments as his centrepiece in their efforts to cohere; in the other case the writer sees the body of society as healthy and consolidated, so that the outsider is a sad, often potentially tragic exception, desperately asserting himself where individualism is strange and unwelcome. Neither type of protagonist chooses his basic position. One is born into a disjointed society and yearns for real human contact. The other is ordained to live in a contentedly conforming group and finds himself restless within it.

In Africa, whatever forces of disintegration may be at work, there is still felt to be a close-knit fabric of society which the majority consciously form part of and contribute towards. The social machine is only just beginning to exist as something separate from the individuals who make up society (I do not refer to southern Africa). So a novelist like Ngugi, seeing this beginning to happen, may still be able to stand out like a social prophet to warn against the folly of pursuing the Western path towards dehumanising the communal structure; and ask whether a rapidly modernising Africa cannot try to find a new road between the pitfalls that the West has exposed. But Ngugi seems to me to be one of the most complex African writers on this whole question, with one of the most constructive attitudes, and I return to a discussion of his writings at the end of this chapter.

In the closely-meshed network of a coherent group the problem for the creative, self-aware, sensitive human being is, then, how to separate himself sufficiently from his (or her) group to be able to assert individuality.

The individualist may be submerged, day in day out, by insistent group attitudes which others share willingly; and his only recourse may be to rebellion. Similar tensions are experienced by the so-called man of two worlds (like Obi Okonkwo) who, having been emancipated by education, discovers the loneliness of being free and seeks to re-establish contact without loss of independence, not always an easy compromise.

Okonkwo in *Things Fall Apart* meets his destiny at the turning point of a society which is just beginning to forego its unified pattern. Achebe is not the writer to sentimentalise or over-simplify traditional life. *Things Fall Apart* makes it clear that forms of acquisitiveness and obsessive self-assertion exist in the village. Already, before there is any confrontation with the white man, Okonkwo shows himself to be an individualist and the odd-man-out in his community. His clansmen, while approving his more moderate ambitions, are not slow to criticise him for his excesses and deviations in urging him to comply with generally accepted social restraints and expectations. The process of falling apart could be seen as a breaking into groups rather than into individual units, since Nwoye is arguably absorbed into a new social pattern which owes its solidarity more to pagan forerunners than to one or two white missionaries and a few detribalised trained converts. Certainly the book is about a clan which at the beginning, in the words of Aigboje Higo's introduction,[15] 'thought like one, spoke like one, shared a common awareness and acted like one'. During the course of the story alarm is expressed that society may soon disintegrate as outside forces play on the new generation. 'I fear for you young people,' says one of the oldest members of the *umunna*,[16] 'because you do not understand how strong is the bond of kinship. You do not know what it is to speak with one voice.'

Okonkwo's otherness, however, is peculiar to himself, not a by-product of a communal sense. 'Although Okonkwo dominates the book,' says Gerald Moore,[17] 'he is presented as a tragic rather than a typical figure. Our feeling of the village life as a whole is given far more through Achebe's terse reporting of its ceremonies, festivals and daily rituals.' The psychological need that Okonkwo feels to assert himself is carefully described to us. And his final act of protest is made in defiance of majority feelings since the society is determined to adapt itself rather than resist change. The exact words that Okonkwo uses to his close friend, Obiereka, about Egonwanne at the climax are most significant: 'I do not care what he does to *you*. I despise him and those who listen to him. I shall fight alone if I choose.' Fateful words of the individualist who will not bend with the majority:

'I shall fight alone if I choose.' Because we see this stand as untypical (rather than representative on a grand scale of what all men are likely to experience), the end of the book can, I feel, be regarded as epic or heroic in conception rather than tragic, and I return to this line of thought in Chapter 3.

The Arrow of God searches into the limits of individual power in a system controlled by tradition:[18]

> If he should refuse to name the day there would be no festival – no planting and no reaping. But could he refuse? No Chief Priest had ever refused. So it could not be done. He would not dare. . . . His mind still persisted in trying to look too closely at the nature of power. What kind of power was it if everybody knew that it would never be used?

The only fault that Ezeulu's mother remembered of her husband was that he wanted to be surrounded by yes-men: 'He forgot the saying of the elders that if a man sought for a companion who acted entirely like himself he would live in solitude.' Whatever wily ideas he has of letting his son pick the brains of the new religion, when this scheme brings him into open conflict with Akuebue, Ezeulu responds as a man accustomed to stand alone, apart from his kind:

> 'But if you send your son to join strangers in desecrating the land you will be alone. You may go and mark it on that wall to remind you that I said so.'
> 'Who is to say when the land of Umuaro has been desecrated, you or I?' Ezeulu's mouth was shaped with haughty indifference. 'As for being alone, do you not think that it should be as familiar to me now as are dead bodies to the earth?'

It is here absolutely clear that Ezeulu's isolation, whether we see it as ordained or self-appointed, is particular to himself and sets him apart. And when he is detained by the white man the real confrontation is clarified:

> for the moment his real struggle was with his own people and the white man was, without knowing it, his ally. The longer he was kept in Okperi the greater his grievance and his resources for the fight.

So that when he leaves he reminds himself, 'I am going home to challenge all those who have been poking their fingers into my face.' Ezeulu is in conflict with the corporate members of his village, not with an abstract administration. Even after his god reminds him that he has no right to use his religion to fight his personal battles – 'I say who told you that this was your own fight which you could arrange to suit you?' – Ezeulu still rejects the elders' offer to let the abomination 'be on the heads of the ten of us here.' And when he is destroyed, the community sees this as judgment on the man who opposes the spirit of his group by upholding the letter of their tradition:

> To them the issue was simple. Their god had taken sides with them against his headstrong and ambitious priest and thus upheld the wisdom of their ancestors – that no man however great was greater than his people; that no man ever won judgment against his clan.

Ezeulu makes it easier for Christianity to strengthen its hold on the community by weakening his own god's standing at a crucial and difficult time. Perhaps Okonkwo's stubborn resistance to the new power was equally ill-conceived as a means of preserving the old order. There is little to suggest that either of these individualists was taking effective action on behalf of a cherished way of life or that the clan was weakly submissive to the new forces. Achebe is more concerned in these books to capture a situation than to make judgments. Much the same is true of *No Longer at Ease*.

Obi well knows that he has been cut off from his background by his sophisticated experiences and finds this knowledge bitter:[19]

> 'You know book, but this is no matter for book. Do you know what an *osu* is? But how can you know?' In that short question he said in effect that Obi's mission-house upbringing and European education had made him a stranger in his country – the most painful thing one could say to Obi.

But he knows also how unfair it is to expect him to shrug off these benefits which had been granted him precisely in order to make him different:

> Obi admitted that his people had a sizeable point. What they did not know was that, having laboured in sweat and tears to enrol their kinsman among the shining élite, they had to keep him there. Having made him a member of an exclusive club whose members greet one another with 'How's the car behaving?' did they expect him to turn round and answer: 'I'm sorry, but the car is off the road . . .'?

Umuofia regards Obi's scholarship as 'an investment which must yield heavy dividends' and Obi himself as 'an invaluable possession'. So they are horrified when he claims the rights of a private individual:

> I am not going to listen to you any more. I take back my request . . . don't
> you dare interfere in my affairs again. And if this is what you meet about
> . . . you may cut off my two legs if you ever find them here again.

Obi's belief that 'I can handle them' proves idle. But when the crash comes
they close ranks with him as they would with any other of their number,
showing that in the city they have not yet let things fall finally apart:

> He was, without doubt, a very foolish and self-willed young man. But this
> was not the time to go into that. The fox must be chased away first; after
> that the hen might be warned against wandering into the bush.

Achebe captures the contradictory situation in which the young educated
African finds himself. Obi has been specially trained to be an outsider, an
independent man. And he is then expected to think and feel and act like
an insider whose will is readily subject to communal pressures. So crucial is
this work to the larger issues I am concerned with that I have chosen it for
detailed analysis later.

A Man of the People is an ironic novel. It is aware that modern trends are
disintegrating trends which can be combated: Mrs Nanga is resolved that
her children shall go back to the village regularly:[20]

> 'Don't you see they hardly speak our language? Ask them something in it
> and they reply in English. The little one, Micah, called my mother "a dirty
> bush woman".'

But the book concerns itself more with the cynical attempt by political
opportunists to make use of the tradition of unity to their own ends:

> We had all been in the rain together till yesterday. Then a handful of us –
> the smart and the lucky and hardly ever the best – had scrambled for the
> one shelter our former rulers left, and had taken it over and barricaded
> themselves in. And from within they sought to persuade the rest through
> numerous loudspeakers, that the first phase of the struggle had been won
> and that the next phase – the extension of our house – was even more
> important and called for new and original tactics; it required that all
> argument should cease and the whole people speak with one voice and that
> any more dissent and argument outside the door of the shelter would
> subvert and bring down the whole house.

Wole Soyinka gives his commentary on what in significant respects is a
similar situation in *Kongi's Harvest*. In Achebe's novel the general reaction
is dryly realistic:

He took the view (without expressing it in so many words) that the main-
spring of political action was personal gain, a view which, I might say,
was much more in line with the general feeling in the country than the
high-minded thinking of fellows like Max and I.

The irony is turned not only against Nanga, the great opportunist, but also
against the 'high-minded' Odili, the small opportunist who goes into politics
to pay off a private grudge and has very little idea of the forces he is playing
with.

Achebe expresses the important view that there are limits beyond which
the communal will cannot operate meaningfully – a view supported by
the parallel of true democracy breaking down when it tries to operate in
units larger than the Greek city states. This line of thought is developed
through a recurrent proverb:

> I thought much afterwards about that proverb, about the man taking
> things away until the owner at last notices. In the mouth of our people
> there was no greater condemnation. It was not just a simple question of a
> man's cup being full. A man's cup might be full and none be the wiser.
> But here the owner knew, and the owner, I discovered, is the will of the
> whole people.

But such sanctions break down in a modern nation, which is too big:

> My father's words struck me because they were the very same words the
> villagers of Anata had spoken of Josiah, the abominated trader. Only in
> their case the words had meaning. The owner was the village, and the
> village had a mind; it could say no to sacrilege. But in the affairs of the
> nation there was no owner, the laws of the village became powerless.
> Max was revenged not by the people's collective will but by one solitary
> woman who loved him. Had his spirit waited for the people to demand
> redress, it would be waiting still.

Thus it is evident that in *A Man of the People* Achebe is doing something
new. He is exploring the situation in a modern African state which is in
the process of breaking completely with its past; and the result is that the
country enters the age of the isolated individual confronting a mechanical
administration, such as we have been deploring in the company of certain
European novelists, the most important difference being that in *A Man of the
People* this is a new situation, which is just dawning on the protagonist,
not an inherited problem to be taken more or less for granted.

There is, as I have said, much common ground between African and

Western novelists, since they are both concerned with human experience. In attempting to define the significant difference between them, I do not want to overstate the case. Though this distinction is important, it is easily blurred by the existence of many common features. My scope allows me now only a very brief survey of a number of other authors. To perceive the elements which concern us here, the following quotations need to be reviewed selectively to distinguish what is immediately relevant.

The power of ancestral beliefs and attitudes is made very plain. We are reminded of the group vision at the beginning of Legson Kayira's *The Looming Shadow*:[21]

> to the old ones, tempered by tradition, weak to challenge its occasional fallacy, nothing in their universe could be dismissed with the shrug of the shoulders, for the ordered universe never told jokes, and the death of the sun could only foretell the death of their chief or someone from that rare species of men called great.

Elechi Amadi's *The Concubine* illustrates more fully the whole shape of my argument. Patterns of behaviour are well defined in the clan:[22]

> Omokachi village was noted for its tradition, propriety, and decorum. Excessive or fanatical feelings over anything were frowned upon and even described as crazy. Anyone who could not control his feelings was regarded as being unduly influenced by his agwu. Anyika often confirmed this, as in Ahurole's case.
>
> Even love and sex were put in their proper place. If a woman could not marry one man she could always marry another. A woman deliberately scheming to land a man was unheard of.

It is illuminating to compare this passage with the opening chapter of *Pride and Prejudice*: from remarkably similar premises almost opposite conclusions are drawn. In the event Ihuoma is willing to modify her passions to conform to the customs of her society:

> That was Ihuoma's world and she behaved true to type. Ekwueme's father had played his part if even over-zealously; Ekwueme had been dutiful; Ahurole had turned out well; it was up to her to avoid behaving in a way that might disrupt this perfect setting. She had had her chance and if the gods had been rather cruel there was nothing she could do about it. She threw herself into the business of switching her mind from whatever had gone before.

Only one person refuses to conform to these conventional restraints, the spoilt, charming, quiet young man Ekwueme, and it is his abnormal determination to follow his heart despite all social proprieties that eventually shapes the story along lines prepared for earlier:

> 'I tell you it is almost an abomination to break off an engagement like this. It is unheard of. No one would ever side with you.'
> Ekwueme's heart jumped into his stomach. A sickening sensation assailed him. His father was right, of course. Worse, tradition was decidedly against him and the thought of kicking against it unnerved him. It would be sensational news in the village. Then he thought of Ihuoma. Suddenly his father was no longer there. In his place Ihuoma stood smiling wistfully, a deep affection glowing in her eyes. Energy surged through him and his eyes shone.

Ekwueme stands alone. His kindred stand together, against him.

The theme of the divided world is constantly present. Oyono puts it like this in *Houseboy*:[23]

> 'There are two worlds,' said Baklu, 'ours is a world of respect and mystery and magic. Their world brings everything into the daylight, even the things that weren't meant to be . . . Well we must get used to it . . .'

Thus, like Obi, an individual may find himself torn between a co-ordinated society which forms his background and other parts of his nature developed by education and situation, as is also the case with several of Mongo Beti's young protagonists. Medza becomes less and less divorced from his earlier environment, though he will never be able to identify with Kala after his town education; while Kala, on its side, is very far from falling apart into isolated units. Beti's two other major novels suggest that while the missionary may very well be an island, this is above all because he has failed to attach himself to the mainland of African culture. We have every hope at the end of *The Poor Christ of Bomba* that Denis has not been permanently fixated. King Lazarus returns to the comforts of polygamy and the rebuilding of his society.

The individual may be driven to the point of renouncing his own roots completely, as does Lawino's husband:[24]

> He despises Acoli dances
> He nurses stupid ideas
> That the dances of his People
> Are sinful,
> That they are mortal sins,

but, quite rightly, it never occurs to Okot's singer that she herself could
be regarded as an isolated or separate existence:

> In our village
> When someone is going
> On a long journey,
> When there is a hunt
> Or communal hoeing
> People wake up early

and,

> The Acoli did not
> Set aside a special day
> For *Jok*;
> When misfortune hits the homestead
> The clansmen gather
> And offer sacrifices
> To the ancestors.

Ocol has even brushed aside his closest relatives:

> And when his mother
> Comes to visit him,
> Ocol locks the doors
> And says
> He has an important meeting
> In the town!

while politics have severed him from his brother:

> Ocol does not enter
> His brother's house.
> You would think
> There was homicide between them
> That has not been settled.

Lawino and her folk, on the other hand, still honour Ocol's ancestors:

> Your grandfather was a Bull among men
> And although he died long ago
> His name still blows like a horn,
> His name is still heard
> Throughout the land.

Lawino sums up the whole position in one question to Ocol:

> I do not understand
> The ways of foreigners
> But I do not despise their customs.
> Why should you despise yours?

Ocol has cut himself off from the all-embracing life of the community which Lawino celebrates.

At the opposite extreme African society may be able to call back the lost soul from human exile, as it does in the case of Clarence in *The Radiance of the King*.[25] Because Clarence accepts, he can be accepted. For all his inadequacy, he finds a place in this inclusive world. It is no accident that Laye elects Clarence, the European, to be the prototype of alienated man, nor that the society into which he must learn to blend himself is an African community.

Wole Soyinka's *The Interpreters* is of particular interest. In spite of their various inner turmoils, the main characters, a mixed group of Nigerians, break down the barriers between them. Though they come together by chance, drift apart at the end, and experience serious internal rifts meanwhile, when they are together they are really together: they make contact with each other.

The husband in Elvania Zirimu's skilful little one-act play 'Keeping Up with the Mukasa'[26] is jolted back into a real relationship with his wife by a sudden glimpse of the state of bourgeois detachment that exists between a neighbouring married couple, so similar, he now realises, to the division which he has allowed to develop in his own household. The play dramatises an escape, not a submission. The hierarchical organisation of the Baganda (and of a very limited number of other groups) with its basic class system, arguably places them midway between a more generally typical African society and the European situation as outlined by G. H. Bantock, and so it is of special interest that Mrs Zirimu has dramatised this contrast of attitudes within a Kiganda environment.

Generalisations must admit of exceptions: Okello Oculi is one of the few African writers who suggest that traditional society itself is at worst a collection of separate particles held together by a dead and impersonal mass of habit and imposed conventional behaviour. Anyone who has read fairly widely may at first be puzzled by the mixture of familiarity and strangeness in this work. Where have we come across this sense of utter isolation before? – surely in a host of European writings. Why is it so unexpected here? – because, surely, it is now being experienced in an African village setting. The very title of *Orphan* identifies a figure whom the poet sees as inevitably alone:[27]

> Orphan boy, wake and face life's
> Twisted humour!
>
> Learn the alphabet of life,
> That we are born with the indelible
> Sin of Isolated Selves,
> To remain perpetual tourists
> To each other
> Along life's pathways!

Neither the village elder, nor the woman whose husband is of Okello's clan, nor Okello's stepmother, nor his father have much hope or compassion to spare for the motherless child:

> Tenderness, humility and decency
> By man to man in honour of manness;
> All are burnt on the altar of Isolation
> And on the worship grounds of aggressive
> Selfishness when a mother dies.

Okello Oculi's angry irony is wide-ranging; but it should be added that he saves his bitterest attacks for the familiar targets:

> All of them in the Exclusive Club
> Are allergic to my village simplicity,
> To my crude pride in myself and my nativity.

Individuality is likely to be of painful and difficult birth. To become fully oneself without cutting one's roots may be the real challenge. This is the challenge which Ngugi is facing. At the same time he is a writer from a country which has had a white settler community; where external forces of change have therefore bitten more deeply and have operated for a longer period than in neighbouring lands; and where non-African vested interests have more obviously influenced modern political development, festering into a desperate period of violence in Ngugi's own homeland.

His full-length play, *The Black Hermit*, written in 1962, is certainly not his most polished piece of work but develops characteristic patterns of ideas. The hero had found himself inside the tribal design:[26]

> Remi was not the husband of Thoni, alone.
> Remi was also the new husband to the tribe.

He is brought back from his college world to become the husband, according to tradition, of his elder brother's wife after the brother has died in an accident: 'They had obeyed me. Now they were asking me to show similar obedience. Finally I agreed to live with her.' And he was on the verge of giving up his political ambitions 'Because I was trapped by the tribe.' But Remi revolts and goes off to the city: 'I wanted to be myself. . . . How then could I take another man's wife? I wanted a woman of my own.' But it is Remi who describes himself as a 'hermit' because he knows he has turned his back on an essential part of himself:

> Seclusion from what was formerly around you is solitude.
> To be a hermit means escaping from what's around you.
> My tribe was around me.

Yet already in this play Ngugi is insisting that the roots of the modern young African reach out in a number of directions: that it is false to make a simple opposition between tribal tradition and sophisticated detachment. Remi puts this to the apparently rather characterless white girl whom he has taken up with in the city when he decides to leave her, and return to his village in a new spirit:

> You are different from me, from us, from the tribe. You cannot know what I know . . . you have not experienced what I have experienced. Your background is a world from mine. How can we be the same? How can the call of the tribe be your call? To you tribalism and colonialism, the tyranny of the tribe and the settler are an abstraction. To me they are real. I have felt the shaft here. Yes, they have made a wound here, a wound that made me run to the city. To you, African nationalism and what it means to us who suffered under colonial rule for sixty years can only be an intellectual abstraction. But to me, my whole being – I am involved in it.

In fact Remi fails to judge all the forces within himself accurately. He rears back to the village obsessed with his personal mission:

> I must now rise and go to the country.
> For I must serve our people,

> Save them from traditions and bad customs,
> Free them from tribal manacles.

He is determined to cut loose from all past ties, without adequately distinguishing between them:

> I will no longer be led by woman, priest or tribe. I'll crush tribalism beneath my feet, and all the shackles of custom. I was wrong to marry her who was another's wife, a woman who did not love me.

The tragic outcome (dramatically somewhat contrived) modifies this fanatical crusade and brings him to some sense of humility. He admits that his grand vision has blinded him to what was at his feet, and acknowledges the difference between pruning a plant and cutting its roots, since under the latter treatment the stock dies:

> I came back to break Tribe and Custom,
> Instead, I've broken you and me.

The first novel that Ngugi drafted (though it was radically rewritten later), *The River Between*, opens with a restatement of ancestral solidarity, which Nyobi in *The Black Hermit* sees beginning to pass away:[29]

> These ancient hills and ridges were the heart and soul of the land. They kept the tribe's magic and rituals, pure and intact. Their people rejoiced together, giving one another the blood and warmth of their laughter. Sometimes they fought. But that was among themselves and no outsider need ever know.

The white man with his religion and his usurpation of the land, was already, in the period in which the novel is set, undermining this pattern:

> The white man was slowly encroaching on people's land. He had corrupted the ways of the tribe. Things would now change.

The two ridges facing each other represent the world of the tribe and the world of the missionaries respectively: 'Joshua was identified as the enemy of the tribe. He was with Siriana, with the white settlers.' Whereas Waiyaki is identified with Gikuyu traditions:

> Waiyaki was becoming the pride of the hills and the pride of Kameno.

Already they had started calling him the champion of the tribe's ways and life.

Waiyaki was superstitious. He believed the things that the people of the ridges believed. Siriana Mission had done nothing effective to change this.

'You are the symbol of the tribe, born again with all its purity.'

And 'The people remained conservative, loyal to the ways of the land.' Is the river between to unite or divide the two ridges? Waiyaki has gone far beyond Remi. He is not satisfied with being the figurehead of one faction established in opposition to another:

He also wanted a reconciliation between Joshua's followers and the others. The gulf between them was widening and Waiyaki wanted to be the instrument of their coming together.

This is a far more difficult task than the one he had been given by the traditionalists. He is aware of his own difficulties in sorting himself out, even before he tries to reunite his tribesmen:

Besides, however much he resisted it, he could not help gathering and absorbing ideas and notions that prevented him from responding spontaneously to these dances and celebrations.

He struggles against this growing sense of separation, brought about in his case not so much by his education as by the difficulty of his self-appointed task of reconciling all his people to each other:

Waiyaki's heart sank with heaviness because of this unrest. Where was his place in all this? He felt a stranger, a stranger to his land.

Education, indeed, is seen in this community as a possible remustering of the corporate strength of the tribe, since the Gikuyu themselves started their own system of education independent of the colonial administration:

Schools grew up like mushrooms. Often a school was nothing more than a shed hurriedly thatched with grass. And there they stood, symbols of people's thirst for the white man's secret magic and power. Few wanted to live the white man's way, but all wanted this thing, this magic. This work of building together was a tribute to the tribe's way of co-operation. It was a determination to have something of their own making, fired by their own imagination.

Waiyaki is foiled in his design by the tribal establishment which, rather like Okonkwo, rejects any idea of reconciliation:

> Kabonyi and the Kiama were asking him to stand by their beliefs, beliefs that would destroy his mission of healing the rift between Makuyu and Kameno.

The two sisters share Waiyaki's vision. As she is dying from her circumcision wound, Muthoni unites the two approaches to life (perhaps rather too simply): 'tell Nyambura I see Jesus. And I am a woman, beautiful in the tribe.' Waiyaki does not succeed. *The River Between* is a warning, an exhortation, rather than being comforting or complacent. But it suggests that traditional solidarity need not be opposed to modern adaptation; that true wisdom might absorb what is good from wherever it comes and reject suicidal last-ditch stands. On the other hand, it insists that education and sophistication present a challenge to the young to use them in the service of ancestral society, not as an excuse for self-pitying withdrawal:

> For Waiyaki knew that not all the ways of the white man were bad. Even his religion was not essentially bad. Some good, some truth shone through it. But the religion, the faith, needed washing, cleaning away all the dirt, leaving only the eternal. And that eternal that was the truth had to be reconciled to the traditions of the people. A people's traditions could not be swept away overnight. That way lay disintegration. Such a tribe would have no roots, for a people's roots were in their traditions going back to the past, the very beginning, Gikuyu and Mumbi. A religion that took no count of people's way of life, a religion that did not recognize spots of beauty and truths in their way of life, was useless. It would not satisfy. It would not be a living experience, a source of life and vitality. It would only maim a man's soul, making him fanatically cling to whatever promised security, otherwise he would be lost.

When he writes about the Mau Mau period, Ngugi is well equipped by virtue both of his vision and technique to observe and record the full complexity of the situation. The conflict splits again the already divided tribe, so that the task of reamalgamation is made even more intricate. At the end of *Weep Not, Child* even the youthful Kamau is filled with a despair he can barely define; but he is not allowed to renounce the task ahead in suicide and must face up to his heavy responsibility. In this book the all-important differences in attitude towards the land between the African and the settler as a time-honoured heritage or a personal possession is economically defined:[30]

For Ngotho felt responsible for whatever happened to this land. He owed it to the dead, the living and the unborn of his line, to keep guard over his *shamba*. Mr. Howlands always felt a certain amount of victory whenever he walked through it all. He alone was responsible for taming this un-occupied wilderness.

Violence breeds violence and hatred breeds hatred. The young men like Boro have fought in foreign wars and are now involved in bloodshed in their own homes. Painful tension develops between Boro and his father. When the old man is dying, having sacrificed himself futilely for another son, Ngotho bursts out bitterly to Kamau, 'Your brothers are all away?' 'They'll come back, father.' 'Ha! At my death. To bury me.' But when Boro does return at great personal risk, he at once kneels: 'Forgive me, father – I didn't know.' And this child of the present solemnly listens to his father's last words: 'All right. Fight well. Turn your eyes to Murungu and Ruriri. Peace to you all. . . .'

A Grain of Wheat ends with reconciliation between Gikonyo and Mumbi which clearly implies that they are again at one with their whole environ-ment: the symbol of the carved stool is to bear the image of a pregnant woman. The hopeful ending is far less tentative than in George Eliot. So complex is *A Grain of Wheat* and so involved with issues which have been raised in this discussion that I will treat it fully in a later chapter.

Wole Soyinka may be seen as often concerned with a challenge compar-able to that which preoccupies Ngugi. It is, I believe, in terms of such a challenge that the blind beggar and the younger son understand each other at the end of 'The Swamp Dwellers', as I shall also be arguing at greater length when I come to discuss the *Three Plays*. It is in the rejection and persecution of a man who seeks to reassert a total harmony in contemporary terms that the tragic intensity of 'The Strong Breed' lies.

The same might be said of Gabriel Okara's *The Voice*. We are still concerned with the single individual's struggle to express his personal vision in an environment which submerges him. But in both 'The Strong Breed' and *The Voice* we are most likely to feel that the majority are in the wrong, since the protagonist is seen as a healer, rejected though he may be, who is trying to minister to a sick tradition, a tradition which is failing to adapt itself in ways which might enable it to survive in changing circum-stances.

Actual people in twentieth-century Europe may in fact be aware of no sense of alienation; many African villagers may, as Okello Oculi points out, be intensely lonely. Contrasts encourage oversimplifications; we have glanced at both the good and the bad in ancestral Africa; and, of course, there are brighter aspects of European experience. But we are here discussing certain attitudes shared by groups of writers in their total view of their respective societies; and even then we are enquiring only whether there is a significant difference of emphasis.

The creative artist is, among other things, the expression of a society's self-awareness. Just as George Eliot or Conrad, T. S. Eliot or Graham Greene can plead with their fellows to reassert human understanding in an environment alien to it, so contemporary African writers are speaking to their generation very seriously indeed. In considering the main streams of Western and African writing, we have become aware of the opposite poles of man's social dilemma. In all human affairs there is a tendency to follow the path of least resistance and so to move from one extreme to the other. If this violent alternation is to be moderated, new influences must come into play. The creative artist often has a vision of a society which can be affected by positive human endeavour as well as by the inevitable pressures of history. Obi and Waiyaki, in almost opposite ways, force upon us the momentous task of seeking ways and means to prevent the transformation of African society from a closely-knit community pattern, within which the individual is perforce submerged, to an efficient, soulless, mechanical structure which holds individuals apart, prevents them from making real contact, and isolates them in private frustration.

There is every reason to fear that in this computerised age African communities may follow faster and faster along the bleak path towards total alienation of individuals by the social machine, a transition chronicled already in works such as *A Man of the People*. Whether Africa takes warning from the dreary European and American experience of this process may depend to a large extent on influences which are difficult to measure, and perhaps not least on her novelists, playwrights and poets, far as most of them may be from centres of political power.

NOTES

1 Jomo Kenyatta, *F.M.K.*, p. 119
2 Penguin Books, 1961, pp. 13–49. Verbatim quotations from G. H. Bantock from pp. 13, 18–19, 23, 32, 35, 38, and 47. Quotations borrowed from this source are from Beatrice Webb, *My Apprenticeship*, Longman, London, 1926, pp. 51–2; H. G. Wells, *Experiment in Autobiography*, Gollancz and Cresset Press, London, 1934, I, p.17; D. H. Lawrence, 'Over-Earnest Ladies', *Evening News*, 12 July 1928, reprinted as 'Insouciance' in

Assorted Articles, Secker, London, 1932, pp. 34–5; Barbara Wootton, *Social Science and Social Pathology*, George Allen and Unwin, London, 1959; Alexis de Tocqueville, *De la Démocratie en Amérique* (1835/40), translated by Henry Reeve as *Democracy in America* 1835/40), particularly relevant are Part I, Chapter XV, and Part II, Book VI, *passim*; Hannah Arendt, *The Human Condition*, University of Chicago Press, 1958, p. 322.

3 P. E. D. Hardy, *Life of Thomas Hardy*, Macmillan, London, 1962, pp. 206–7.

4 Thomas Hardy, *Tess of the D'Urbervilles*, Macmillan, pocket edition, 1906, pp. 154–5; the two following quotations are from pp. 93 and 49-50.

5 Thomas Hardy, *The Return of the Native*, Macmillan, pocket edition, 1906, p. 351.

6 Thomas Hardy, *Jude the Obscure*, Macmillan, pocket edition, 1906, 259; the quotation below beginning, 'And then again he uneasily saw . . .' is from p. 211.

7 George Eliot, *The Mill on the Floss*, Blackwood ed., 1874, p. 464.

8 George Eliot, *Daniel Deronda*, Blackwood ed., 1871–80, p. 169.

9 George Eliot, *Middlemarch*, Blackwood ed., 1874, p. 316; the quotation below beginning 'There is no general doctrine . . .' is from p. 459; and that beginning 'I never could do . . . ' from p. 609.

10 *The Mill on the Floss*, p. 404; the quotation below beginning 'Retribution may come . . .' is from p. 459, and that beginning 'All people of broad, strong sense . . . ' from p. 463.

11 George Eliot, *Romola*, Blackwood ed., 1880, p. 279; the next quotation is from p. 435.

12 Joseph Conrad, *Victory*, Methuen, London, 1915, fifteenth ed. 1926, p. 162.

13 E. M. Forster, *A Passage to India*, Edward Arnold, London, 1924, concluding paragraphs.

14 Graham Greene, *The Heart of the Matter*, Heinemann, 1948 and *The Burnt-Out Case*; *Jagua Nana*, Hutchinson, 1961.

15 Chinua Achebe, *T.F.A.*, 1965 ed., Introduction, p. v.

16 Chinua Achebe, *T.F.A.*, p. 152; the quotation below beginning 'I do not care' is from p. 181.

17 Gerald Moore, *Seven African Writers*, O.U.P., 1962, p. 60.

18 Chinua Achebe, *The Arrow of God*, H.E.B. A.W.S., 1964, p. 4; the next seven quotations are from pp. 114, 166, 217, 221, 240, 260 and 287.

19 Chinua Achebe, *N.L.A.E.*, pp. 71–2; the following five quotations are from pp. 98, 32, 83, 75 and 5.

20 Chinua Achebe, *A Man of the People*, H.E.B., A.W.S., 1966, p. 44; the following four quotations are from pp. 42, 128, 97, 166–7.

21 Legson Kayira, *The Looming Shadow*, Longman, London, 1967, p. 12.

22 Elechi Amadi, *The Concubine*, Heinemann, 1966, p. 165; the two following quotations are from pp. 166 and 139.

23 Ferdinand Oyono, *Une Vie de Boy*, Julliard, 1960, trans. John Reed as *Houseboy*, Heinemann, 1966, p. 93.

24 Okot p'Bitek, *Song of Lawino*, E.A.P.H., Nairobi, 1966, p. 41; the following six quotations are from pp. 88, 98, 152, 183, 206, 29.

25 Camara Laye, *Le Regard du Roi*, Plon, Paris, 1954, trans. James Kirkup as *The Radiance of the King*, Collins, Fontana Books, 1965.

26 Elvania Namukwaya Zirimu, 'Keeping Up with the Mukasas', *Origin East Africa* ed. David Cook, H.E.B., A.W.S., 1964, pp. 140–51.

27 J. Okello Oculi, *Orphan*, E.A.P.H., Nairobi, 1968, pp. 36, 41; the following two quotations are from pp. 98 and 55.

28 Ngugi wa Thiong'o (James Ngugi), *The Black Hermit*, H.E.B., A.W.S., 1968, p. 8; the following nine quotations are from pp. 35, 31, 32, 34, 46, 47, 45, 65 and 76.

29 Ngugi wa Thiong'o (James Ngugi), *R.B.*, p. 3; the following thirteen quotations are from pp. 107, 125, 81, 83, 127, 32–3, 104, 46, 69, 79, 147, 61 and 162–3.

30 Ngugi wa Thiong'o (James Ngugi), *Weep Not, Child*, Heinemann, 1964, p. 35; the following three quotations are from pp. 139, 140 and 141.

CHAPTER 2

The Craft of Poetry

In turning from the novel to poetry, I feel it would be out of place in the present context to limit the discussion to a strictly literary critical approach. The novel in Africa is, for better or for worse, a generally accepted fo rm, with an assured readership. It is picked up and read by anyone with the appropriate skills without fear or hesitation, as something they expect to understand and enjoy. If one novel proves somewhat hard-going, a reader will turn to another without assuming that novels in general are out of his reach or his range of interest.

The same is not true of poetry. Though reference to any traditional society will confirm that poetry is an essentially popular as well as a universal form of public expression in words, and though it is still readily accepted by most village communities and by children, education seems to have laid a dead hand on this most vital and expressive of the verbal arts. Generations have emerged from African schools afraid of poetry because their teachers have been afraid of it, so that it is seen all too often as a tedious and fearsome obstacle-course which no one would enter upon again of their own free will. It is appalling how often trained enthusiasts for literature arrive at university from secondary school begging to be allowed to continue their literary studies without having to read any more poetry, which by this stage they are convinced is beyond them – beyond their comprehension, their enthusiasm, and their critical grasp.

On the other hand, nothing is more encouraging than the enthusiasm with which the new generation of African teachers of English welcomes the prospect of teaching poetry. I know of many young teachers from widely differing backgrounds who regard poetry lessons as the highspots of their week, and find that their students constantly demand more. At this possible educational turning-point, it might be helpful to look into the causes of the blockages that have occurred in the teaching of poetry. No doubt the main explanation lies in the very idea that poetry can or should be mechanically taught in a way that makes it objectively examinable. Teachers who are themselves inhibited through their own training no doubt find it easier and less demanding to give instructions about spondees and dactyls and the sonnet form than to set out on the high seas of poetic experience and enjoyment. Teachers who are not so inhibited may well find the exact opposite to be true.

The creative and critical problems, which have been discussed, for instance, by John Reed and Gerald Moore with regard to East African poetry, are closely inter-related with the educational issues. And each may throw light on the other. The confusions that have twisted pupils' reactions to poetry are nowhere more apparent, in my experience, than in the falterings of would-be apprentice East African poets, including some who have got themselves into print – as John Reed discovered in his rather narrowly-based commentary.[1] Similar bewilderment is also apparent in the seemingly perverse anger expressed by non-poets at meetings of young writers against what they regard as the wilful obscurity of their contemporaries who are trying to write poetry.

This discussion will involve my going once again over certain matters which may appear fairly obvious to the initiated. But the root of much failure in understanding lies in the rarity with which basic principles are either expressed or grasped. And I therefore do not offer any apology for reiterating some of these basic premises in my own way, based in the first instance on an East African experience, with the hope that they may also find wider relevance among teachers and apprentice poets elsewhere, as well as perhaps among those who are concerned to evaluate the first phases of African anglophone poetry critically.

If you ask somebody who has attempted a few English poems, or a group of secondary or university students, what they regard as the most basic and essential feature of poetry in English, the first answer is almost invariably 'rhyme'. If you can then establish, as is usually possible, that they have read some African poems in English and ask if they can think of one which is rhymed, there will most often be a puzzled and amused answer in the negative. A dogma has been instilled about the nature of poetry which is unshaken by what is actually experienced. A rough equivalence has been established between, say, the writings of Shelley and Keats and what poetry 'ought' to be. In English-speaking Africa, many expatriate teachers of English belonged to generations reared in the tradition which took the 'romantics' to be the apotheosis of poetry (with or without training in

Latin poetry in the background). No doubt in most cases unconsciously, they passed on their inherited prejudices, which inevitably came to be understood in a narrow or confused form, either through their own fault or in the process of transmission. The consciousness of the African secondary student, who was quite often to become a teacher of English, was thus for long schooled to conceive the norms for all poetry in terms of certain particular types of repetitive pattern, emphasised by rhyme and marked lyrical rhythms.

In view of the strength of this misconception, it is not surprising that so many teachers spent their time 'teaching' poetry as external form, draining it of all vitality and significance for their students, and turning it into a mere set of difficult and boring terms to be crammed; nor that many would-be poets at first set out upon the dead-end road to becoming latter-day British romantics. This explains why the craft of poetry is so often presumed to lie essentially in inversions, archaisms, regular stanzas, rhyme, a steady beat and so on, in defiance of contemporary evidence. So that a poet of some real talent like John Mbiti could fall into such lifeless contortions as these:[2]

> Had I the wings of a honey bee
> To a distant shrub would I retire
> In search of solitude and stillness
> The world too near has been
> And I too near the world
> For a lonely shrub
> In the wilderness
> I long. . . .

Or a young poet with an evident sense of word-magic could allow his determination to rhyme in regular stanzas to murder his natural sense of harmony like this:[3]

> Once when birds of season
>   Circled the lemon-blind sky
> I caught a solitary bird
>   Midflight in my desperate eye. . . .
>
> 'Here with a raging thirst
>   They turned their pale wind-swept
> Faces, and turning grieved with
>   The tides; and naked, they wept. . . .'

In pursuit of irrelevant aims, the whole movement falters.

The poet with any real talent will soon find his or her way out of these confusions, though a good deal of time may have been wasted. And in finding it necessary to turn violently away from such an unpromising beginning, it may prove hard to become tuned to the kind of temporary apprenticeship that has nurtured so many artists. 'It is strange,' says John Reed,[4] 'that with such a taste for literary diction there is so little discipleship. . . . Imitation Hughes or Ferlinghetti or Okigbo may not be what we want to read but to start off under such an influence is a sound way of discovering your own voice.' However, to realise that your first god was a false god does not encourage further creative discipleship. The East African poet may escape from barren decoration to find himself or herself in apparently featureless surroundings. Gerald Moore has observed[5] that 'The range of solutions open to an East African writer is narrowed by the fact that English has never really developed there as a distinctive regional dialect, with its own wealth of idioms, grammatical short cuts and fully-integrated loan-words. The contrast with West African English may be highlighted by considering the range of English speech deployed by Wole Soyinka in a play like *The Road*.' But in these respects the West African dramatist or novelist may have more advantage over an East African counterpart than the poet. West African poetry has not found it so easy to absorb the casual features of colloquial language. Okigbo had to recognise that his feeling for T. S. Eliot might be one valid point of departure in the quest to find himself, and Richard Ntiru has done likewise. Gabriel Okara found 'initial impetus *into* English'[6] from his own language, and it is arguable that Okot has dived even deeper by leaping more vigorously from his own springboard.

Furthermore, the fact that talented poets escape from the wrong sort of entanglements, even if with some delays and bearing certain scars, does not mean that their potential readership will do likewise. Once confused, an uncommitted reader will give up the pursuit of poetic satisfaction far more quickly than will the rarer individual who carries a private poetic generator. And if a teacher is merely made nervous or bored by the idea of presenting poetry to a class, few of his or her students will trouble to revive for themselves the delicate life of poetry which has been dissected before them in the schoolroom. Such a dismembering may seem very final. In any true revival the teacher needs to become the ally of the creator, so that the old roadblocks are down and there is free passage between artist and audience.

The first need on all sides is to reject false assumptions. Impinging on the wrong kind of craftsmanship may do more harm than good, and it might be better if poets and readers alike referred only to their own intuitions, and clung to just a few simple facts about poetry. Firstly, that whatever else a poet is, he is honest and does not lie to himself or to others about his feelings; secondly that a poet must be prepared to expose his inner self so that to play safe is a denial of his role; thirdly that a poet uses words more precisely than any other writer or composer, and until he has learnt to do so, no verse will deserve attention. However, this does not mean that we cannot venture further than these basic principles in discovering a more suitable basis for discussing poetic craftsmanship.

To avoid possible misunderstandings, let me clarify my initial position. In art nothing belongs to anybody. Any successful use of any form is a real success. All artists react to all their environment which includes all their reading. To deplore the influence of one writer or group of writers upon another is to regret that men affect each other, or that a writer is a man. One may well feel that an evidently capable writer is failing to use his talents to the best advantage if he always employs forms and mannerisms which smack of another time and another place: this is not to say that the result is necessarily bad poetry – though it often is. Certainly it is not to regret occasional forays into the past or into distant parts to bring back spoils for here and now.

Of course a modern African poet may use rhyme effectively as an intensifying device provided it is not employed by rote; rhyme is no signature tune of a particular age or culture, and may even be part of the poet's first language tradition. Acquah Laluah, a Sierra Leonean who lived and died in Ghana, employs a lush romantic form to reflect her own lush romantic emotion which she and we now experience in her terms in the slight but pleasant poem entitled 'Rainy Season Love Song',[7] whether or not we recognise its affinities with modes more familiar in other places and other times:

> Out of the tense awed darkness my Frangipani comes,
> While the blades of Heaven flash round her and the roll of thunder drums.
> My young heart leaps and dances with exquisite joy and pain,
> As storm within and storm without, I meet my love in the rain.

The criterion for acceptance or rejection must always be feeling, not formula. Similarly Rose Mbowa can employ inversion significantly at the end of each stanza in her poem 'Ruin'[8] to depict agonised holding back, as her extended metaphor explores the experience of a young girl's reluctant approach to physical sexual experience: 'But on she walked', 'Still – on she moved', 'Through them – she pushed', 'To the door – she stepped'.

The proper starting point for all formal discussion of poetry is from a fact so simple and obvious that lovers of poetry often imagine that it is immediately self-evident to all readers. On the contrary considerable skill may be needed in leading a discussion with, say a group of students so as to elicit this point. To ask people who have been reading and enjoying a variety of poetry what is the only technical feature which all poems share and which readily distinguishes every one of them from prose usually provokes a lively variety of suggestions, each of which can be readily dismissed by reference to obvious examples, from rhyme to rhythm (the latter is incredibly widely assumed to be an attribute of poetry alone). The simple answer to the question is, of course, that the *poet* has decided where the lines end and not the printer. This is true of all verse but never of prose, except at the end of paragraphs.

This glimpse of the obvious is momentous in its implications, and forms a sound basis for grasping the true nature of all poetry. In rhymed poetry, or poetry with any clear-cut repetitive form, there is an evident equivalence between line-endings and sound patterns when the poem is read aloud. The parallel between written and spoken effects is more difficult to define in unrhymed irregular verse, but certainly exists. A good reader will be differently influenced by the arrangement of line-endings in different contexts, but influenced he or she will be in both pausing and intonation, quite as much as by punctuation where it exists. If ever one feels that there is no connection at all between the exact point where each line ends and the way it is to be spoken, the verse arrangement must surely appear to be affected, a fad, a wilful trick, or at best a naive failure in the poet to hear and recognise his or her own melodic (or deliberately dissonant) groupings. Even in an established poet's work, like that of Lenrie Peters, there are moments when one is at a loss to interpret a certain arrangement of lines aloud, particularly when invited to emphasise a normally unstressed word at the end of a line:[9]

> Senghor extols the beauty,
> the African beauty. The
> chocolate icing and mascara 'selves'
> along the ports and river's edge.

I cannot find any way of reading the second line as it stands here meaningfully, with 'The' stressed as is demanded by elevating it to a position of emphasis; nor do I find any increase in significance in the third line, since, put in its normal place before its noun group, 'The' would carry no stress and so 'chocolate icing' would retain its force. It is true that a slight pause after 'The' might well be telling, but this has been achieved at the expense of the second line, which to my ear and eye falls apart; and so the loss is greater than the gain. In reading this poem I find that it must be rendered – with or without a pause after 'The' – as

> Senghor extols the beauty,
> the African beauty.
> The chocolate icing and mascara 'selves'
> along the ports and river's edge,

but this could not be perceived at first sight.

The verse line, then, is the one essential feature of poetry which does not exist in prose. Sentence patterns and all they imply in terms of intonation, rhythm, meaning and emphasis are available to poetry whenever it wishes to take advantage of them, as it normally does in ways proper to itself. Of what, then, is the line a unit? Since the structure of prose already provides a means of expressing all aspects of communication, there is nothing new that the poetic line can offer. Its contribution is not to introduce any feature unknown to prose, but to offer additional means of exploiting the resources normally available to all language – a further system of rhythms, more points of emphasis in a more complex design, further arrangements of pausing, intonation, meaning.

Among these most notable is rhythm. To the complex rhythmic organisation of prose (and we should be aware that words cannot communicate at all without rhythm) is added the powerful new dimension of the line unit, which sometimes runs parallel with the sentence system, re-enforcing it further, and sometimes runs across it producing the fascinating counter-rhythms which provide one of poetry's essential strengths. We might compare prose rhythm to a single drum being played with an intricate beat, and poetry to two drums being deliberately played together in different rhythms, an effect which is indeed characteristic of African music:[10]

> Agosu if you go tell them,
> Tell Nyidevu, Kpeti, and Kove
> That they have done us evil;
> Tell them their house is falling
> And the trees in the fence
> Have been eaten by termites . . .

> By this well,
> Over-hung by leafy branches of sheltering trees
> I first noticed her.
> I saw her in the cool of a red, red evening.
> I saw her
> As if I had not seen her a thousand times before.

Certain of the natural sentence groupings and pauses are now weighted against the others, and new alignments are also set across those already inevitable in prose structure ('the trees in the fence/Have been eaten' or 'I saw her/As if I had not seen her . . .'). How right Taban lo Liyong is to insist on the primacy of rhythm in the art of poetry:[11]

> assonance
> rhythm most
> rhyme least
> and
> consonance . . .

In providing further possibilities for balance and contrast in wording, phrasing, tonal groups, and emphasis, the arrangement in lines (or their spoken equivalent) alerts readers and listeners to a more intense form so as to prepare us for a more intense response to overtones and implications. A greater pressure of imagery and metaphor is acceptable in this more measured medium. In the relatively casual haste of prose, such richness would seem cloying, and would slow us down when we believe that our concern is to press ahead: but the poet has signalled in the form that we are to expect concentration and complex significance, and so we are more ready to linger, to contemplate and savour phrasing which might weary or overwhelm us elsewhere:[12]

> And my blood ripples, turns torrent,
> topples the years and at once I'm
> in my mother's lap a suckling . . .
>
> Listen to the hunting drums
> And the hunting horns
> Mingling with the howls
> Of hunting dogs,
> See the river of pain
> On the face of the singer,
> The anguish of rape
> Bloodshed and death . . .

Poetic drama, that most popular medium in so many societies, reveals again how the poetic form releases poet and audience alike from the limits of mundane expectation and of restricted emotion, without embarrassment or apparent overstatement:[13]

> Will all great Neptune's ocean wash this blood
> Clean from my hand? No, this my hand will rather
> The multitudinous seas incarnadine,
> Making the green one red.

How many people are there who know the third of these lines by heart and yet would never have agreed to read through such words at first encounter in prose? A young East African playwright, Tom Omara, learnt early how, through incantation, rhythmic patterning and control, poetic form can elevate everyday speech to a new dramatic significance, and can allow one language to play against another with a new intensity:[14]

> We have been brought up in the wilderness.
> Our mother reared us in the forest wilderness.
> But the forest, the wilderness I met was different.
> There dwelt beasts of every tribe.
> Snakes venomous, big-headed vipers, night adders,
> Lions, buffaloes, wildebeests, gazelles,
> Rhinoceroses with horns
> That would make the skin of a cow itch in fear and wonder . . .

Just as all writers employ intuition and craftsmanship in determining the length and structure of their sentences, so a poet has additional opportunities and responsibilities in choosing, and perhaps varying the length of his lines in order to relate the emotional impulses more exactly to external form. We accept such manipulation whenever it echoes feeling in the pauses, the modulation, and the timing:[15]

> I shall sit often on the knoll
> And watch the grafting.
> This dismembered limb must come
> Some day
> To sad fruition.

> There was a time when meadow, grove, and stream,
> The earth, and every common sight,
> > To me did seem
> > Apparelled in celestial light,
> The glory and the freshness of a dream.

If poetry creates expectation of greater concentration of effects, it will be most widely employed when a writer is aware of having a heightened and intense experience to express. The greater technical complexity of a poem makes it capable of bringing together many aspects of an experience, not one after the other, but at the same time. Certain forms of prose, of course, make the same attempt, but it is predominantly the role of poetry to explore the limits of expressing many different matters simultaneously. Twisting the many threads of reality together, as they actually come to us in the workaday world, will make this form of expression by definition more difficult, but at the same time more rewarding if successful. After all, we rarely receive a single sensation in life isolated from all others. Even at a moment of passionate closeness to another human being, one may also be aware of the fly that settles on one's nose, of the hope that the weather is not going to spoil our next plans, and perhaps the need to decide what to have for supper. Experience is always multiple. Our normal prose attempt to relate things one after another is a necessary device to simplify most of what we want to say; but poetry seeks to put all these elements back together as a complex whole. So it cannot be simple; or very seldom so: it needs a great master to say very complicated things simply.

In the following short complete poem the writer is running to catch a bus, and in doing so glances at his reflection in a puddle, feels the rain, sees some old men huddling under a tree away from the storm near the stop, waiting perhaps for a different bus, and he hears or assumes that they are talking, in the midst of their laughter, about death. All these impressions rush together in his consciousness, till he fixes them in a pattern which expresses movement of both body and mind, so that all these fragments of experience blend together in a coherent design, asking questions about the relationship between life and death, movement and stillness, youth and age, laughter and sorrow:[16]

> Old men wait at the stop
> Huddling from rain
> Under a tree
> As I pass
> Running to catch up
> With my reflection
> In a puddle
> They laugh
> And talk of death.

Although I had the poem to work from, my outline of it conveys less in more words than the poem itself. Yet without the careful attention induced by the poetic form itself, we might not fully observe the significance of these delicate impressions.

However, the form cannot itself create what is not inherent in the words. Having keyed ourselves to expect a supercharged statement (whether comic or serious, passionate or detached), we shall feel let down if what we find is flat and insipid; there is anticlimax, bathos. Prosaic writing in poetic dress will therefore seem pretentious and inflated. On the other hand, if we are faced by passages which are difficult in expression but have nothing subtle or high-powered to say, simply because the writer delights in impressive difficulty for its own sake, then we shall certainly feel cheated after exerting our minds and feelings upon the poem. Poetry is an exacting medium, not an easy way to impress a gullible public.

Once the nature of poetry is grasped, intuitively or intellectually, it is evident that the poet has a wide selection of technical devices from which to choose in building up this heightened form of expression. It also becomes clear that all such devices are artistic conventions, or customs, which will appeal variously to different societies in different places and times. Rhyme and regular stanzas will then be seen as helpful according to the response they evoke from particular writers and readers.

However, the poet must employ some devices. And poets will therefore do well to be aware of the vocabulary of techniques current in their society, so that if they choose from outside this range, they will not do so in ignorance, through a misunderstanding of what is appropriate, but by deliberate choice for their own purposes.

As I have already suggested, it might be more obvious in an African than a Western context that poetry is potentially a popular art, a fact which the West has to some extent tried to relearn over the past decade. With a rich store of oral tradition in the African atmosphere, we have no excuse for looking at poetic form as the rarefied possession of an intellectual elite. Almost all societies find occasions when prose expression is inadequate to achieve the required intensity, when more meaning is demanded in concentrated form:[17]

> The spear with the hard point,
> Let it split the granite rock;
> The spear that I trust,
> Let it split the granite rock;
> The hunter has slept in the wilderness,
> I am dying, oh;

> The spear that I trust,
> Let it split the granite rock;
> The spear with the sharp point,
> Let it crack the granite rock;
> The hunter's spear is sharp,
> I am dying, oh;
> The hunter has slept in the wilderness,
> I am dying, oh;
> The spear that I trust,
> Let it split the granite rock.

It is natural that poetic forms should be popular not only at times of public ceremony and ritual, but on most occasions when the community is involved in verbal expression. In so-called developed societies, the printing press has tended to compete with communal song till the latter has retreated from its public functions, leaving poetry to limited groups of creators and audience.

It is a matter of great concern that in African society, which is so open to a wide variety of verse forms as a means of intense communication, misguided education has formed false views among the highly literate minority, so that it is all too readily assumed to be natural or indeed inevitable for printed poetry to be both written and read almost exclusively by what at worst might be labelled an aesthetic clique. This process may rapidly form a vicious circle. If poets write self-consciously for their peers alone, they will seem to confirm their own assumptions that poetry is by nature a minority taste or a piece of group display. Thus the gap between the poet and a more extensive potential audience is easily widened.

Clearly it is not too late to reverse this process. Okot's songs, particularly *Song of Lawino*, are among the very few works that might be called East African best-sellers, and they demonstrate therefore that the traditional popularity of poetry can survive into the age of print. *Song of Lawino* satisfies all the essential criteria of concentration and intensity mentioned earlier, conveyed through patterns which set all Okot's faculties at work, and are apt in the society that hears them: the urgent verbal communication in short lines, heightened by dramatic monologue; the subject matter of immediately vital concern:[18]

> My mother
> Was a well-known potter,
> She moulded large pots,
> Vegetable pots,
> And beautiful long necked jars.
> She made water pots

And smoking pipes
And vegetable dishes.

The sensuous imagery is rooted in the environment:

The tattoos on her chest
Are like palm fruits,
The tattoos on her back
Are like stars on a black night;
Her eyes sparkle like fireflies,
Her breasts are ripe
Like the full moon.

We hear a double set of rhythms; complex emphases, repetitions, contrasts
direct our attention as the poet wishes; the faint ironic humour and the
quizzical realism define the personality of the speaker and weight the
presentation of the subject to the reader by the placement of precisely chosen
words, for the most part words simple in themselves, in a form which provides maximum opportunity for highlighting particular items in the
language, and setting them deliberately against each other:

When Skyland was not yet there
And Earth was not yet moulded
Nor the Stars
Nor the Moon,
When there was nothing,
Where did the Hunchback live?

Where did the Hunchback
Dig the clay for moulding things,
The clay for moulding Skyland
The clay for moulding Earth
The clay for moulding Moon
The clay for moulding the Stars?
Where is the spot
Where it was dug,
On the mouth of which River?

By now we have become ourselves involved in this chant of doubt – doubt
above all on our part as to which indeed is the less sophisticated, this un-
supported creation myth or the questioner.

Not that I am subscribing to the heresy which suggests that because poetry
can rightly be seen as a popular art in many of its finest manifestations (Shakespeare's plays, for example), there is something reprehensible in the writing
of poetry which is not at once easy to understand. Indeed it is deplorable to

find antagonism too often expressed in urban societies towards poetry (and indeed all art) which is 'difficult', impressionistic, non-naturalistic, symbolic or surrealist. This antagonism seems to be based on a very strange assumption, that it is the poet's duty to render even the most subtle, paradoxical and complex experience in a significant and concentrated form and yet with the utmost simplicity; as if readers and listeners who are concerned about the more involved and intense aspects of living will tolerate their expression on paper only in the manner of *The Reader's Digest*. This is a peculiarly bourgeois and middle-class approach to art, not shared by the sturdier imaginations of peasants, children, nor the majority of those who actually enjoy what artists produce. Traditional spoken literature is, of course, heavily reliant on suggestion, imagery, metaphor, symbolism, innuendo, double meanings and all aspects of mystery. Such modes are natural to people who are aware of ritual, ceremonial, and the mystical nature of existence, who do not suppose that experience can be reduced to logical formulas, and who are close to the origins and essence of at least one religion, whatever it may be.

I myself was brought up among people who resented the work of Picasso and Stravinsky, Henry Moore and T. S. Eliot, even though no one ever suggested that they were expected to take note of it. Such an attitude, which is current in some African university circles,[19] might easily frustrate and discourage certain of our best young poets, such as Richard Ntiru and Jared Angira, were it not for the fact that the creative urge has to be fairly strong in the first place for a writer to expose his poetry publicly (unless he is a charlatan); and so he can perhaps withstand the onslaught of those who actually get angry with him for writing what they do not effortlessly understand after they have chosen to spend time reading it of their own free will. I have already excluded from such a defence those who are too lazy to say something simple simply, or who conceal confused or elementary ideas under a mere welter of words.

For instance, Richard Ntiru is well aware that the metaphysical preoccupation with the relationship between life and death is rooted in village consciousness as expressed in much ritual; and that those who have learnt to accept life confidently through facing the implications of death are to be found in all communities. These perennial issues are linked in his poem 'To the Living'[20] with an awareness of the continued presence of the ancestors, and with complex traditional ceremonies relating to mortality:

> Only they
> Have the inner knowledge
> Of the numbing nutation
> On gravestill nights when nude priests,
> In mortal ecstasy,
> Bless multicoloured antiamulets
> On virgin pelvicbone amphorae
> And celebrate prenatal deathdays
> To the rhythm of the drum of death
> Struck with the thighbone
> Of him who died on his bridal night. . . .

Through his own intellectual and imaginative experience he associates these insights with Plato and with their modern urban restatement in T. S. Eliot, creating in this amalgam his own unique and honest perspective:

> Who but they
> Who walk beyond the twilight glimmer
> Between sleep and waking,
> Who bask in nocturnal sunlight
> And breathe the cool diurnal darkbreeze,
> Who have experienced
> The realization of the inevitable dream,
> Know the revitalizing power of the stilled blood?

Ntiru can now conclude (my quotations are extracts) by contrasting with this vision the barren and desperate questioning of those of us who have learnt to accept and comprehend nothing. Through his images he parallels the bewildered village sceptic with his counterpart elsewhere; while he rejects any attempt to sentimentalise either the agnostic peasant or the alienated intellectual:

> But we,
> We who clutch at tattered totems
> And turn away from solar solace
> When the innocence butter
> Melts in our hands at the ordeal,
> We who raise open hands in supplication to Nyabingi –
> Hands that would embrace –
> What dream are we capable of?

It would be idle to imagine that such a poem could be put in uncomplicated terms and remain either truthful or illuminating.

The freer forms of English poetry, without rhyme or regular metrical groundbase, which have proved particularly attractive to many twentieth-century writers, including those working in English as a second language, appear at first sight to be easier to handle than more formalised structures. And it is true that it is possible to write bad poetry in free verse with even less effort than it takes to write bad poetry in stricter conventions. However, once these conventions are perceived not as hindrances to the poet but as a set of compass points by which he and his audience can find their bearings on the vast sea of human emotion (on which it is so easy to get lost or to wander idly without sense of direction), then it will be seen that it is in fact harder to write significantly with fewer and less distinct guidelines, not easier. In this less obviously disciplined medium, it may be simpler to satisfy oneself than to satisfy others and communicate with them.

This is the difficult task which most African poets in English set themselves. It demands a very great awareness of words to induce multiple interpretations all of which are relevant to one's purpose without any structured focus. It is not easy to achieve the authority which is one of the few qualities shared by the following openings to four poems. Nor is it easy to identify the factors that hold us and draw us to read on in each case. We can observe the exact placing of the unexpected yet precise word – 'fraudulent', 'scooped', 'sharp', 'grave'; but beyond this there is a rhythmic control which bespeaks the poet's sure grasp of his elusive form, something to be judged by our ears and our senses, not our intellects:[21]

> Sitting down
> An old man is like a rock, rough hewn,
> Which a god shaped –
> Shaped here and scooped there
> With sharp eagerness. . . .

> > Watching someone die
> > is a fraudulent experience
> > The deep significance is felt
> > the meaning escapes. . . .

> > > We are the solitary street travellers,
> > > Fearing death
> > > And wearing masks of fear. . . .

> > > > It is the constant image of your face
> > > > framed in my hands as you knelt before my chair
> > > > the grave attention of your eyes
> > > > surveying me amid my world of knives
> > > > that stays with me. . . .

It is not surprising, therefore, that a number of writers in poetic form make play with visual effects, such as the omission of punctuation and capital letters or the lacework arrangement of words on the printed page. Such details express an understandable reaction against the outward signs of a different poetic convention which had to be cast off; apart from acting as a further deterrent to the unpractised reader, these visual tricks are harmless provided they do not appear to be rejecting what poetry *is*. Indeed an expert craftsman – let alone a past master like e. e. cummings – can play a game with words which turns out to contribute to the powerful and serious effects of the poem: after all there is an element of play in all art. In 'The Street' Jared Angira maps out his roadway with pavements on either side and traffic in the middle, a setting which is essential to the ideas he is conveying:[22]

Worms crawling   Worms crawling

mercedes slides past
blue shadow

garbage

swinging   swinging
boozing   boozing

zephyr slides past
green shadow

garbage
black shadow

Wananchi   Wananchi. . . .

Unfortunately these devices, which may on such occasions be very meaningful, can readily turn into verbal acrobatics which divert the poet from the 'intolerable wrestle with words' which is his real business, and will then simply irritate the reader in not seeming purposeful.

Yet it is hard to play a game in which you have to establish your own rules; and it becomes even harder when you have to bring in other players who need both to learn the rules and to acquire the skills to play well at one and the same time. But this is precisely what the reader of poems in free verse must do, since the next game we play together will have subtly different rules again. And yet there may be no choice. The poet working in a second language cannot employ a rhyme system which has no emotional resonance for him; nor a stanza form which, instead of feeling like a comfortable garment, seems more like a straitjacket.

The important thing in this situation is for an apprentice writer to have the opportunity to read and think about and discuss a wide range of forms, so that in choosing to write short stories, or to compose in a dramatic or poetic mode, he has some idea why he has chosen a particular genre, and is aware of some of its possibilities and pitfalls. Likewise it is to be hoped that the young poet will be in a position deliberately to select free verse or a more stylised manner, rather than just happening to stumble across a convention, becoming mesmerised by it, and employing it for want of any other to hand. In terms of subject matter, an apprentice poet will certainly do well to write what he feels he 'must' say rather than woodenly choosing a topic before he has found his voice or is sure that he has anything to say at all. The deliberate selection of a worthy subject may for the moment be the death of a potential poet, since above all at this stage the would-be artist in words must discover some fire, some fierce preoccupation within himself or herself which is seeking an outlet. This makes it all the more important that there should be no arbitrary prescription as to form.

In East Africa at present poetry in English is still perhaps somewhat limited in matter and manner. To a large extent it lacks the blaze of vision, the passion of strongly felt personal experience, the sequential development of ideas in terms of images and verbal designs. But it is at once possible to qualify such a sweeping statement in each of these respects:[23] East Africa flares up not only in Okot's 'Song of Prisoner', but also in poems by David Rubadiri and Jagjit Singh and Jonathan Kariara to add to the West African voices of Kofi Awoonor, Gaston Bart-Williams and Soyinka. The labyrinths of the inner self are explored in poems such as Laban Erapu's 'I Beg You', William Kamera's 'Poem in Four Parts' or Parvin Syal's 'Defeat' which we might set beside Kwesi Brew's 'The Two Finds', Dipoko's 'Autobiography' and J. P. Clark's 'Olokun'. The sinewy and coherent development of John Ruganda's 'Barricades of Paper Houses', of Yusuf Kassam's 'The Recurrent Design', of Henry Barlow's 'My Newest Bride', or of many of Ntiru's and Angira's poems may match that of Gabriel Okara's 'Piano and Drums' or Lenrie Peters' 'Parachute' and at least the occasional poems of Christopher Okigbo. There are no doubt many reasons for the directions that poetry in English in East and West Africa has taken, but if we have to pause and think before adding to the examples just given, this may be in part because certain types of inspiration have not often enough been matched by the creation or adaptation of suitable forms of poetic expression.

For all the problems that they face, there are significant compensations for African poets writing in English. Those who spend any significant amount of time bewailing their difficulties in having to write poetry in a second language would do better to turn to their first language, or try another form, or both. Indeed the successful writer in English may well be the man or woman who is already rejoicing in the possession of two or more language heritages and is allowing these to react upon each other so that integral new possibilities are created in each.

It is sometimes assumed that the only possible relationship between a first and a second language must be either in terms of translation or clumsy imitative confusion between the two sets of structures. But surely when a writer confidently takes possession of two languages, they will play upon each other in his subconscious in very subtle ways, so as to produce quite new rhythms and forms in each which could probably be evolved only by someone who is the child of that particular language partnership, and which are nevertheless perfectly attuned to the inner nature and harmony of the language being employed.

Okot p'Bitek's songs are a case in point. I cannot pronounce on the relationship between the Acoli original and the English outcome, but one can readily perceive that the total effect of the songs is essentially new in English. The strong two-beat base, shifting into three- and occasionally one-beat lines, with the pattern sometimes being varied when a pair of two-beat groups is linked in a single line, or when the base itself shifts for a passage to a single or triple beat, is firmly established in *Song of Lawino*: as are also the sturdy rhetorical manner, and the free repetition of refrain lines and structures binding together a highly visual and sensuous narrative and descriptive manner. G. A. Heron has rightly defined one of the fundamental problems of working in a second language as deriving from the fact that[24] 'Every language has its own stock of common images expressing a certain people's way of looking at things.' Okot has done much to help establish a stock of images in East African English which express an East African way of looking at things, an achievement of great importance and complexity: for other writers it may be easier to build from this nucleus than it would have been to start creating their own base. Okot's pumpkin image, of course, derives from an Acoli concept, but it is already a common idea, a common point of departure for most literate East Africans and perhaps already for some beyond the limits of East Africa, because of the English version of *Lawino*.

The descriptive content of the first two songs is in the main relatively simple so that Okot's poetic authenticity is above all dependent on an absolutely right judgement in selection of the part which is to represent the whole – or at least more than itself; and the selection and placing of the occasional unexpected word so that it has maximum effect, and of the common word so that it may be restored to a new purity of meaning – essential activities of poetry. Consider the very last lines of *Lawino*: the word 'wealth' is so obviously the right word that it would never be questioned, yet how exact it is in the range and precision of all its overtones; while the slightly unusual word 'uproot' is so completely at home here in the rhythmic pattern, so clear in meaning, that few readers will hesitate at it, even if they have never in fact come across it in print before this work, and so its freshness is entirely positive:[25]

> Let me dance before you,
> My love,
> Let me show you
> The wealth in your house,
> Ocol my husband,
> Son of the Bull,
> Let no one uproot the Pumpkin.

And yet *Song of Ocol* and 'Song of Prisoner' show this form to be capable of great variety and flexibility:[26]

> I plead fear,
> I plead helplessness,
> I plead hopelessness.
> I am an insect
> Trapped between the toes
> Of a bull elephant. . . .

The emergence of one-beat groups as a frequent feature; the increase in the proportion of three-beat groups; the greater concentration of stresses into briefer patterns with no unstresses between, work together to produce a different tone of voice, a more staccato manner for Ocol in his own song: when Okot sought to express a different set of tensions, he found his medium pliable:[27]

> There is a large sack
> In the boot
> Of the car,

> Take it
> Put all your things in it
> And go!

or

> Tell me
> You young man
> From Masailand . . .
> Would you let a man
> 'Borrow' your wife
> Yet kill him
> For taking your *shuka*?

Too many critics have assumed over-readily that this form has already been worked out. Whether it has as many openings to provide as the blank verse line once offered to British poets I do not know, but it would be a great artistic wastage to overlook the wide range of possibilities inherent in this and other forms of African English poetry which are beginning to emerge.

One needs no very intimate knowledge of traditional orature to recognise its strong formal conventions, in word groupings and repeated refrains for instance, or to realise that as African poets begin to search for more controlled styles in English within which to operate, as they are doing, one powerful source of inspiration must be oral tradition. This may prove to be the basis of conventions more in tune with the ways these poets and their readers feel things than mannerisms derived from past periods of the English language which cannot now be given new life even in Britain or America, let alone in a second language context. At the same time, these new modes may on occasion offer interestingly close parallels with earlier styles, possibly giving new life to intricate patterns of rhyme, assonance, onomatopoeia, alliteration and so forth:[28]

> Belching steam the miner's train pulled out
> and in the pistons a voice sang
> João-Tavasse-went-to-the-mines
> João-Tavasse-went-to-the-mines
> João-Tavasse-went-to-the-mines
> João-Tavasse-went-to-the-mines.

> Child: River bird, river bird,
>   Sitting all day long
>   On hook over grass,
>   River bird, river bird,
>   Sing to me a song

> Of all that pass
> And say,
> Will mother come back today?

Bird: You cannot know
> And should not bother;
> Tide and market come and go
> And so shall your mother.

This new life can be embodied even in an imaginative transliteration–
I use this word to suggest the creation of a poetic counterpart in another
language as opposed to a mechanical translation. In 'A Mother to Her
First-born',[29] transposed from Didinga or Lango, we find a 'translation' in
which English is made the instrument of new sounds and effects which are
powerful and intriguing, though I do not claim to speak for its authenticity
as a representation of the original. Of course no language can mirror another
identically; but I do not think this praise-song could be as fresh and truthful
as it is in English if were not honestly and meaningfully related to the
Lango version: it can thus remain African in its English form – (I quote
a short passage near the end):

Be splendid and magnificent, child of desire.
Be proud, as I am proud.
Be happy, as I am happy.
Be loved, as now I am loved.
Child, child, child, love I have had from my man.
But now, only now, have I the fulness of love.
Now, only now, am I his wife and the mother of his first-born.
His soul is safe in your keeping, my child, and it is I, I, I, who made you.
Therefore am I loved.
Therefore am I happy.
Therefore am I a wife
Therefore have I great honour.

You will tend his shrine when he is gone.
With sacrifice and oblation you will recall his name year by year.
He will live in your prayers, my child,
And there will be no more death for him, but everlasting life springing
> from your loins.

But how much more powerful it can be when the creative impulse flows
across from one language to another more spontaneously, as in this little

lyric re-created in English from a Rutooro source by Ralph Bitamazire under
the title 'I Love You, My Gentle One':[30]

> I love you, my gentle one;
> My love is the fresh milk in the rubindi
> Which you drank on the wedding day;
> My love is the butter we were smeared with
> To seal fidelity into our hearts.
> You are the cattle-bird's egg,
> For those who saw you are wealthy;
> You are the papyrus reed of the lake,
> Which they pull out with both hands.
> And I sing for you with tears
> Because you possess my heart:
> I love you, my gentle one.

This is even more effective when the poet exercises his own creative force
in the process of transformation, as does Okello Oculi in *Orphan* whenever
he lets his rhythm run free, making an original work with a complex
ancestry:[31]

> Let us go and dare the bush ghosts
> With our youth,
> And tease the guardian shadow of bird with
> Traps. . . .
>
> Let us live out ourselves
> Before the sun sets again
> And sleep cajoles and lulls us to the mercy
> Of the witch doctors of Darkness –

(though it is true that it is hard to find a passage in this very vigorous and
challenging work which has no trip-wires in the rhythm or the wording
or the line arrangement).

When the wheels catch fire, the poet dissolves all boundaries and makes
distinctions unimportant:[32]

> Seed
> A bowl of dark unblemish
> A chancel closed in forest
> Silences
> Repletion for earth's own regenerate need

A wind's
Dark mantle brushes past
A quiet prelude to the stir
Of germ
A cycle's ether sieve for pollen hair

Fall seeds
Then, to mineral hands
Flush out in your green
And gentle blades
Awaken minds and grow to cosmic shades.

When we are as close to the roots of inspiration as here in one of Soyinka's 'Animistic Spells', all self-consciousness about being poetic, or being African is forgotten in the final confidence of knowing that such words must by definition be both.

In East Africa we are now in danger of our own models being themselves used as mechanically as the British romantic poets have been emulated in the past. It is the principle behind the work of the writers I have mentioned that should stir their contemporaries and successors: the disciplined originality deriving from the mutual cross-fertilisation of languages, not the mere imitation of the success of others.

With regard to the development of imagery, metaphor, symbolism, and reference, the argument rages. Should the African writer militantly restrict himself or herself to indigenous influences; or should these be allowed free interplay with experiences which are general and may have been absorbed from uninhibited reading? The problem tends to solve itself for the genuine poet whose creative forces merge into a new form of expression which is at once personal and individual. We have surely now reached a stage of self-awareness when allusions by African poets to daffodils or countryside covered in snow will raise a smile rather than serious discussion. But how far it is desirable to go in the opposite direction so as to become self-consciously African is debatable. The celebrated Argentine author and writer, Jorge Luis Borges, has expressed himself forcefully on similar issues, for instance in his essay 'The Argentine Writer and Tradition', which I quote in a translation by James E. Irby:[33]

> Besides, I do not know if it is necessary to say that the idea that a literature must define itself in terms of its national traits is a relatively new concept; also new and arbitrary is the idea that writers must seek themes from their own countries. Without going any further, I think Racine would not even have understood a person who denied him his right to the title of poet of France because he cultivated Greek and Roman themes. I think Shake-

speare would have been amazed if people had tried to limit him to English themes, and if they had told him that, as an Englishman, he had no right to compose *Hamlet*, whose theme is Scandinavian, or *Macbeth*, whose theme is Scottish. The Argentine cult of local colour is a recent European cult which the nationalists ought to reject as foreign.

Some days past I have found a curious confirmation of the fact that what is truly native can and often does dispense with local colour; I found this confirmation in Gibbon's *Decline and Fall of the Roman Empire*. Gibbon observes than in the Arabian book *par excellence*, in the Koran, there are no camels; I believe if there were any doubts as to the authenticity of the Koran, this absence of camels would be sufficient to prove it is an Arabian work. It was written by Mohammed, and Mohammed, as an Arab, had no reason to know that camels were especially Arabian; for him they were a part of reality, he had no reason to emphasize them; on the other hand, the first thing a falsifier, a tourist, an Arab nationalist would do is have a surfeit of camels, caravans of camels, on every page; but Mohammed, as an Arab, was unconcerned: he knew he could be an Arab without camels. I think we Argentines can emulate Mohammed, can believe in the possibility of being Argentine without abounding in local colour.

The African village minstrel has no more problem about local colour than Mohammed. He is a craftsman who makes no false distinction between his craft and his art. He thus has complete integrity of intent. Techniques are available to him, at the tips of his consciousness, for the purpose of communicating exactly what he wants to communicate in exactly the ways he wants to communicate it. Content and process are indivisible. In finding their own answers on such questions, contemporary African poets – unless they are to rely solely on spasmodic inspiration and unpolished intuition – must willingly become conscious craftsmen in order to serve what has to be said and do justice each to his or her vision.

Similarly, in exploring the art and the craft of the poet, student, teacher, and critic must first have responded to the poem, and must then be seeking to grasp it more completely, to possess it and experience it through perceiving its form, which is the expression of its inner life. To say that this must needs be African craftsmanship is not to suggest that any writer or reader or student of poetry will be much better at their task for being ridden by African theories, any more than by an ill-defined collection of borrowed and archaic criteria. Nevertheless, effective answers and effective responses will most often develop in the light of moods and attitudes which grow simultaneously in the individual and his or her contemporary society through interaction.

NOTES

1 John Reed, 'Poetry in East Africa', *Mawazo*, i, 4, Dec. 1968, pp. 31–6; the article is an extended review of *D.B.*

2 John Mbiti, 'Solitude and Stillness', *Poems of Nature and Faith*, E.A.L.B., 1969, p. 9.

3 K. A. Kassam, 'Once when birds of season', *D.B.*, pp. 52–3.

4 John Reed, *ibid.*, p. 35.

5 Gerald Moore, 'The Language of Literature in East Africa', *Dalhousie Review*, liii, 4, Winter 1973–4, pp. 694–5.

6 *Ibid.*

7 *Our Poets Speak*, ed. Donald St. John-Parsons, University of London Press, 1966, pp. 30–1.

8 *New Voices of the Commonwealth*, ed. Howard Sergeant, Evans, London, 1968; as corrected in *Poems E.A.*, p. 100.

9 Lenrie Peters, 'You Talk to Me of "Self"', *African Voices*, ed. Howard Sergeant, Evans, London, 1973, p. 107.

10 Kofi Awoonor (George Awoonor-Williams), 'Songs of Sorrow II', *W. A.Verse*, p. 75; Henry Barlow, 'The Village Well', *Poems E.A.*, p. 20.

11 Taban lo Liyong, 'The Best Poets', *Frantz Fanon's Uneven Ribs*, H.E.B., A.W.S.90, 1971, p. 39.

12 Gabriel Okara, 'Piano and Drums', *Mod. Poetry*, pp. 93–4; Okot p'Bitek, 'Song of Prisoner', *Two Songs*, E.A.P.H., 1971, p. 115.

13 William Shakespeare, *Macbeth*, II, ii, pp. 59–62.

14 Tom Omara, 'The Exodus', *Short East African Plays in English*, ed. David Cook and Miles Lee, H.E.B., A.W.S. 28, 1968, p. 60.

15 Wole Soyinka, 'Requiem 5', *Mod. Poetry*, p. 114; William Wordsworth, 'Ode: Intimations of Immortality from Recollections of Early Childhood' (1806), opening lines.

16 Amin Kassam, 'Waiting for the Bus', *Poems E.A.*, p. 76.

17 Okot p'Bitek, 'Tong ma lake tek': 'The spear with the hard point', Songs of the Spirit Possession Dance, *The Horn of My Love*, H.E.B., A.W.S. 147, 1974, p. 91

18 Okot p'Bitek, *Song of Lawino*, E.A.P.H., 1966, p. 138; the following two are from pp. 34–5 and 139.

19 Ali Mazrui sets out his views clearly in 'Abstract Verse and African Tradition', *Zuka* 1, Sept. 1967, pp. 47–50. He is not opposed to difficult poetry of which 'the *right* meaning' can be stated; but to what he calls 'abstract verse' which 'is calculated to leave a good deal to the reader's imagination'. He assumes that poetry which can be interpreted in more than one way has *no* meaning since it offers 'sheer imagery as a substitute for meaning'. Images such as Okigbo's often succeed 'in forming a pattern' but 'fall short of forming coherence'. And so Mazrui demands that 'the canons of literary creativity in the English language' should be 'Africanized' to exclude 'poetry which is totally abstract' – apparently all poetry for which 'a *right* meaning' cannot be specified.

20 Richard Ntiru, 'To the Living', published almost simultaneously in

Poems E.A., pp. 116–17 and *Tensions*, E.A.P.H., 1971, pp. 90–1; the 2nd, 4th and final sections are here quoted.

21 Jonathan Kariara, 'Age and Experience', *Origin East Africa*, ed. David Cook, H.E.B., A.W.S. 15, 1964, p. 99; Lenrie Peters, '6', *Satellites*, H.E.B., A.W.S. 37, 1967, p. 12; John Mbiti, 'Wearing Masks of Fear', *Poems of Nature & Faith*, E.A.P.H., 1969, pp. 24–5, slightly revised by the poet in *Poems E.A.*, p. 99; Dennis Brutus, *Sirens Knuckles Boots*, Mbari, Ibadan, 1963, unpaginated and *A Simple Lust*, H.E.B., A.W.S. 115, 1973, p. 24.

22 Jared Angira, 'The Street', *Poems E.A.*, 10.

23 Five of the poems named are in *Poems E.A.*, Erapu, 'I Beg You', p. 40; Kamera, 'Poem in Four Parts', pp. 60–1; Syal, 'Defeat', pp. 168–9; Ruganda, 'Barricades of Paper Houses', pp. 143–5; Yusuf Kassam, 'The Recurrent Design', p. 82; Kwesi Brew, 'The Two Finds', *The Shadows of Laughter*, Longman, London, 1968, p. 21; Mbella Sonne Dipoko, 'Autobiography', *Black & White in Love*, H.E.B., A.W.S. 107, 1972, p. 33; John Pepper Clark, 'Olokun', *Mod. Poetry*, p. 85; Henry Barlow (Y. S. Chemba), 'My Newest Bride', *D.B.*, pp. 26–8; Gabriel Okara, 'Piano & Drums', *Mod. Poetry*, pp. 93–4; Lenrie Peters, 'Parachute', *A Book of African Verse*, ed. J. Reed and C. Wake, H.E.B., A.W.S. 8, 1964, pp. 51–2.

24 *Song of Lawino & Song of Ocol*: combined school edition, E.A.P.H., 1972, Introduction, p. 6.

25 Okot p'Bitek, *Song of Lawino*, p. 216.

26 Okot p'Bitek, 'Song of Prisoner', *Two Songs*, E.A.P.H., 1971, pp. 33–4.

27 Okot p'Bitek, *Song of Ocol*, E.A.P.H., 1970, pp. 9–10, 52.

28 José Craveirinha, 'Mamana Saquina', *When Bullets Begin to Flower*, trans. Margaret Dickinson, E.A.P.H., 1972, pp. 49–50; John Pepper Clark, 'Streamside Exchange', *W.A. Verse*, p. 56.

29 James Herbert Driberg, *Initiation: Translations from Poems of the Didinga and Lango Tribes*, The Golden Cockerel Press, Great Britain, 1932, pp. 16–17; reprinted in *The Unwritten Song* I, ed. Willard R. Trash, Cape, London, 1969, pp. 105–7.

30 *Poems E.A.*, p. 23.

31 Okello Oculi, *Orphan*, E.A.P.H., 1968, pp. 60–1.

32 Wole Soyinka, 'Animistic Spells XI', *Poems of Black Africa*, ed. Wole Soyinka, H.E.B., A.W.S. 171, 1975, p. 72.

33 Jorge Luis Borges, *Labyrinths*, ed. Donald A. Yates and James E. Irby, Penguin, 1970, pp. 214–15.

PART II

Close-up Studies

CHAPTER 3

The Centre Holds

A study of Chinua Achebe's *Things Fall Apart*

ON rereading *Things Fall Apart* I have been struck by the fact that the impression the book as a whole leaves on the mind is different from that gained by breaking off mid-way and considering one's immediate reactions. The book looms large in our memories as a well-proportioned structure, weighty and deliberate, economical in style, impressive in conception. A close-up view shifts the emphasis. Under detailed scrutiny the economy may scale down to spareness; while the large scope may seem to result in ruggedness, even roughness of texture. The plainness which the author was evidently seeking then seems for the moment not far from aridity.

Literary analysis is meaningful only in the service of a new synthesis. Close study of a passage from *Things Fall Apart* out of context is particularly likely to lead to pedantic fault-finding and to have little relation to the full impact the novel makes upon us, since, as I wish to argue in this chapter, the achievement of this work is essentially an epic achievement in which the whole is greater than the parts; and in which the parts cannot be appreciated properly when separated from the whole. Naive praise of *Things Fall Apart* can sometimes lead to an exaggerated reaction which underestimates the significant role that this novel plays in the chronological sequence of African writing in English. It has become an early landmark not only because of its point in time (though such a book could hardly have been written later) but because it is a worthy archetype.

It has not been uncommon to discuss *Things Fall Apart* in relation to Greek concepts of tragedy. In reference to this work and to *Arrow of God* Abiola Irele declares that[1] 'In two of his novels, at least, Achebe succeeds in striking a profoundly tragic note' and identifies Okonkwo's 'inflexibility' as his tragic flaw. Gerald Moore speaks of[2] 'the austere tragic dignity of

Things Fall Apart' and refers to its 'classic treatment'. John Povey remarks that[3] 'Okonkwo matches other tragic heroes who in their extremes are simultaneously the most heroic and also the most unreasonable of men . . . . His heroism is based upon his unyielding sense of rectitude.' And G. D. Killam takes up this theme,[4] in saying that Okonkwo's story 'is presented in terms which resemble those of Aristotelian tragedy – the working out in the life of a hero of industry, courage and eminence, of an insistent fatality . . . which transcends his ability to fully understand or resist a fore-ordained sequence of events.'

A. G. Thomson ventures on some analogies with heroic poetry in general[5] but does not find this a very promising parallel: The ceremonies whose repetition is proper to the heroic poetry of people to whom heroic poetry is natural is a little oppressive in this novel, which invites comparison with other novels rather than with saga or epic.' And he soon withdraws from the discussion: 'Neither, perhaps, is there much point in speaking of modes, and in setting some general concept of the novel or chronicle against a concept of heroic poetry.' Thomson assumes that the epic and novel modes are mutually exclusive, and so wisely decides that there is little point in pursuing their relationship in this negative vein. But it is strange that, having observed a heroic manner to be apt for 'a people to whom heroic poetry is natural', he fails to conceive that this might indeed be a positive aspect of a novel by an Igbo about traditional Igbo society.

If *Things Fall Apart* is to be regarded as epic, then Okonkwo is essentially heroic. Both propositions are tenable. The work is epic in that it celebrates the achievement of a heroic personage in earlier times; and through him embodies a people's conception of their past. The story as a whole is heroic in that it concerns action which has recourse to bold, daring, extreme measures in attempting great things. The strength of an epic is in the structure of events it presents in order to depict in imaginative form the history of a society. In achieving this it may become both grand and some- what impersonal, sacrificing warmth and detail of characterisation, but this is rather part of the definition of the 'kind' in which Achebe is writing (to adopt a Renaissance term) than a derogatory assessment.

Okonkwo is a hero in that he shows exceptional bravery, firmness, even greatness of soul. A hero is by definition an exceptional figure and so he does not simply embody the average virtues of his society in a fairly typical form; he is very far from being an Everyman.

Okonkwo, indeed, flouts the norms of his society in significant respects and in doing so brings many of his own ills upon his head. But this flouting is not, in terms of the design of the book, merely incidental or accidental; these deviations are highly significant and are made into major issues, so that in the process the norms are all the more clearly defined. He is twice punished for crimes against Ani, the earth goddess: if the last occasion leading to his banishment is an accident beyond his control, this is certainly not true of his infringement of the Week of Peace, on which occasion we are told that[6] 'Okonkwo was not the man to stop beating somebody half-way through, not even for fear of a goddess,' though his first two wives plead with him volubly. Three days short of the New Yam Festival he shoots at his second wife; and he is reprimanded by Chielo, the priestess of the Oracle, for resisting the demand that his daughter shall be brought into the presence of Agbala. Most telling of all, perhaps, is Obiereka's final reproof for his role in the killing of Ikemefuna: 'What you have done will not please the Earth.' Okonkwo's aberrations serve to emphasise the social and moral framework.

Okonkwo is unlike the prototype epic heroes of Homer and Virgil in one very important respect which has to do with circumstances rather than character. He is not a founding figure in the fabled history of his people, but the very reverse. He makes a final, grandiloquent assertion of the values of his society before the established pattern of that society is changed beyond all recognition: he sings the swan-song of a tradition which is about to be transformed. He is heroic in standing for certain essential qualities in this long-established social pattern that made it strong, significant and enduring. Every society is unique in the precise balance of values and assumptions that maintain it. Some of the positives of one group may not necessarily be positives in codes of behaviour elsewhere. As Ajofia, speaking for the *egwugwu* of Umuofia, declares:

> We cannot leave the matter in his [Mr Smith's] hands because he does not understand our customs, just as we do not understand his. We say he is foolish because he does not know our ways, and perhaps he says we are foolish because we do not know his.

I do not myself believe that *Things Fall Apart* is concerned to pass judgment on social systems, nor to assert dogmatically that one is better or worse than another. What it does, in a lordly, objective, incontrovertible manner, is to demonstrate that every society depends on a fairly rigid set of conventions which can only be lived as a whole and can therefore only be evaluated as a whole – ideally from the inside. For foreigners to arrive extolling their

own familiar social values and habits more or less uncritically and indiscriminately as 'civilised', and dismissing in contrast a different way of life
demanding different conformities as 'primitive' was patently arrogant,
prejudiced, uninformed, unintelligent. This does not mean that Achebe is
bent on bettering their example by creating a mirror image of their bigotry.
He prefers to reveal the darker side of both traditions as well as the better
side and leave us to draw our own conclusions. He does not romanticise
Igbo society nor vilify Christian European behaviour as a whole. There is
little point in oversimplifying highly developed systems of human intercourse and labelling those of one's choice 'good' and the rest 'bad'. 'Facile
rejection and facile acceptance,' says Ezekiel Mphahlele,[7] 'cannot stand
"ironic contemplation".' Achebe is neither arrogant nor simplistic in *Things
Fall Apart*: he takes a very long perspective.

As Professor Stock, among other critics, has pointedly observed,[8] for all
his non-conformity, Okonkwo accepts the traditional values of his society:
when he is banished, for instance, he does not kick against the judgement,
but accepts it without question. And indeed he sets about overcoming the
problems he has himself created in his life-pattern by methods proper to
the very same tradition that has defined his misdemeanours.

What Okonkwo is really opposed to is history, or the inevitability of
change resulting from converging forces which cannot now be diverted.
These forces include not only the colonialists' self-righteous determination
to rule and to impose conformity with their own conventions, backed by the
power of guns, but also the counter-force of the oppressed within the
traditional society; and the universal tendency of all human beings to want
what they see; and yet again the inherent generosity, hospitality and mis-
placed pity that the Igbo expressed to wandering strangers. It is the whole
complex of historical facts that Okonkwo stands against. The goodness
or the badness of what is intruding and taking over is not for the moment
the essential issue. Achebe is objective in *Things Fall Apart* not because he is
indifferent – far from it; but because he is looking beneath the surface of
things at the play of forces in a historical context. His refutation of pompous
alien critics of Igbo society is incidental: they are the more effectively
crushed because this is treated as a fairly elementary issue. Achebe's full
subject is much larger and of more lasting significance. An epoch is reviewed
in terms of the last-ditch stand of a great champion of that epoch.

His stand can be seen as futile since he is opposing the inevitable. It can
also be seen as desperately heroic (a better word than 'noble' since Okonkwo
is in fact not noble, nor, incidentally, particularly intelligent). This is a fine,

hopeless, ultimate assertion that something that is about to disappear existed, was absolutely itself, and embodied certain great positives which can hardly be recreated exactly in a different context. In part we share the grand, objective viewpoint of the novel as a whole. But the purpose of a powerful objective writer is very often to leave us asking key questions for ourselves, and this surely is true of the author of *Things Fall Apart*. In terms of this work, modern African society can meaningfully review one set of its roots and origins, without sentimental idealising, but attributing proper value where it is due. And we are then bound, surely, to go on to ask how far these values can be properly and appropriately retained, or restored and reasserted in the different context of our own times.

In considering Okonkwo as a heroic figure in an epic framework, it is helpful to compare him to other protagonists whom Achebe has created. The differences between Okonkwo and Obi are numerous, but what interests me for the moment is to observe that when we set them side by side, Obi, in his complex set of dilemmas, is unmistakably a small man in contrast to Okonkwo. Ezeulu in *Arrow of God* is in an intermediate position, but his setting offers him large opportunities, and he is in kind, at least potentially, more similar to Okonkwo than to Obi; and yet this further comparison makes it all the more obvious that the hero of *Things Fall Apart* towers above his successors.

With some irony, Okonkwo's return to Umuofia is referred to as 'the warrior's return';[9] but at this moment the irony is not so much directed against the protagonist himself as against the society which no longer values, or even recognises, a warrior's qualities. Nothing demonstrates more clearly how things have degenerated in his absence in Mbanta than the virtual irrelevance of Okonkwo's stature, and of his very concepts, when he steps in over-confidently to rally the wavering spirit of his people.

Okonkwo has always been known as Roaring Flame. We are told at the very opening of the book that he 'was clearly cut out for great things'. He is a figure with a destiny, who in the proper course of events is ordained to set his mark on the history of his clan. He has the appearance of a hero: 'He was tall and huge, and his bushy eyebrows and wide nose gave him a very severe look.' A symbolic, ritual figure must look the part. Even in appearance, of course, these heroic qualities are not necessarily attractive in the mellower sense – they are grand and austere. Bravery, the quality which is to be assumed in any hero, is admirable but not in itself specially likeable. It is not for his humane endowments that the fighter is adulated. From the outset the tone employed in describing Okonkwo's pre-eminence is amusingly ambiguous. Immediately after the introductory set-piece description of his imposing appearance, the very next thing we learn is of his mighty snoring, which is upon the same scale:

> He breathed heavily, and it was said that, when he slept, his wives and children in their out-houses could hear him breathe.

On the other hand, Unoka, Okonkwo's father, who is despised by his son, has many amiable traits which are fully consistent with tradition: he is a companionable drinker; he loves the flute; he has a talent for good fellowship. We are specifically told that Okonkwo is not convivial – indeed his scorn of his father is increased by the latter's possession of these sociable qualities. At festivities Okonkwo goes through the motions, as a dutiful child of Umuofia, but he does so mechanically, without enthusiasm:

> But somehow Okonkwo could never become as enthusiastic over feasts as other people . . . he was always uncomfortable sitting around for days waiting for a feast or getting over it. He would be much happier working on his farm.

First he looks down upon his father because of his mildness, and then he comes later to spurn his own eldest son, Nwoye, for the very same characteristic. Though grandfather and grandson are in many respects very different, Unoka and Nwoye have in common a hatred for war, the event above all others in which Okonkwo shines. It is a familiar fact about *Things Fall Apart* that in rejecting his father for disgracing him and failing to give him a start in life, Okonkwo comes to hate and fear 'gentleness' to a psychopathic degree:

> Perhaps down in his heart Okonkwo was not a cruel man. But his whole life was dominated by fear, the fear of failure and of weakness.

John Povey is right, then, when he says,[10] 'In spite of our general sympathy Okonkwo is not a lovable man.' He refuses to show the affection that he actually feels. This neurotic repression of his softer emotions is comprehensible, and could have engendered a good deal of sympathy for him as a man tortured by this conditioned self-concealment. But the book gives the reader little encouragement in such reactions. He even throttles into silence the mutual affection between himself and his daughter:[11] 'Okonkwo was specially fond of Ezinma. . . . But his fondness only showed on very rare occasions.' For the most part he treats her sternly, and, with characteristically stubborn rejection of all the warmer contacts within his reach, he broods perversely on his wish that she were a boy.

We see Okonkwo, then, as brusque, impatient, self-sufficient. His lack of humility is demonstrated by the haughty way in which he perpetually finds fault with others, which occasionally leads his fellow elders to reprimand him and demand that he apologise to his victim. If we feel for Okonkwo, it is in his public capacities, not as a private individual. The very first paragraph of the novel sings his praises as a man of action in a context, in this society, which provides one of the great positive opportunities for a man to show his prowess – wrestling. As a successful member of his group Okonkwo – to employ a Western praise-term – is very much a self-made man, and he has much of the thick-skinned self-assurance which that phrase implies.

We should note that our attitude to a successful fighter in the inter-tribal contests of Okonkwo's heyday is determined by the scale upon which these wars were fought in traditional circumstances. Twelve men were killed on the enemy side in a great victory, and two from among the conquerors. Numbers do not, of course, affect the gravity of violent death in itself, one way or the other; nevertheless our attitude is affected by the fact that an action such as this does not run beyond our imagination; it does not dwarf the idea of Man himself; he is not ironically belittled as in the widespread carnage and destruction of modern warfare.

However, much of Okonkwo's self-assertive activity occurs in contexts in which we are not asked to admire him. 'Okonkwo's way of conforming,' says Abiola Irele,[12] 'besides being an inverted sort of nonconformity, is a perversion. The meaning that he attaches to manliness amounts to fierceness, *violence*.' He insists, as we have noted already, on participating in the killing of Ikemefuna, contrary to determined advice; he beats Ojiugo in Peace Week, thereby scandalising the community; he tries to kill his second wife and fails only because he is a bad shot – a scene which is ludicrous but far from amusing. His ferocity alienates his eldest son and drives him into the arms of the Christians. 'It is not Christianity and the world of the whiteman that has broken up Okonkwo's family,' says John Reed.[13] 'It has merely given the disruptive passions within that family their chance.' Looking back from the vantage point of hindsight, his contemptuous dismissal of those who have not succeeded in life is ironic:[14] 'He had no patience with unsuccessful men.' In the last resort how successful is Okonkwo himself? His wilfulness actually earns him the dislike of his clansmen:

people said he had no respect for the gods of the clan. His enemies said his good fortune had gone to his head. They called him the little bird *nza* who so far forgot himself after a heavy meal that he challenged his *chi*.

Nevertheless, he is punctilious in the niceties of tradition even to his own disadvantage: he will not return to Umuofia before the very day on which the full seven years expire. And when he leaves Mbanta, in spite of his own dislike of public festivities, he surpasses expectation in the feast that he throws as a farewell gesture:

we expected a big feast. But it turned out to be even bigger than we expected.

Indeed, when one considers how much there is potentially to weight our feelings against Okonkwo, it speaks much for Achebe's achievement in his chosen mode that his protagonist retains for us such indubitable heroic stature. It is of vital importance in this connection that the climax of the whole action is a crucial moment of violent drama in which, however ambiguous its implications, we are essentially in sympathy with Okonkwo; the story is shaped to induce our support at this moment for his gesture of defiant opposition to the arrogant presumption of white rule and the calculated degradation of a great tradition. He stands alone in this last expression of stubborn independence. His is an exalted defeat for which his whole career has prepared him.

Things Fall Apart presents us with a fairly full picture of the Igbo society which Okonkwo takes it upon himself to champion. As we have said, there is no romanticising and yet, once it has been shown to us in depth, the idea that this human complex is merely barbarous when compared to others is clearly the result of social attitudes which are themselves unsophisticated. We are shown a coherent and at the same time contradictory pattern of human existence, in these respects very much like most others. It has achieved a system of controls which assure internal order and allow in the main a humane conduct of daily affairs, based on well recognised positive values. Umuofia prides itself on fighting only for a just cause – not out of blood-thirstiness or rash endeavour; and its neighbours are said to acknowledge the truth of this claim. This policy is not a rationalisation of weakness but takes its stand from a position of strength. Their oracle restrains them from engaging in a 'fight of blame'. It is the pressure of society which forces Okonkwo to withdraw when he humiliates an unsuccessful clansman at a meeting. Uchendu blames the Abame group for killing the first white man to appear in their midst: 'Never kill a man who says nothing.' This is not simply a question of self-interest; it is rational response to a new situation. By the time that Okonkwo acts at the end of *Things Fall Apart*, the white group have not only made their negative position disastrously plain, but this attitude is now seen to be irrevocable and permanent.

Within Igbo society there is no ultimate complacency with regard to social mores. Obiereka questions himself searchingly as to the rationale of Okonkwo's ritual banishment, and finds no satisfaction, as he admits himself:

> Obiereka was a man who thought about things. When the will of the goddess had been done, he sat down in his *obi* and mourned his friend's calamity. Why should a man suffer so grievously for an offence he had committed inadvertently? But although he thought for a long time he found no answer.

A mature perspective is struck between different life-patterns. Uchendu declares,

> There is no story that is not true. . . . The world has no end, and what is good among one people is an abomination with others.

Complex ironies are involved in the missionaries' rejoicing at Nwoye leaving his parents in the name of the true church. This is orthodox enough Christianity – 'Come thou out from among the unbelievers' – but at one and the same time it is counter to the most positive principles not only of the Igbo and of almost all African societies, but also to good middleclass British Victorian morality which found blood to be a good deal thicker than water. Time and again it is the values of traditional society, with its non-materialistic base and its absence of vested interests in any commercial sense, that are stressed – virtues to which most Europeans would surely be bound at least to pay lip-service:

> We do not pray to have money but to have more kinsmen. We are better than animals because we have kinsmen.

These positive values are frankly set against the inhuman practices and irrational taboos that are part and parcel of the conventions and assumptions of the Igbo, epitomised very specifically in the treatment of the osu and the abandonment of twins. Both these items of conduct are mandatory within the Igbo system; nevertheless they have haunted Nwoye's mind long before he finds his own escape route into the new church, as an over-sensitive refugee from his own environment. Nwoye, as Professor Stock well observes,[15] 'was the kind of youth to whom personal feeling meant more than public spirit, which was one reason that he was a nonentity in Umuofia'. Outcasts, misfits and malcontents formed fertile ground for the new breed of spiritual sowers.

Yet there is no question whatever of holding up Christianity as an untarnished alternative. It embraces anomalies which are even more fundamentally paradoxical than Igbo tradition. Not only does the new religion sing hallelujahs when it succeeds in wrenching child converts from 'pagan' parents, but it supports and in turn is supported by the oppressive rule; each basks in the approval of the other:[16] 'Mr Brown's mission grew from strength to strength, and because of its link with the new administration it earned a new social prestige.' It is good avowed respected members of the flock who perpetrate the worst abuses:

> They were beaten in the prison by the *kotma* and made to work every morning clearing the government compound and fetching wood for the white Commissioner and the court messengers. Some of these prisoners were men of title who should be above such mean occupation.

The six elders are captured by a calculated piece of dishonourable treachery; and are thereafter treated altogether inhumanly by men who profess both the virtues of Christianity and of white administration, not always distinguishing between the two.

And so the total effect is one of balance. In the argument between Mr Brown and Akunna, we see little to choose between the two religions in the light of objective analysis: needless to say Mr Brown himself does not entertain such a heretical view, but the honest reader who accepts the validity of the novel finds such a reaction inescapable.

Thus, while it is plain that both systems can be and are in some respects corrupted and oppressive, and while the new white rule is totally blind, on the other hand, to the many excellences of the established system, the main emphasis is not on the stupidity or bigotry of the new order, but on the fact that with it, for better or for worse, lay the inevitable stream of history at the time in question:

> The elders consulted their Oracle and it told them that the strange man would break their clan and spread destruction among them.

74

This Okonkwo does not or will not believe. He has a blind, superb faith in the possibility of maintaining the past unchanged into the future: 'God will not permit it.'

But the oracle speaks for the gods more fittingly than Okonkwo, who is steadfastly swimming against the strengthening tide, refusing to acknowledge that he is already losing ground in the face of forces which are beyond his control, regardless of whether or not it is desirable to oppose them. Okonkwo's clansmen see their dilemma as more complex and they accept Mr Brown's counsel: 'If Umuofia failed to send her children to the school, strangers would come from other places to rule them.' They are caught in a situation which seems to offer no meaningful choice: they have to play out a game wherein they have no chance either to determine or to challenge the rules. Obiereka attributes their position to the wiliness of the Europeans:

> The white man is very clever. He came quietly and peacably with his religion. We were amused at his foolishness and allowed him to stay. Now he has won our brothers, and our clan can no long act like one. He has put a knife on the things that held us together and we have fallen apart.

This is true in more than one sense, and yet it overestimates the foresight of the invaders. The whites did not have a concerted plan in this way to take advantage of the factors which Obiereka's speech identifies. They were self-infatuated empiricists with a consuming sense of mission who were lucky to have guns and history on their side, forces too great for Okonkwo to have stood against even if he had succeeded in rallying his people. But this is the last moment that heroic protest will be possible, not only against the alien power but against all extra-human forces that seem to support it; and Okonkwo seizes that moment.

Since the appearance of *A Man of the People* the sceptics who could not believe Achebe's claim that his style in the 'trilogy' was deliberately chosen, but presumed that this was the only style he could master, have been silenced. The contrast with *A Man of the People* may encourage us to exaggerate the similarity between the three earlier novels. But while such similarities can be overstated, the three works have a likeness of purpose and a likeness of manner which confirm their identity as a group.

The style, in its 'epic', heroic, objective manner, rests its strength on firm overall structure. The plan of the three books – especially *Things Fall Apart* – is grand, powerful, fully successful in outline. The 'fable' (to use what still seems to be the best translation of an Aristotelian term) is altogether adequate. The spare style of the first novel with its bare vocabulary, its fairly simple structures, and its restraint in imagery apart from the special kind of colouring provided by proverbs, has (like most other styles) its advantages and disadvantages. It is direct, uncloyed, classically stark. Achebe has succeeded in his stated attempt to escape from an essentially British manner in phrasing.

On the other hand, a style which Anne Tibble has joined Gerald Moore in describing as 'laconic' before adding the additional epithet 'flat',[17] may be found to be lacking in texture. As I said earlier, for all one's constant rediscovery of the scope and scale of *Things Fall Apart*, there is a level at which immediate satisfaction falters. The language is plain to the point of losing at later readings intense minute-to-minute interest. The occasional imaginative phrase, which is not directly descriptive or proverbial, emphasises rather than relieves this manner, reminds us of the deliberate rarity of such usages: kites 'hovered over the burning field in silent valediction';[18] 'It was a tremendous sight, full of power and beauty'; 'And whenever the moon forsook evening and rose at cock-crow the nights were as black as charcoal'. These occasional embellishments are for the most part in keeping with the stylistic manner, and do not break the general tenor.

The power of this style is above all cumulative in its effect, especially because of its utter suitability to the whole literary mode that I have been attempting to define, 'a prose', as Margaret Laurence puts it,[19] 'which is plain and spare and at all times informed with his keen sense of irony'. To say that this work is always more impressive as a whole in the mind, in completed retrospect, than in terms of our immediate reaction in mid-paragraph, is not negative praise. It is arguable that the permanent impression that a serious and memorable book leaves with us is the most important thing of all concerning our critical reactions. *Things Fall Apart* is built in such a way that nothing is likely to dislodge it from its place in our memories or in any consideration of the development of anglophone African writing. Artistic stoicism is clearly more appropriate to this ruggedly constructed masterpiece than any purely external fancifulness or richness would be.

It is interesting to observe in passing that Achebe, in escaping from British stylistic clichés and mannerisms, has employed, aptly enough, what is often theoretically declared to be a normal feature in constructing English prose, but which on closer analysis appears to be something of a rarity among well-known British writers. It is asserted in certain types of textbook and guide that there should be, or indeed that there always is in good

writing, a 'key' sentence in every paragraph, either at the beginning an-
nouncing the subject which is then developed in the body of that particular
paragraph, or at the end to bring together the points that have been raised.
In practice one can search through writer after writer without distinguishing
such a key sentence in each paragraph as a norm (though examples can be
collected). Achebe has adopted in *Things Fall Apart* a style which is tightly
trussed up and carefully modulated; and to suit his purpose he has employed
a rather more formalised conception of the paragraph than many English
writers.

There are strong patterns in the structuring of *Things Fall Apart*. Although
the design is simple, being centred upon one character, with in the main
a linear time progression and a clear placing of the short passage in Mbanta
between the two major sections in Umuofia – the whole expressing a clash
between two major social forces, there is a rightness about the scheme
which suggests the imprint of a master craftsman and artist who can return
to first principles and achieve the most difficult of all artistic effects: significant simplicity. From first to last the work gives the impression of having
been soundly planned and of being under firm control. The organisation of
the chapters defines meaningful spans of the novel: the ending of the first
chapter with Okonkwo becoming Ikemefuna's guardian is one of many
pointers to the book's planned proportions: and Ikemefuna is the subject
of the final paragraphs of both Chapters 2 and 4, just as his name is the last
word of Chapter 7, in which he has been killed.

One piece of description of traditional society – the coming of the locusts –
turns out to be imaginatively and ironically significant:[20]

> I forgot to tell you another thing which the Oracle said. It said that other
> white men were on their way. They were locusts, it said, and the first man
> was their harbinger sent to explore the terrain.

An example of particularly careful patterning of an incident on many levels
is to be found after the occasion on which Enoch has violated one of the
ancestors:

> That night the Mother of the Spirits walked the length and breadth of the
> clan, weeping for her murdered son. It was a terrible night. Not even the
> oldest man in Umuofia had ever heard such a strange and fearful sound,
> and it was never to be heard again. It seemed as if the very soul of the
> tribe wept for a great evil that was coming – its own death.

Once a proverb is deliberately repeated to link two parts of the novel –

a tautening device which Achebe was to develop in *Arrow of God* and *A Man of the People*.

Things Fall Apart is so clearly an important work that it is easy to forget how early it came in its author's career. In assessing its strengths we may also become aware that certain opportunities have been lost. In this novel Achebe seizes upon a special creative opportunity which lay before him, such as is seldom offered even to the perceptive artist more than once. In later works he learnt to depend on a more complex development of techniques. The intimate display of the whole life of the Igbo is an integral part of the subject of *Things Fall Apart*, yet this does not have to be recounted in disconnected incidents, such as we sometimes find, with little part to play in the development of plot or characterisation or other aspects of the novel. Gerald Moore is right when he says,[21] 'The boredom of daily routines in an isolated forest village must be felt, but not suffered, by the reader, in order that he may feel also the excitement of the festival and the thrilling fear of the unheralded event.' However, the scenes needed to establish our awareness of the way of life that is threatened might more constantly have served other purposes at the same time, for instance the incident in which the elders give judgement in the case of the runaway wife, the long wrestling scene in which Okonkwo is not involved, or the description of the ceremonies in overture to marriage.

Even the tale that Ekwefi tells in Chapter 11 appears to have been selected at random. A traditional fable is essentially a story which can be applied to actual circumstances in a current situation, and so the embedding of such a narrative in *Things Fall Apart* would seem to offer an admirable opportunity to link one aspect of the novel to another by implication at various levels. But I have been unable to perceive any relevance in Ekwefi's tale to the novel at large, and I am not aware that anyone has done so.

When one turns a deliberately critical eye on the book one can see possible cross-references in the subject-matter which seem to cry out for some patterned recognition. For example, upon studied consideration one is struck by the fact that Okonkwo is exiled for his gun going off accidentally and killing someone, whereas earlier he misses his wife when he deliberately shoots at her with the same weapon with intent to kill. Eldred Jones does not convince me,[22] however, that this conjunction has been significantly planned. It may be suggested that since a reader can see a possible ironic linkage here, the author can be said to have deliberately scattered these contradictory events throughout the book with the aim of making the reader search out a connection. This strikes me as too arbitrary a method with too random an effect to be thought of as meaningful structuring.

There are limitations also in the characterisation. Okonkwo is the only individual in *Things Fall Apart* who is presented to us in any detail. Other characters are introduced convincingly enough but are developed only as far as the bare needs of the plot demand – that is to say sketchily at most. Even Ekwefi and Ezinma are slight portraits, and Eldred Jones has rightly complained of the virtual disappearance of the latter from the scene before the climax.[23] Okonkwo is the only character whom we can consider in the round though the novel aspires at this level to be a realistic work.

In many of the respects in which we discover such restrictions in *Things Fall Apart*, *Arrow of God* is a more mature, a less chancy work of art. It is a fine, polished novel, which satisfies us more at each new reading. And yet it still misses something of the happy, rugged strength of *Things Fall Apart* which derives from the self-confident handling of the strong basic structural idea. Nowhere is this clearer than in the ending which is placed so exactly and surely and is handled with such fine restraint, confirming as we close the book the indelible impression that it will leave upon us.

The well-known final ironic paragraph at the D.C.'s expense is a neat rounding out in key with the controlled distancing of the whole novel. That the D.C. perceives this action as a small, intriguing vignette in the autobiography which is to glorify his image in the eyes of what can only be a petty and uninformed circle of provincial English readers, finally epitomises his own smallness, the narrowness of his vision and the pathetic inadequacy of his ambitions, for all the inflated image he has of himself and his role. But at this stage in the work the D.C. is a fairly easy target within the wide perspective of Achebe's canvas; the author's deeper concern is with the more powerful structural irony which takes shape in the last two pages and provides the serious conclusion to the novel at its most profound and permanent level.

Okonkwo has broken the final taboos of his own society in committing suicide:[24]

> It is an abomination for a man to take his own life. It is an offence against the Earth, and a man who commits it will not be buried by his clansmen. His body is evil, and only strangers may touch it.

How has Okonkwo been brought to deny in his death all that he has lived for? The answer is clear enough. He has reached the point of absolute disillusionment. In the betrayal by his clansmen his life disintegrates; and so the values he has striven to maintain no longer have any meaning. His death is a physical expression of his knowledge that things have irrevocably fallen apart. He, and through him his clan, have been denied three times, but the shame is heaped upon Okonkwo himself: his people will not bury him. In the depth of his chagrin Obiereka musters his spirit to put the blame upon the white man to his face, and there is truth in the accusation, just as there is truth in the assertion that Okonkwo has himself committed an abomination:

> That man was one of the greatest men in Umuofia. You drove him to kill himself; and now he will be buried like a dog.

This speech expresses the paradox. The aliens are responsible for Okonkwo's death and yet he is to be buried like a dog. And why? The clansmen will not so far break the laws of tradition as to cut down Okonkwo's body and bury it. Yet they have not lifted a finger to support Okonkwo when he alone made a stand in the name of that very tradition. 'We shall make sacrifices to cleanse the desecrated land.' Yet was not Okonkwo's act in killing the messenger itself a deliberate sacrifice with precisely the aim of cleansing the desecrated land? Obiereka's words to the D.C. confirm this – yet at that moment those who are now so nice about social proprieties as to leave the body of their champion in strangers' hands had hung back and left Okonkwo naked. Which is the real desecration – Okonkwo's stoic death, or the meek acceptance of humiliation at the hands of the white man?

After this the irony of the last paragraph takes on a new dimension. It is not just that the D.C. plans to reduce the heroic death pangs of a way of life to a patronising paragraph: it is that the clansmen have allowed themselves to be diminished in this way without resistance. The only figure who escapes this final irony is the dead Okonkwo.

NOTES

1 Abiola Irele, 'Tragic Conflict in Achebe's Novels', *Black Orpheus*; reprinted in *Introduction to African Literaturé*, ed. Ulli Beier, Longman, London, 1967, p. 167.

2 *Seven A.W.*, p. 60.

3 John Povey, 'The Novels of Chinua Achebe', *Introduction to Nigerian Literature*, ed. Bruce King, Univeristy of Lagos/Evans, 1971, p. 101.

4 G. D. Killam, *The Novels of Chinua Achebe*, H.E.B., 1969, p. 17.

5 A. W. Thomson, 'The Political Occasion: A Note on the Poetry of John Pepper Clark', *J.C.L.*, vii, 1, 1972, pp. 84–5.

6   *T.F.A.*, p. 27; the following two quotations are from pp. 60–1 ('What you have done. . .'), and 172.

7   Ezekiel Mphahlele, *The African Image*, Faber, London, 1962, p. 202.

8   A. G. Stock, 'Yeats and Achebe', *J.C.L.*, v, 1968, 107.

9   *T.F.A.*, p. 165; the following five quotations are from pp. 7 ('was clearly cut out. . .'), 3 ('He was tall. . .'), 3, 34, and 12.

10   John Povey, *op. cit.*, p. 100.

11   *T.F.A.*, p. 41.

12   Abiola Irele, *op. cit.*, p. 169.

13   John Reed, 'Between Two Worlds', *Makerere Journal* 7, 1963, p. 13.

14   *T.F.A.*, p. 4; the following six quotations are from pp. 28, 152, 126 ('Never kill a man. . . '), 113, 127, and 151.

15   A. G. Stock, *op. cit.*, p. 108.

16   *T.F.A.*, p. 164; the following five quotations are from pp. 158, 125, 128 ('God will not permit it. . .'), 164 ('If Umuofia failed. . .'), and 160.

17   *Seven A.W.*, p. 59; Anne Tibble, *African-English Literature* (Peter Owen, London, 1965, p. 107.

18   *T.F.A.*, p. 29; the following two quotations are from pp. 50 ('It was a tremendous. . .'), and 86 ('And whenever the moon. . .').

19   Margaret Laurence, *Long Drums and Cannons*, Macmillan, London, 1968, p. 107.

20   *T.F.A.*, p. 125; the following quotation is from p. 168.

21   Gerald Moore, *The Chosen Tongue*, Longman, London, 1969, p. 152.

22   Eldred Jones, 'Academic Problems and Critical Techniques', *African Literature and the Universities*, ed. Gerald Moore, Ibadan University Press, 1965, p. 94.

23   *Ibid.*

24   *T.F.A.*, p. 186; the following two quotations are both from p. 187.

CHAPTER 4

Men Fall Apart

A study of Chinua Achebe's *No Longer at Ease*

READERS of fiction resist any attempt on the part of a writer to play on their emotions. Only the most unsophisticated enjoy having tears wrung from them. Certain kinds of narrative situation put us on our guard; when an emotional trap is closing round characters whose experience we are apparently expected to share, we feel on the defensive. If we are left to watch an inevitable sequence unfold from a relatively objective view-point, as in classical tragedy, we may be willing to endure the sadness of a god's-eye view; but if an author is clearly intent upon putting us through the emotional mill subjectively by way of direct involvement, we draw back.

There are moments during a first reading of *No Longer at Ease* which fill us with trepidation. One is the foreseeable loss from the parked car of the money Obi has borrowed from Clara. We expect this to happen and we suspect that we shall be inescapably caught in an emotional snare. There is something of the same foreboding with regard to the central theme of accepting a bribe. In British Victorian schoolboy fiction there were swathes of pages during which the uncritical reader was titillated by agonies of doubt while the (eventually exonerated) hero was proved, apparently beyond doubt, to have stolen a watch. Are we to be subjected here to the same kind of helpless suspense?

Needless to say, Achebe avoids the pitfalls of easy emotionalism with skill and care. Once we are assured of this, we follow through a second reading of the book in a more untrammelled and easier frame of mind. But there are other reasons why *No Longer at Ease* improves upon closer acquaintance. If a first quick reading leaves us with the impression of fairly obvious and familiar problems in modern African society being competently but rather simply restated, even over-simplified, we realise upon closer perusal that this was a shallow assessment, and that there are levels beneath levels in the book which together make up a complex analysis of the issues. Indeed the width of perspective achieved is at length virtually as extensive as that of *Things Fall Apart*, though we have reached our point of vantage by a very different path.

Our first reaction to the story as it unfolds is to blame Obi. The brash and arrogant young man who has had every advantage nevertheless takes a bribe: he is corrupt: he has succumbed; he has betrayed his educated standards, and has disgraced the people who raised him. But from the very start the structure of the novel discourages this simplistic response of shocked surprise. The opening page or two of *No Longer at Ease* yield a very subtle picture of Obi Okonkwo to careful observation, epitomising his weaknesses and also the reasons why we sympathise with him in spite of, even because of, these negative traits. His carefully prepared pose of brazen, worldly-wise indifference attempts (not very successfully) to conceal a basic sensitivity and naivety. The fact that he has to make such an effort to achieve this stance shows that he is not sophisticated enough, nor perhaps clever enough, to be really vicious: 'Obi tried to do what everyone else does without finding out how it was done.'[1] Nor, on the other hand, is he mature enough to be unconcerned about the impression he makes. His whole problem has been that he has not the strength of personality to jump off the social band-waggon, nor the wit and ease to find a comfortable seat on it. He is at a disadvantage both in front of the Umuofia Progressive Union and with his professional acquaintances; his gaucheness, which spurs him just so far along a certain path and then leaves him stranded, unable to go forward or back, evokes our consciously tolerant sympathy. In absolute contrast to his grandfather, Obi is something of a pathetic figure. He thinks he is hardened against the clichés that he is subjected to in court, but is betrayed by tears, tears of self-reproach, and irritation that he has lost the substance of his ideals, as well as of his bribe, for the shadow.

The opening of the novel deliberately robs the bribery theme of real suspense. Almost the first thing we know about Obi is that he is guilty; and so in following through the processes that lead up to this day in the dock, the book insists on our considering cause and effect – the real motivation lying beyond vulgar greed or a callow attempt to escape from a painful situation by the simplest means. And so we are led further to the complex question of responsibility.

Quite soon we react along very different lines. Obi has been educated out of his own background into a highly competitive elite. If he is to maintain his success, he must 'keep up', and this consumes his high salary. And he is expected to keep up not only by his fellows, but also by those who have externalised their dreams in him. As a member of the senior civil service, thanks to the support he has gained from his clan, he is expected to represent the group and raise its prestige by living like a European, driving a car and dressing well at the office, while at the same time providing his brother's school fees, repaying his loan and, of course, helping his brethren to get jobs.

Obi is a man not just of two but of several worlds: in Nigeria apart from the traditionally orientated village and the Christian community of his parents, there are the 'two cities in one' – Ikoyi and the slums, while beyond lie his ventures in Europe; and so *No Longer at Ease* requires a different structure in terms of setting from *Things Fall Apart*. In the latter, the interlude in Mbanta is sufficient to allow new developments to have proceeded just so far by the time that Okonkwo returns home to create a dramatic confrontation: that is enough, since this confrontation is contained within one place, Umuofia. But *No Longer at Ease* demands more movements between the separate milieux in order to present them perpetually in uneasy relationship.

What, then, was Obi educated for by the elders of his clan? For his own good, or as a vested interest – 'an investment which must yield heavy dividends'? Perhaps the fairest way to put it is to say that he was educated by a group for the good of the group, including himself. 'They wanted him to read law so that when he returned he would handle all their land cases against their neighbours.' But the process of education is more complex than that. Not only has it raised his status, it has done something more radical to the whole structure of his personality, something which he cannot reverse even if he would: it has made him see himself as an individual. The dual worlds are not simply those of the village and the rich elite, or of the educated and the uneducated; Obi has also to commute between the corporate world of an integrated society and the lonely world of the individual consciousness, a polarity which I have already discussed in Chapter I.

Are not his people to blame, then? They have treated him as something to barter with in the game of life: 'Every town and village struggles at this momentous epoch in our political evolution to possess that of which it can say: "This is mine"'; and they have lost their bargain because they did not understand the market. In the process they have surrendered Obi to social and mental bondage. Having had him trained for one thing, they now demand something totally different from him, which he is far less in a position to give them than before he underwent his expensive grooming. The ironic confusions and misundertandings involved are epitomised in attitudes and reactions to corruption. Above all, in the eyes of his own people, Obi's crime lies in being found out; while they feel further humiliated by the small sum for which he has been disgraced: 'But we have a saying that if you want to eat a toad you should look for a fat and juicy one.' Insofar as they also feel some degree of shame because he has contravened the public code which maintains the outward face of this society, they are altogether unaware that in refusing to find jobs for his kinsmen, Obi would have been maintaining that code and for a while turning his back on the very corruption to which at length he falls victim in a manner which chagrins them.

But the analysis is not complete. In what sense, we must go on to ask, are the village elders 'wrong' in what they expect and demand of Obi? Are they 'wrong' to seek education for their children? If their urge to do so can be held as a virtue, can they in any way be expected to conceive of the new attitudes that education must inevitably lead to? Have they any alternative but to evaluate education in the light of the best that they already know? Does it then make any sense to lay the responsibility for Obi's dilemma at their door?

Who, then, is in a position to evaluate both worlds and make some attempt to bring them together – those with or those without formal education? In spite of the fact that Obi has undoubtedly been put in a false position, he has been put there in good faith, and it is only he who could hope to make coherent sense out of this new and complex situation: but he fails to do so. If we can imagine that a reconciliation between the two worlds is possible, and if we admit that the only candidate for the role of go-between is the educated man, Obi has not lived up to the challenge.

Inevitably, a study of *No Longer at Ease* becomes to a considerable extent a character study of Obi, since the whole development of the novel hinges on his lack of faith in himself. The most perceptive and subtle analysis I have seen of Obi Okonkwo is by Abiola Irele:[2]

> Obi's dilemma is contained in the conflict between his developed intellectual insight and his lack of moral strength to sustain it. . . . His weakness of character is reflected in his inept handling of his human relationships and of his material problems; he is an individual with no sense of order. . . .

Obi is never really prepared to engage in any sort of sustained effort, with the result that he flounders through his life.

This study, some aspects of which are reflected in Killam's later sketch,[3] is part of Irele's search for classical tragic heroes in Achebe's novels, and consequently he regards the character of Obi as being to a large extent a creative failure. This to me illustrates the dangers of criticism which aims at classification, since I do not think that Achebe is trying to make Obi a tragic hero in a stoic mould, and so the fact that he has not done so is beside the point. And I find some contradiction in Abiola Irele's assertion that Obi is 'a pathetic figure' followed almost at once by the statement that 'the emotion that he inspires is not pity but antipathy'.[4]

One of the weaknesses of *No Longer at Ease*, however, is that, while it presents characters with whom we can sympathise, we are not allowed to get very close to them nor to care about them very much as individuals. Obi is in fact rather a cold fish, and we are not invited to regard any of the other personae from the inside. This would be a more serious fault if the book were essentially about private personalities and clashes; but, like *Things Fall Apart*, its real concern is with movements and confrontations within the fabric of society. Obi and the Umuofia Progressive Union represent two different social orders, two different sets of assumptions as to what society is and should be.

Both these concepts are shown to be deeply faulted. It is not difficult, with the help of Achebe's earlier novel, to conceive of the kind of life that the members of the Union think they are standing out for. But the things that they would claim to be defending have not only fallen apart, the pieces have been taken and built up into shoddy, jumbled structures bearing little resemblance either to coherent tradition or to ordered modernity. On the other hand, Obi pins himself to a half-baked intellectualism, with grand but vague ideals supported by little precise thinking. He would no doubt shine in a debate about principles but is hardly even a beginner in the art of the possible.

Christopher scorns Obi's literary arguments, not 'based on factual or scientific analysis':[5] his own hard-bitten realism, we learn later, excludes the possibility of marrying an osu. Obi maintains – it is a major thread of structural irony – that the only way to get rid of corruption is to replace the old men, 'who have no intellectual foundations to support their experience' and who get to the top through 'an ordeal by bribery', by university men (' "I didn't say *straight* from the university" '); not on the grounds that they are more pure at heart, but because 'they can afford to be virtuous' and 'even that kind of virtue can become a habit'. Obi has all the right sentiments: 'Education for service, not for white-collar jobs and comfortable salaries'. Indeed, he quite genuinely is not a snob and eagerly moves out of the hotel to stay with Joseph (hurting his patrons' pride in the process). He despairs of popular education as a means to salvation, however, since it takes effect too slowly:

> 'Where does one begin? With the masses? Educate the masses?' He shook his head. . . . 'It would take centuries.'

But Obi's stock of idealism is supported by no real concern for other human beings as people. He asserts himself, not his fellowship with others. He slights the feelings of his kindred by arriving at his reunion in his shirt-sleeves, but learns nothing from this blunder, since he repeats it in attending his first union meeting. He is intemperate, ineffectually high-minded at his interview for a job. He had once imagined himself combating alien politicians by shouting, ' "Go away, you are all bloody hypocrites!" ' His heart glows with pride in hearing Umuofia praised and he longs to return – but contrives to stay only four days on his visit home. He realises that 'Sometimes a lie was kinder than the truth' but does not act on this knowledge.

What makes Obi's lack of tact so alarming is that such thoughtlessness characterises the complete absence of any serious initiative by either side to try and understand the other or to seek to comprehend its problems. The Union does not attempt to work out the simple arithmetic of its conflicting demands upon Obi, which are at the root of his dilemma at the practical level, a starting point which they could certainly reach. Similarly, when Obi goes home, we surely feel that he must have been in his time a very poor student of literature if he now understands so little of the human problems that confront him, and fails to sense the need of him, the love for him – however obsessive – with which the air is charged. He is callow and entirely occupied with his own concerns, which ensures that he will never be able to resolve them, since they involve others.

But what chance does Obi really have? This question, I believe, is linked to the reasons why Achebe makes the position of the osu even more crucial in this second novel than in his first. His purpose in doing so is not immediately obvious. As long as one conceives the central theme of *No Longer at Ease* as being whether 'the man of two worlds' can resist temptation in the form of bribes amidst the complex economic pressures which are the result of his divided responsibilities, the question of traditional taboos is largely beside the point; and we may even suspect the author of seizing upon it as an opportunist device to swell his material since in this perspective whether Clara is an osu or not must appear at best to be a side-issue. And so our respect for Achebe's craftsmanship increases as we come to grasp the intended place of this element in the thematic structure.

As in *Things Fall Apart*, there is a deep-seated contradiction in the people's retention of tradition, since far from 'clutching at their gods', they have adopted the imported religion, in all its external forms at least. The Umuofia Progressive Union starts its meetings with a Christian prayer and sends Obi off to England in the odour of sanctity. They stand in danger of getting the worst of both worlds, as does Isaac Okonkwo in uncompromisingly asserting Christian dogma (' "Here is a little child returned from wrestling in the spirit world and you sit there blabbing about Christian house and idols, talking like a man whose palm-wine has gone into his nose" '), and yet upholding the ancient tribal abhorrence of marriage to an osu. 'When two cultures meet,' said Chinua Achebe to Robert Serumaga during a broadcast in February 1967, 'you would expect, if we were angels, shall we say, we could pick out the best in the other and retain the best in our own, and this would be wonderful. But this doesn't happen often. What happens is that some of the worst elements of the old are retained and some of the worst of the new are added on to them.'[6]

However great Obi's personal responsibility may be, there are certain points at least upon which reconciliation between the two generations and the two sets of experience is impossible: conflicting assumptions, convictions and standards of right and wrong are too deep-seated on either side. Surely we must agree that Obi has some obligation to try to balance his way of life so as to accommodate the feelings and wishes, within reason, of the traditional community in which he has his roots. If we go on to ask whether Obi ought to give in to them on this point of prejudice against the osu, when such submission would radically alter both his life and hers, we come to the heart of the matter. Yet what hope is there that the elders will compromise on a question such as this, or that Obi's mother will ever comprehend his point of view, or even be able to conceive that he has a tenable point of view at all? To her it cannot seem other than that he is being wilful and stubborn, even so far as to be prepared to sacrifice his own parents. At the very core of *No Longer at Ease* we find the same awareness of the complementary, and indeed inter-dependent, good and bad features in the very fabric of both ways of life that exists at the centre of *Things Fall Apart*.

Yet at the last we remain uneasy about Obi's place in this confrontation, less because he refuses to submit on a matter of principle which has serious implications in specific human lives, than because when all is said and done he himself is not sufficiently committed either to his family or to Clara herself. Obi handles every attempt to lay before his people his determination to marry an osu extremely badly, both through cowardice and arrogance. He allows his parents to hear the news from Joseph's letter instead of breaking it gently himself. Each time the matter is raised in the homestead, it is his father or mother who start the discussion, so that Obi is left on the wrong foot, on the defensive. He reacts to their opposition by sulking, and insulting the neighbours by refusing to see them. His own attitudes are expressed to his father in coldly intellectual terms; he behaves like an outsider and never begins to explain the reasons for his choice in positive or intimate terms which might influence the older folk. The Christian resistance to marrying an osu is, of course, illogical, but Obi has foreseen it and when the time comes behaves nevertheless more like a cross-grained schoolteacher than a mature and devoted son trying to win over his family through love and affection. 'His mind was troubled not only by what happened but also by the discovery that there was nothing in him with which to challenge it honestly.' His education fails him utterly at this time of real test. He runs to the city early, confirming his complex inability to cope with the human situation. We are actually told that he gets pleasure from overbearing his father:[7]

> He waited for his father to speak that he might put up another fight to justify himself. . . for it was true what the Ibos say, that when a coward sees a man he can beat he becomes hungry for a fight.

In rather the same way, once Joseph expresses hostility to the idea of his proposed marriage, 'Obi felt better and more confident in his decision now that there was an opponent.'

Obi does not have any great emotional subtlety or depth, and he turns out to be an inadequate lover (except at a purely physical level) or protector of the social outcast. His early clumsiness in dancing is characteristic of his general lack of grace. It is far from incidental that the first sequence of the novel tells us that 'he had recently lost his mother, and Clara had gone out of his life.' There has been little justification for breaking his mother's heart over his choice of a fiancée when immediately afterwards he alienates and rejects Clara more finally than even traditional society had done. 'Against an irrational caste system,' as Abiola Irele puts it,[8] 'that demands of him a firm rational stand, against the pressure of a moral problem that calls for individual resolution, Obi has nothing to offer but abdication.' If Obi had had a richer relationship with Clara and with his own family, instead of remaining ultimately detached from both, he would have had a much better chance of reconciling the opposed sets of attitudes in his fragmented environment. 'His submission on the issue of Clara, and his subsequent betrayal of her (and the cause involved in her problem) opens the wide road to his moral decline. He knows what is right, but is unable to stand up for it.'[9]

Obi takes no one into his confidence. He dithers and lets everything go by default. When he decides to stop making repayments to the Union, he is convinced that 'Everyone understood family commitments'[10] yet he decides against making a clean breast of it. If they didn't sympathise 'it was just too bad', but how could they sympathise if they were told nothing? He confides in Christoper about Clara's pregnancy, and then determines also to tell the Hon. Sam Okoli, but changes his mind because of the need for secrecy and rushes to the telephone to ensure that Christopher will preserve their anonymity. This indecisiveness is something we can well sympathise with since it is a failing we all share to some extent. But with Obi it extends so far as to affect the nature and quality of his commitment to Clara. As he watches her being driven away by the doctor who is to undertake the abortion, Obi feels the urge to dash out of his car and shout, ' "Stop. Let's go and get married now," but he couldn't and didn't' – though an emotional display of some sort to support his supposed love for her would, we feel, be very appropriate. But once the car is out of sight he can and does follow it in a wild-goose chase which is as abortive as every aspect of this affair.

Clara has been more graceful and tactful than Obi in the way she lends him money as compared to his conventional and self-proud rejection of her gesture; and she is generous in the way she accepts the theft while he crumples up. When they talk together at the crisis of their relationship, there is no doubt who has the positive personality and who has not:

> 'Come and sit down, Clara. Let's not be childish. And please don't make things more difficult for me.'
> 'You are making things difficult for yourself. How many times did I tell you that we were deceiving ourselves? But I was always told I was being childish. Anyway, it doesn't matter. There is no need for long talk.'

When he tries to save this situation, which is the real test of his character, 'Obi began to say something, but gave it up after three words or so.' They sit in silence for ten minutes and then part. Obi is prepared to let his mother turn her face to the wall in the belief that he will marry an osu since 'for him it was either Clara or nobody', but at a moment of emotional crisis he can do nothing to express or consolidate his passion. We sympathise with Clara at almost every move (with perhaps one exception, when she expresses her 'been-to' snobbery). In Obi Achebe seems sadly to be depicting the educated elite as spineless. He has studied English literature but seems to have learnt surprisingly little in the process. He does not trust Clara; and treats her like a child in pretending that there has been only a temporary set-back between himself and his parents (which she has the sense to recognise at once as an untruth). He does not seem to have moved very far forward from the brief and trivial affairs he had graduated on in England during which he 'seemed to stand outside it all watching the passionate embrace with cynical disdain'.

In all these delicate relationships Obi contrasts unfavourably with the elders of the Union. Whatever reservations we may have about the consistency of their attitudes, the basis of their action in the last resort is human solidarity, at least in so far as the extended family is concerned. Considering the extreme manner in which Obi has reacted to their criticisms, with a determination to slight and humiliate them by his indifference, the deliberate way they rally round when he is in trouble is more than a mere closing of ranks. It expresses a moral maturity and human warmth which must excite our admiration:

> as the President pointed out, a kinsman in trouble had to be saved, not blamed; anger against a brother was felt in the flesh, not in the bone.

Obi, on the other hand, although he was fully aware of the traditional opposition he would meet in marrying an osu, does not make even a single attempt to reason with members of his clan or to modify their predictable but quietly expressed views. Instead, he flounces out of his first meeting with them like a spoilt child at the very first sign of opposition. This way deadlock lies.

The death of Obi's mother again reveals all the protagonist's weaknesses. He thinks only of his own grief and rationalises his refusal to go to the funeral, without thought for the way this will increase the burden upon his father and family, or of the final indignity that he is inflicting on his mother's memory. Once more, he is exposed by the relatively generous humanity of the Union members who, if they cannot restrain themselves from criticising him, at least come together to comfort him by their presence.

So at the last Obi begins to take bribes after the emotional pressures upon him, which might have offered some reason, if not excuse, in our eyes, have been allowed to produce their worst effects with very little resistance on his part. His mother has died in bitterness and been buried ignominiously; Clara has been sacrificed to the abortionist's knife and has retired to a new loneliness. At the nadir of his fortunes, events overcome Obi; his principles prove to be shallow-rooted; he succumbs and falls.

In James Ngugi's *The River Between* secular education is shown, potentially at least, to have a crucial role in the relationship between the world of tradition and the world of more modern ways: Waiyaki's school is not neutral, but is a meeting ground, socially and intellectually inclusive, part of a new dispensation and yet able to respect and even nurture inherited culture, and provide it with peaceful channels through which to assert its rights and its survival value. It is true that Waiyaki is caught out by his own shortcomings, and even more by the contradictions in popular emotional attitudes, swayed by the wiles of a traditional demagogue who is as dangerous to future unity as is the sophistical voice of Siriana or the seductions of the big city. But this lapse, for all that it is in part Waiyaki's own, far from being conclusive, contains the seeds of hope.

In *No Longer at Ease*, on the other hand, the central conflict seems to offer no openings for conciliation, no meeting ground: 'Real tragedy is never resolved. It goes on hopelessly for ever.' We sympathise with Obi because we see the causes of his confusion in the divergent modes of life which he must attempt to co-ordinate, but we still observe his complete failure to make any effective contribution towards establishing a new harmony. If there is to be a coming together, there must be a radical transformation in Obi himself, who surely at his most lucid moments would welcome such a rapprochement. Yet his education seems to have made him less rather than more flexible; it has made him more conscious of his status than his humanity, more anxious to assert his rights than to honour his responsibilities. But a change is also vitally needed on the part of the elders with regard to certain crucial issues which are left untouched by their general humanitarianism: yet there is no indication within the bounds of the novel that such a change is at all likely.

And so *No Longer at Ease*, for all the limitations that may strike us at first acquaintance, opens out in our minds, and reveals layer beneath layer of meaning and understanding. At the last, it offers no solutions, but brings us rather to a point at which we lose interest in simply blaming various groups and characters, since we discover that all are culpable; and that each may in their various ways be exonerated. If at first glance we are willing to join the accusers when we see Obi standing in court, eventually this formal, depersonalised indictment seems irrelevant.

And yet we do not end in vagueness. To understand all is not necessarily to forgive all. We do not forgive the failure in Obi's education, though this novel is not concerned to look into the nature of this breakdown, nor to ask how far the fault lies with the pattern of education itself, how far with Obi, and to what extent the educational process has been corrupted by the social conditioning of the student. Nor do we forgive the petulance with which Obi brushes aside the concerns of others when they are in conflict with his own wishes and intentions. If a new beginning is to be made, someone must make a start. Both from childhood experience and adult study Obi is better placed than others to cross the dividing lines in this sectionalised society.

Yet his personal failure is not necessarily an invitation to despair; it can be seen rather as a direct challenge to a wide sector of Achebe's audience. G. D. Killam rightly claims[11] that Achebe 'causes the reader to identify with the actions and reactions of the characters and make the same discoveries about the nature of things as the characters themselves.' Thus many of those who find in this novel a living experience may feel themselves implicated when it becomes evident that Obi is no more able to minister to the needs of his time than was his grandfather, Okonkwo. He is in a real sense typical: as Gerald Moore remarks,[12] 'Obi Okonkwo is a well-intentioned young man, no weaker-willed than most and anxious to please everybody.' What may have started as a conventional study of a stock character, has grown under Achebe's hands into a disturbing and fully recognisable portrait from our times. So the ending of *No Longer at Ease*, like that of *Things Fall Apart*, has ramifications far wider than the case study of an isolated individual. If at the last, unlike his grandfather, Obi goes out not with a bang but a whimper, in effect a whole educated generation is being thoughtfully called to account.

NOTES

1 *N.L.A.E.*, p. 6; the following four quotations are from pp. 32 ('an investment. . .'), 7 ('They wanted him to read law. . .'), 32 ('Every town and village. . .'), and 6 ('But we have a saying. . .').

2 Abiola Irele, 'The Tragic Conflict in Achebe's Novels', *Black Orpheus*; reprinted in *Introduction to African Literature*, ed. Ulli Beier, Longman, London, 1967, pp. 172–3.

3 G. D. Killam, *The Novels of Chinua Achebe*, H.E.B., 1969, pp. 50–1: 'The core of the novel is the moral dilemma in which Obi finds himself and the conflict in the novel is produced by the clash between the strength of his moral awareness on the one hand and his almost total lack of moral courage in sustaining it . . . he oscillates at critical moments.'

4 Abiola Irele, *op. cit.*, p. 174.

5 *N.L.A.E.*, p. 20; the following nine quotations are from pp. 20 ('who have no intellectual foundations. . . '), 20 ('I didn't say straight. . .'), 21 ('an ordeal by bribery'), 21 ('even that kind of virtue. . .'), 32 ('Education for service. . .)', 43–4, 56 ('Go away. . .'), 57 ('Sometimes a lie was kinder. . . .'), and 51 ('Here is a little child. . .').

6 *African Writers Talking*, ed. Dennis Duerden and Cosmo Pieterse, H.E.B., 1972, p. 13.

7 *N.L.A.E.*, p. 137; the two following quotations are from pp. 72 ('Obi felt better. . .'), and 2 ('he had recently lost. . .').

8 Abiola Irele, *op. cit.*, p. 173.

9 *Ibid.*

10 *N.L.A.E.*, p. 156; the following six quotations are from pp. 149 ('Stop. Let's go. . .'), 143, 75 ('for him it was either Clara. . .'), 70 ('seemed to stand outside. . .'), 5, and 39 ('Real tragedy. . .').

11 G. D. Killam, *op. cit.*, p. 11.

12 *Seven A.W.*, p. 67.

CHAPTER 5

A New Earth

A study of Ngugi wa Thiong'o's *A Grain of Wheat*

ONE of the things a serious novel, or any work of art, must concern itself with to some extent is discerning connections and patterns amid the apparently shapeless mass of day-to-day experience, and examining the relationships between one event and another. *A Grain of Wheat* is even more involved in this searching and questioning than many works. Ngugi realises that human beings are reluctant to acknowledge any design in existence:[1]

> Previously [Mugo] liked to see events in his life as isolated. Things had been fated to happen at different moments. One had no choice in anything as surely as one had no choice on one's birth. He did not, then, tire his mind by trying to connect what went before with what followed after.

After all, to admit that one thing proceeds from another in a related sequence is also to accept that we might have some influence on this sequence, to accept responsibility. And men fear responsibility. This is why Warui resents the old woman's claim that her son has returned to her. 'Things of yesterday,' he insists, 'should remain with yesterday.' But Ngugi does not want us to run away so easily. Karanja, the man who betrays his people by becoming a chief and working with the white man during the emergency, is the character in the novel whose life most obviously amounts to waste and failure, swayed as he is by the impulse of the moment, living only in the present situation, solving only the immediate problems which disturb his comfort; and so it is Karanja who at last walks out of the novel aimlessly, heading nowhere:

> Thompson has gone, I have lost Mumbi. His mind hopped from image to image, following no coherent order. Incidents in his life would pop up and then disappear.

95

Mugo, on the other hand – Mugo, who is also a betrayer, weighed down by an insupportable sense of guilt – resolves the meaningless muddle of his life. The moment at the trench when, beyond all reason, he makes his futile attempt to protect the pregnant woman from being beaten by the guard, is a moment of moral commitment. Again, there is his ironic and profoundly sad vision of himself atoning for his guilt by becoming the awaited saviour:

> It was he, Mugo, spared to save people like Githua, the old woman, and any who had suffered. Why not take the task? Yes. He would speak at the Uhuru celebrations. He would lead the people and bury his past in their gratitude.

Inevitably he abandons this brave project when he discovers that his uhuru speech is to be the occasion for the public accusation of Karanja for the crime Mugo himself had in fact committed. But the vision reveals to us the man buried within Mugo.

These earlier occasions lead up to the simple, stark, carefully prepared, yet breathtaking climax, when Mugo voluntarily confesses himself before the uhuru congregation. And Ngugi emphasises that, for all its terror, this is the moment when the events in Mugo's life fall into place. It is a brief experience, but time enough for the metal of his existence to run into a new mould:

> As soon as the first words were out, Mugo felt light. A load of many years was lifted from his shoulders. He was free, sure, confident. . . . He was conscious of himself, of every step he made, of the images that rushed and whirled through his mind with only one constant thread: so he was responsible for whatever he had done in the past, for whatever he would do in the future. The consciousness frightened him.

The fear is justified. The acceptance of responsibility is fatal to Mugo. 'Your deeds alone will condemn you,' says General R., '. . . No one will ever escape from his own actions.' Mugo does not escape. But his dignified acceptance, his calm facing of his actions, changes the whole significance of his life.

Throughout the novel Ngugi weaves for us a pattern in time, with the present as the warp and the past as the woof. It would be quite wrong to refer to this interplay between different periods as 'flashbacks'. A flashback is a rather worn-out mechanical technique for overcoming a narrator's problems in telling his story. But the interlocking of different phases of

time is essential to all that *A Grain of Wheat* has to say to us. To see someone as a hero or a villain is always an over-simplification: it is to see him
at one time, in one set of circumstances only; but a man is more than one
thing. In counterpointing various aspects of his characters' lives in *A Grain
of Wheat*, Ngugi calls on us to moderate callow judgments of the individuals
with a more profound human compassion; not least because in a true summary we ourselves are in desperate need of this same compassion. This is
his major theme. And secondly he begs us to move out of a period of simple
heroics into the much more baffling and complex realities of our independence, where we have again to face the hard facts of human greed, selfishness,
deceit and self-deceit, where the enemy is now ourselves, but where we
can still find love and community if we will only stop shouting slogans
and living in the past.

The links across time which play such an important part in the whole
structure of the novel are of many kinds. There are the parallels and contrasts between similar events at different periods. The two races in which
Karanja and Gikonyo meet are an obvious example. The first race brought
Gikonyo and Mumbi passionately, idyllically together. Both are now aware
of the alienation between them; and yet the second race and the broken
arm are to be the means of their reconciliation. Karanja sees the second race
over-optimistically as a chance to right the balance that went against him
in the first. The trains that rumble across so many scenes pull many images
and counter-images behind them. Retributive footsteps echo inexorably
behind the guilty.

In the opening scene we see Mugo preparing his morning uji.

> But whenever he took it, he remembered the half-cooked porridge he
> ate in detention. How time drags, everything repeats itself, Mugo thought;
> the day ahead would be just like yesterday and the day before.

So at the outset we meet with mockery of the whole sense of pattern and
purpose which the novel sets out to rediscover. 'Where,' wonders Mugo
as he sits eyeing his shamba,[8] 'was the fascination he used to find in the soil
before the emergency?'

Eventually, however, the carving of the stool which Gikonyo plans in
detention ties the final hopeful stroke of the novel to the whole past;
optimism grows out of despair: it has roots.

The first, short division of the book has a very special function. It introduces, as a collection of disjointed hints, themes which are later to be

explored in depth. In this first part the sadness, confusion, fear and bewilderment of the characters is deliberately unexplained, and so, as far as we are concerned at this stage, their conduct is unrelated to any scale of praise and blame. Ngugi activates our sympathies in this unknown context for these crushed and lost human beings – Mugo, Gikonyo, Mumbi, Kihika, General R., Karanja.

Later the uhuru celebrations will be brilliantly employed as a focus to bring all these individuals together in terms of actions and consequences; but for the present they are evoked as feeling entities without our grasping coherently any narrative sequence. Rather we recognise their motivations as springing from the way they are trapped (like all of us) in a complex set of controlling circumstances and emotional tensions, and for this purpose we do not neeed to know exactly what these circumstances are. And so when the plot emerges – and a powerful plot it is – those whom we might have pilloried as 'guilty' are already within the ambit of our sympathetic concern, and we are in a position to compare, in their favour, the pressures upon them and the struggles they have undergone with those of externally 'blameless' characters. And when we hear of Gikonyo in 'ghost-ridden Rung'ei' on his return from detention, we already know these ghosts – they are our ghosts too. From the very start the novel is not to be concerned with judgment, but with understanding, though its own values are made apparent both subtly and forcefully.

Some of these memories depend on the same place being seen at two different times. Mugo wanders along the derelict trench as uhuru approaches and it is this that recalls the violent scene of his arrest. Particularly suggestive is the recurrent image of Mugo stopping outside the old woman's house, hesitantly compassionate and yet reluctant to commit himself, a contradiction which is central to his whole character. Indeed when Ngugi first presents this scene it runs in tiers into the past. As Mugo walks by her hut in the present, the Sunday before uhuru, we hear the story of her deaf son being shot down in the emergency; then of Mugo's agitation on seeing the old woman when he returned to the village, and again of his visit to her with provisions; the sight of her sleeping place reminds him of his own terrifying childhood (of which we are soon to hear more); we move once more to the end of the first visit and so again to the present, when his resolution to enter falters. 'There was a bond between her and him, perhaps because she, like him, lived alone.'

This bond of loneliness and reluctant compassion runs right through Mugo's life. So there is symbolic significance when he makes his final visit to her – the only person to greet her on uhuru day – and she dies in the act of mistaking him for her own son come back to her, the deaf son butchered by the emergency forces.

Again, the visit of the elders which causes Mugo so much terror at the end of the first chapter is echoed by the last visit of General R. and Lieutenant Koinandu in which that fear is fulfilled and resolved. The first visit brought the invitation to speak at the uhuru gathering; the last visit is the result of Mugo's having spoken.

Finally there are those events in the novel which are seen from more than one point of view. What Kihika's meeting with Mugo was thought to be like, and what it was really like. The villagers dancing around Mugo's hut and hymning his heroism; and our later glimpse of Mugo inside the hut abject with fear and remorse. Thompson's brusque memorandum of having spat in an informer's face; and Mugo's memory of the traumatic meeting. The two accounts of Lieutenant Koinandu's raping of Dr Lynd. An event is thus not to be regarded as something absolute which can be observed, neatly recorded and judged. Ngugi is a creative technician in fiction, providing his own method for presenting the same scenes in different ways to reveal to us the many-sidedness of experience.

It is General R. who passes the last sentence that we hear upon Mugo: 'Your deeds alone will condemn you.' Yet General R. himself in his youth had had to leave his village because he attempted to kill his own father. Who then is guiltless? Gikonyo confesses the oath and his own footfalls haunt him. Mumbi submitted to Karanja. Lieutenant Koinandu raped Dr Lynd. Thompson betrayed his own cause as well as humanity's in Rira; and Mrs Thompson betrayed her husband. The list could be lengthened. And, while the emergency was a unique situation, we do not feel that these individuals are exceptionally or unbelievably evil. We can explain psychologically – and sympathetically – the state of mind that led to these doings in each case.

Certainly all are guilty – perhaps only one major character can be seen as free from guilt, but I will return to this exception. Man is a potentially violent and dangerous animal, whether he is black or white, young or old; whether he manipulates great or little power: Mugo's aunt and General R.'s father go to the limits of their tyrannical means. If deaf Gitogo is callously mowed down; then Mugo harbours in his heart the passionate desire to kill his aunt. Each of us has a coiled spring within him; if most of us can deliberately direct this pent-up energy into positive channels and release any surplus at worst in daydreams, we should rejoice that we have the opportunity to do so; and we must recognise nevertheless the potentially destructive force within ourselves if we are to understand the pressures existing inside other people and thereby find ourselves in a position to minister to our society. Self-righteous condemnation of those whose latent savageness un-coils viciously when exploited by circumstances will do nothing to improve the human condition.

There are, it is true, extremities of conduct which must be regarded as the outcome of mental sickness, and can be compared only to the random force of chance. Fate leaving a child without parents or letting a life be crushed by a passing train can be paralleled by the reckless and senseless savagery of men: Robson, the guards in the detention camp or at the trench, Karanja's gun-lust. Yet in the main *A Grain of Wheat* presents guilty humanity to our compassion not our righteous anger, since we are all seen as partaking of a common corruption. In T. S. Eliot's *The Cocktail Party*, Reilly, who is both psycho-analyst and, by implication, father confessor, tells his patients,[2]

> Your business is not to clear your conscience
> But to learn how to bear the burdens on your conscience.

In the same way Ngugi, in effect, reminds his readers that it is not for human beings to claim innocence, but to face up to the implications of our shared guilt. So we feel concern for Ngugi's characters not because they suffer undeservedly, but because they are both guilty and self-aware. It is much more terrible to know that you are guilty than to be unjustly accused. The latter is someone else's miscarriage of justice; the former is like your own vote of no confidence on yourself.

And so *A Grain of Wheat* can guide our feelings along that difficult path: partial identification with people whom one does not readily like, and with confused characters whose conduct in some part we repudiate. In the former group we can count the naif idealist Thompson whose vision crumbles in the face of a reality he cannot contact; and his wife, whose sordid affair with Van Dyke evokes not so much disgust as pity, or even a sort of grudging admiration for her defiant gesture against life's dismal disillusionments.

Even Karanja is alarmingly comprehensible: we recognise so many of his minor actions and reactions from our own self-awareness. As he sits nauseated, unable to eat, in the greasy restaurant in Githima on uhuru day, the day he did all he could to delay, we are pained at the sight of this fellow human being slumped amid the ruins of his life, which he has wrecked through his own actions, so that he has not even the wry consolation of blaming forces outside himself. Step by step he has created this situation; by his selfish neglect of his mother; his over-confident, careless delay in wooing Mumbi; his desperate embracing of the colonialists' cause because he convinces himself they are invincible; his abject clinging to the coat-tails of the white man at Githima. Yet for all our loathing of his cruelty towards his own people as a chief, we are not asked to stand up at the last and utter judgment upon him in holy anger. Instead we are presented with a broken, self-defeated man whose moral plight wins our pity, if he can never hope to gain our respect.

Through penetrating human sadness, the novel encourages us to adopt a tolerant perspective on man's delinquency. If we comprehend how men suffer, we shall not want to gloat even over a Karanja in his fall. And it is the other characters in the book who anticipate us in this sympathetic understanding. A miniature example is General R.'s reaction to the discovery that Githua has for years been playing upon their charity by pretending to have been shot by the security forces. General R. has no blame for Githua:[3]

> 'It makes his life more interesting to himself. He invents a meaning for his life, you see. Don't we all do that? And to die fighting for freedom sounds more heroic than to die by accident.'

'Don't we all do that?' – this is the hidden refrain of the book. Who can exonerate himself when all are guilty? A sense of our own guilt induces in us understanding and sympathy for the backslidings of others.

It is this concern, perhaps, more than anything else which elects Mugo as the central figure of the novel. We know a great deal about his shrivelled, frightened, unfulfilled existence before we guess at his crime. His guilt creeps into our consciousness on waves of his perpetual terror, a terror which brings us close to him in the melting pot of raw human emotion. This guilt, then, does not come to us as in a newspaper report which we can assess objectively, but as a gnawing awareness of self-shame. We are not Mugo's judges but his equals. And this too is how the other characters see him, the very people he has betrayed most deeply and have most reason to recoil from him. 'He seems to be a courageous man,' admits Karanja; and Mumbi agrees: 'Yees!' Wambui, utterly steadfast in her devotion to the cause, at length has doubts after Mugo has paid both for his deed and for his final honesty in confessing it: 'Perhaps we should not have tried him.'

But it is Gikonyo, in one of the key passages of the novel, who really pronounces Mugo's funeral oration:

'He was a brave man, inside,' he said. 'He stood before much honour, praises were heaped on him. He would have become a chief. Tell me another person who would have exposed his soul for all the eyes to peck at.' He paused and let his eyes linger on Mumbi. Then he looked away and said, 'Remember that few people in that meeting are fit to lift a stone against that man. Not unless I – we – too – in turn open our hearts naked for the world to look at.

Gikonyo is still struggling to come to terms with the knowledge that Mumbi has borne Karanja's child. He is, also, still seething with the awareness of his dishonourable capitulation to the authorities in the detention camp. He hates himself. His self-pride is deeply hurt. And he attempts to reassert this pride by projecting all his own guilt onto Mumbi, making her the scapegoat for his weakness; and so he magnifies her failure. Gikonyo has justified his betrayal of his compatriots in the prison by idealising Mumbi, to whom he wished to return. But Mumbi too has gone through the mill of experience: she is not simple and pure: she has suffered and faltered. In his disappointment, Gikonyo heaps all his inner rage against himself on her – an all too familiar form of self-delusion. He clings obstinately to the hard core of pride within him. He cares more about vindicating himself by condemning Mumbi than he does about her as his wife, or as another troubled and imperfect individual. So he shuts his ears and his mind and his heart to the detailed knowledge of what really happened to her; to know all may be to forgive all, and he does not wish to forgive her, since he has not yet learned to forgive himself.

To accept forgiveness one must admit that one is not self-sufficient. But Gikonyo cannot humble his masculine arrogance so far as to confess his need. A true marriage demands that a husband and wife shall share not only their strengths, but also their fears and their inadequacies. Instead, because Mumbi is not absolutely pure, Gikonyo condemns her as absolutely impure, ignoring mitigating circumstances, admitting no degrees in human responsibility. And so, in our eyes, Gikonyo takes on himself the responsibility for refusing to mend their marriage, which is far from being past repair, given a little understanding and humility on both sides – for who is Gikonyo to set himself up as a righteous man when those accusing footsteps dog his conscience?

Natural and convincing as Gikonyo's and Mumbi's early courtship is, it has also an idealistic quality. It is a real relationship between two human beings, rooted in gentle understanding, consummated in passionate emotion. The scene in Rung'ei woods when the two make love is an image of human union. When it is split, therefore, the situation between them takes on an importance over and above our liking for them as individuals; and their reconciliation makes the proper conclusion to the whole novel. It is genuinely hopeful without being sentimental, since we see the steps by which each finds the way back to the other. Love and understanding must conquer pride. Gikonyo's perception of the true nature of Mugo's self-sacrifice is an important stage in his revaluation of his marriage; but it is Mumbi who first breaks down her fierce and natural resistance to her husband's behaviour. She submits to her mother's entreaties and continues her visits to Gikonyo in hospital. But at first he is choked by all the bitterness within him and cannot respond. 'But after Mugo's confession, he found himself trying to puzzle out Mumbi's thoughts and feelings.' And the symbolic idea of the carving he wished to make for her returns to him. He finds he misses her when she does not come to the ward one day. And so his stubborn, individualistic, arrogant anger slowly melts. He finds himself blurting out not just a tentative call to Mumbi, but words which go to the heart of the thing which divides them: 'Let us talk about the child.' The division is at an end, and the woman's figure on the stool is to be a pregnant mother.

The second major theme in *A Grain of Wheat* is related to public responsibility, just as our discussion so far has emphasised private responsibility.

Are we going to take the benefits of uhuru for granted? Are we going to lean on the achievements of those who fought for freedom without facing the new challenge which their success has created? If so, we shall be bitterly disappointed. We shall find the new power magnate taking over from the old, and acquiring the white man's estate for himself, not helping the co-operative group to purchase it. We shall be saying with Mugo, 'the day ahead would be just like yesterday, and the day before.' We may even find ourselves asking with the deflated Karanja, 'Was death like that Freedom? Was going to detention freedom?'

Ngugi warns us that rallying slogans of the fight become mere empty escapism after the fight is won. We must look forward to the next thing to do, not go through the motions of what has already been well done and completed. The last Biblical quotation introducing the final section of the novel is from Revelation: 'And I saw a new heaven and a new earth: for the first heaven and the first earth were passed away.' And this new world demands a new response. The heroic moment is past. The time has come for less dramatic, more painstaking, detailed, complex thought and effort. We are in danger of opting out into mere cynicism:[4]

> 'In the name of blackman's freedom, I salute you.' Then he bowed several times in comic deference.

This and many other passages have a deeper irony when we reread the novel; but Ngugi himself is not at all sceptical of the value of heroism at a time when heroism is appropriate. I said earlier that only one character in the book appears to be free from guilt, and this is Kihika: it is Wambuku's inadequacy that she cannot follow him, not Kihika's fault that he must pursue his destiny. *A Grain of Wheat* pays tribute to those who fought, however criss-crossed the moral threads may be. Kihika is not in the event tested amid the more complex demands of peace. He dies during Mau Mau while the sort of heroic absolutes of urgent action which come naturally to his extrovert and ambitious nature are still relevant. Ngugi thus preserves him as a model leader in combat. He may be self-assertive, he may be un-compromising and violent, but he is not guilty because his conduct of affairs represents what was necessary in the given situation; and he has no chance to show whether his idealism and dedication could have been tempered by the different requirements of very different circumstances. For the time of clear-cut, unambiguous issues is past once and for all when uhuru arrives: the novel is structured in such a way as to emphasise this. And so Ngugi's main character is an anti-hero. He contradicts any simplification of the moral issues before us. He draws from us compassion, not cheers.

Perhaps both Kihika and Mugo are grains of wheat, each sacrificing themselves in their own fashion so that others may be regenerated. If the Kenya of uhuru has been 'quickened' to life by the death of Kihika and his kind; then the new vision inherent in the reunion of Gikonyo and Mumbi – representative figures in this context whose very names make them arche-types – is 'quickened' by Mugo's readiness to face the final implications of his new-found, hard-won integrity. In *A Grain of Wheat* the military struggle is in the past; the seeds of war have borne fruit; the harvest has been reaped. What, asks the novel, of the next crop? That which must now be sown and tended is to be weathered in the new climate of independence and must feed the demands of peace. The old Kenya is dead: has the new Kenya been 'quickened'? Are the living willing and able to nurture their inheritance?

Mugo is an anti-hero in two senses. First because he himself is taken by surprise by his own defiant bravery in the face of inhumanity – most obviously when he futilely leaps to the defence of Wambuku against the trench guards. And secondly through his being miscast by Rung'ei in the role of hero, an irony which forms one of the main structural features of the novel. His truest moment of heroism is when he publicly confesses his betrayal of Kihika. This is the opposite of the heroism of the battlefield: it is the heroism of admitting our guilt and weakness.

The problems of peace and reconstruction are problems of human relationships. If we approach civil affairs with the heroics of a campaign, we are running away, we are thrusting the responsibility on others; and we shall end disillusioned in the hands of cynics and demagogues.

During the Emergency, Kihika had realised that violence could be justified only if it were seen as a painful necessity, in which one participated as a sort of ritual sacrifice. Though many simply indulged their ruthless passions and were defiled; some at least comprehended the nature of the ordeal:

> how many took the oath and are now licking the toes of the whiteman? No, you take an oath to confirm a choice already made. The decision to lay or not to lay your life for the people lies in the heart. The oath is the water sprinkled on a man's head at baptism.

The theme of violence runs continuously through the book, an endless cycle of mere destruction. Karanja has given vent to his sensual delight in inflicting pain, and is himself pursued by fear of retribution:

> As a boy, once, Karanja saw dogs tear a rabbit. They tore its limbs and each dog ran with blood-covered pieces. Karanja now saw himself as that rabbit.

General R. is left momentarily tongue-tied in his uhuru speech by the memory of the raw savagery of the butchering of the Rev. Jackson Kigondu. But this does not teach him to withhold vengeance when it has ceased to be meaningful or necessary: Mugo dies.

Violence is the most terrifying, but not the only pattern of conduct which is continued after it has been emptied of all positive significance. The villagers gather hopefully for the uhuru ceremony: 'We sang song after song about Kihika and Mugo. A calm united our hearts.' But they are fed with a mechanical, complacent, lifeless representation of the Christian religion in

Kigori's piece of shallow rhetoric. Yet, symbolically, the traditional rituals are also eventually enacted without conviction:

> The field was so empty. Only four (or were we five?) left. We slaughtered the rams – and prayed for our village. But it was like warm water in the mouth of a thirsty man. It was not what I had waited for, these many years.

It is, in fact, Mugo who works the awaited transformation in many hearts, and points the complicated way to peaceful commitment. He makes the difficult transition from chosen isolation to voluntary self-sacrifice. 'Why should Kihika drag me into a struggle and problems I have not created?' he asks after the fateful visit. This same man faces a much surer danger when he accepts his responsibility to other men, even his enemy:

> In his mind, everything was clear and final. He would stand there and publicly own the crime. He held on to this vision. Nothing, not even the shouting and the songs and the praises would deflect him from this purpose. It was the clarity of this vision which gave him courage as he stood before the microphone and the sudden silence.

The insistence on the visionary aspect of his determination is important. This way, if any, lies the new heaven and the new earth. Ultimately public and private responsibility cannot be divided. We know the effect of Mugo's self-exposure on the key characters. Even Kihika's mother is overcome:

> They bent down their heads and avoided his eyes. Wanjiku wept. ('It was his face, not the memory of my son that caused my tears,' she told Mumbi later.)

The novel can therefore end hopefully. The final chapter which resolves the fundamental issues between private individuals, is entitled 'Harambee', symbolising communal dedication. Mumbi and Gikonyo resolve their human misunderstandings in a new harmony. Mumbi has set her face against revenge upon her brother's betrayer, because she is convinced that this is the last thing that Kihika himself would have wished. And Rung'ei, on the verge of gloating over Karanja as the victim of just such a revenge, instead comes away from Mugo's confession with humility and respect.

A Grain of Wheat is a well planned and well constructed novel. In his early writings Ngugi's scenes were too brief and disjointed to allow of truly intimate development of character; though *The River Between* and the short stories show an awareness of the essential interdependence of one situation upon another. In his third novel, without completely breaking with his earlier experiments, he has developed a technique for conveying continuity comparable to a cine-camera following a character from place to place, so that even when the background is constantly shifting, as in the opening chapter, the separate parts are held together by a particular figure.

In deploying language Ngugi has a remarkable ability to get the best of both worlds by combining simplicity with great range and variety. He achieves this by a spontaneous but courageous use of the full spectrum of English structures. If we take as material for detailed investigation the thirteen longer quotations from the novel which I have quoted so far in this chapter (those which have been inset), we shall have a cross-section of samples all chosen for other purposes and yet immediately available for investigation and fairly easy to turn to. These thirteen quotations amount to almost six hundred words which are grouped into more than fifty sentences. The average length of the sentences is thus less than twelve words, and indeed there is only one really long one (of forty-five words in the fourth quotation), while only three others just creep up to or top twenty words.

Ngugi's short sentences use fairly straightforward vocabulary without being self-consciously limited to simple expressions. Most of the longer words are familiar – 'previously', 'incidents', 'celebrations', 'responsible', 'interesting' – while the more specifically literary items are not only infrequent (I found at most no more than fifteen) but are not in fact in the main very remote or uncommon: 'isolated', 'coherent', 'gratitude', 'consciousness', 'heroic', 'linger', 'exposed', 'deference', 'vision', 'clarity'. One such word appearing every four or five lines will hardly deter anyone who is willing to master the difficulties of the book's whole design, yet they ensure that the texture of the writing partakes of the richness of the English language.

If we compare this style with others that also rely on a high proportion of short sentences – Achebe's in the early novels already discussed, or the mode employed by Peter Abrahams – we shall find that the result is very different. For within his short sentences of familiar words Ngugi packs an endlessly varied and sophisticated series of patterns. It is not simply that a fourteen-word sentence is likely to comprise three tightly linked clauses ('But whenever he took it, he remembered the half-cooked porridge he ate in detention'); within the friendly brevity of the units, he unobtrusively introduces highly literary and subtle structures without our consciously noticing that he has done so, and certainly without frightening off even diffident readers. Phrases based on non-finite parts of the verb, especially infinitives, abound ('to confirm a choice already made') and these may even become the subjects of clauses and be balanced against each other ('to die fighting for freedom sounds more heroic than to die by accident' – this instance occurs within convincing colloquial language; or again, 'The decision to lay or not to lay your life for the people lies in the heart').

There are frequent sentence modifiers and sentences opening with subordinate clauses, and we may even find both together as in the sentence just referred to beginning 'But whenever'; or we may have two sentence modifiers ('As a boy, once, Karanja saw dogs tear a rabbit'). Even in lively speech patterns we find unusual ordering of words creating special interest and emphasis ('In the name of black man's freedom, I salute you'). We have grammatically unconventional sentences – 'Only four (or were we five?) left' – an extract which also illustrates the flexible use of punctuation to bring out the full effect of such dramatic arrangements. We find verbal echoes from elsewhere, for instance, most relevantly from the Bible which is a constant point of reference in this novel ('Wanjiku wept.'), as well as rich and telling metaphors and similes. Noun clauses are common. Many verbs are terse and forceful but they range into more complex and meditative tenses (especially 'would' tenses in conveying Mugo's stream of consciousness). Subjects, in keeping with the norms of the language, are usually short, most often being pronouns or names, but, as we have already seen, Ngugi is ready to employ elaborate subjects when this seems apt ('Nothing, not even the shouting and the songs and the praises would deflect him').

These more complex structures are continually clarified and controlled by the use of parallelism and balance at the levels of words, phrases, clauses and sentences: a feature so constant as not to need illustration. Thus Ngugi makes use of all the resources of English, without ever overweighting his sentences or overwhelming his readers. This style is fundamental to the whole achievement of *A Grain of Wheat*.

There are two special difficulties involved in moving backwards and forwards through time, and across from the narrative of one character's experiences to an account of another character, as Ngugi does throughout this novel. Great skill is needed to ensure that the reader is always clear as to which period of time is being referred to. It seems to me that the author has here controlled our movement from past to present and back again, and from one sector of his story to another with great sureness. A young Ugandan teacher-trainee impressed me with his view of the structure of Ngugi's work: he thought of each life-history in the book as a separate petal of a flower, each overlapping with others to form a balanced pattern and each linked at the heart of the design by the action on uhuru day, which serves like the centre of the flower to bind together all the constituent elements. This vision of the work confirms that the patterning of *A Grain of Wheat* is meaningful and satisfying to a wide and varied readership.

Secondly, there is the problem of maintaining interest after a shift in the narrative. The reader may be absorbed in one sequence of events and may be reluctant to be snatched away to another situation by his overlord, the novelist. Where Ngugi falters in *A Grain of Wheat* it does not appear to me to be through inadequate planning but by an occasional abuse of his own techniques. He usually eases us from one scene to another almost imperceptibly, by some connection in place, by the stirring of chords of memory, or by one character confiding in another. However, I would agree with the reviewer who found that the break when Mugo is on the verge of strangling Mumbi leaves us for the moment uneasy at the conduct of the story; though I would deny that time-shifts jar on us more than very occasionally. A more serious objection at that particular point in the story is that for once I find the emotional process to be implausible in its rapidity. There is an almost superhuman readiness on Mumbi's part to forgive Mugo after the physical assault upon her life; and so surely the splitting of this brief scene between pages 210–11 and page 236 makes it all the more difficult for us to grasp and to credit the rapid sequence of feelings which the author is attempting to convey to us in the last of these fragments, which in other respects is most effectively placed. It seems unnatural for a woman to be able to master such a terrifying experience so soon after it has occurred: but if we cannot have more details and if Mumbi is not to be allowed a little more time, then at least it would seem fitting that these tumultuous moments should be related consecutively.

One other important event in the novel which I do not find wholly convincing is Mumbi's surrender to Karanja when he tells her that her husband is at last going to be released. It is not that this is an impossible reaction on her part; but rather that the author seems to take it for granted as natural emotional logic which needs no explanation: I do not find it to be so and expect to see into this psychological paradox more fully.

A sense of loneliness is pervasive in *A Grain of Wheat*, but the causes are various. Mugo's childhood has made him recessive; and he betrays Kihika partly because the latter insists on forcing him uncomfortably out of his obscurity. Gikonyo recoils from the unfamiliar Mumbi into himself, almost with the relief and abdication of despair:[5]

One lived alone, and like Gatu, went into the grave alone. Gikonyo greedily sucked sour pleasure from this reflection which he saw as a terrible revelation. To live and die alone was the ultimate truth.

In the opening pages of the novel Mugo finds that the greyness of everyday existence reminds him of detention; but Gikonyo also has the same reaction more explicitly: 'Thabai was just another detention camp; would he ever get out of it?' And how similar are some of Gikonyo's reflections to what Karanja says to Mumbi in self-justification: 'a time will come when you too will know that every man in the world is alone, and fights alone, to live.' This loneliness may, in fact, be self-appointed, as Wangari points out forcefully to Gikonyo inside his new house; while Karanja leaves his mother alone to go out simply to his own bleak solitariness.

It is our own pain, the novel seems to reiterate, which impels us to hurt others. Both Mugo and Mumbi are romantic dreamers, and at least in moments both achieve their heroic visions. Yet when Mumbi has just opened her secret heart to him,

> Suddenly Mugo wanted to hurt her intensely. He revelled in this mad desire to humiliate her, to make her grovel in the dust: why did she try to drag him into her life, into everybody's life?

When Mumbi returns to her parents, Wangari accuses Gikonyo:

> See how you have broken your home. You have driven a good woman to misery for nothing. Let us now see what profit it will bring you, to go on poisoning your mind with these things when you should have accepted and sought how best to build your life. But you, like a foolish child, have never wanted to know what happened. Or what woman Mumbi really is.

As we have seen, Gikonyo is taking out his own shock and hurt upon Mumbi – a very real shock and hurt which we have experienced with him – and so it is true that he does not want to know the other side of the case: we can agree with what his mother says. But we do not really blame him: blame is irrelevant: the pain he gives Mumbi increases his own.

Dr Lynd treats her African staff badly because she has been ravished in body and mind. Thompson is broken and disappointed and behaves accordingly. Karanja desperately tells Mumbi, as she reports to Mugo, that he had 'saved himself from detention and forests for me', and in his frustration he lets himself go as far as Robson in giving rein to his sadism: walking out on his mother is in some twisted way a salve to his own failure and bitterness.

One form of suffering is guilt, suffering which drives people very hard: Mugo, Gikonyo, General R. over the killing of the Rev. Jackson, Lieutenant Koinandu over raping Dr Lynd, Mrs Thompson over her infidelity, Thompson over the Rira incident.

How, then, is it possible to escape from this vicious circle? If the will to be violent is increased by suffering, punishment will intensify the pattern. In the light of this realisation, on the other hand, perhaps we may acknowledge that since everyone suffers, suffering need not be hugged to ourselves as a unique possession. When Mugo's walking in the rain is explained as being caused by heaviness of heart, another villager replies, 'That's not anything to make himself drench himself ill. Which of us does not carry a weight in his heart?'

Yet it is in the end Mugo who begins to untie the knots. It is he who first reverses the destructive process by confessing in public. We are left in no doubt, as we saw earlier, of the positive nature of this act: 'he was free, sure, confident.' Though it lasts 'only for a moment', the transformation in Mugo is complete. The crowd is overawed by his act and forgets its thirst for revenge. His alienation has been too complete to be healed; but we feel some sense of tragic apotheosis at the end of his story. Mugo has escaped from the spiralling effect of inflicting his own sorrow upon others, and is the catalyst to start the same process of release in Gikonyo. Gikonyo learns to accept some degree of identity with Mugo, what Conrad might have called a 'secret sharing'; and in quite a short space of time this alters first his whole attitude towards himself, then his attitude towards others, and at length his entire course of action. Mumbi is dependent upon the pattern of Gikonyo's suffering and it is therefore of the greatest significance that it is he who eventually initiates the reconciliation between them. The novel thus makes its final point not in tragic terms but in a positive demonstration that some alternative to mutual destruction is possible for human beings. The quiet, happy ending has the full weight of the whole novel behind it.

NOTES

1 G.O.W., p. 195; the following nine quotations are from pp. 198 ('Things of yesterday. . .'), 261, 146, 267, 270 ('Your deeds alone. . .'), 4, 9, 135 ('ghost-ridden Rung'ei'), and 8 ('There was a bond. . .').
2 T. S. Eliot, *The Cocktail Party*, Faber, London, 1950, p. 113.
3 G.O.W., p. 172; the following seven quotations are from pp. 258 ('He seems to be. . .'), 275–6 ('Perhaps we should not. . .'), 265, 278 ('But after

Mugo's confession. . .'), 280 ('Let us talk about the child'), 4 ('the day ahead. . .'), and 261 ('was death like. . .').

4 *Ibid.*, p. 5; the following seven quotations are from pp. 218, 260, 246 ('We sang song after song. . .'), 273, 220 ('Why should Kihika. . .'), 267, and 252.

5 *Ibid.*, p. 135; the following six quotations are from pp. 135 ('Thabai was just. . .'), 165.6 ('a time will come. . .'), 158, 200, 168 ('saved himself from detention. . .'), and 203 ('That's not anything. . .').

CHAPTER 6

Of the Strong Breed

A study of Wole Soyinka's *Three Plays*

SHORT plays by outstanding dramatists seldom receive the critical attention they deserve, and are often relegated to amateur drama festivals, where they may have a vigorous life. A piece of vintage Shaw like 'Overruled' is otherwise little known; fine and unusual pieces of writing such as Christopher Fry's 'The Boy with a Cart' or characteristic miniatures by Pinter such as 'The Dumb-Waiter' are not caught up in the general acclaim of a writer's work when he achieves success. Soyinka, as a leading figure in a new anglophone literature and specifically in the new African drama in English, has perhaps been relatively fortunate in this respect, partly no doubt because when he was first in the ascendant his short works comprised a large proportion of his output. Even so, critics have not always granted their due place in Soyinka's dramatic canon to the contents of the volume that first appeared in print as *Three Plays*, in the same year as *A Dance in the Forest* and *The Lion and the Jewel*. They are elusive writings as far as the reviewer is concerned, having proved hard to describe coherently for the benefit of readers not familiar with them; Soyinka's achievement above all is that he thinks and feels directly in his dramatic medium so that any attempt to abstract themes or 'plots' from these plays is like breaking open an egg to see if the embryo is alive.

These short plays are as intensely disturbing and as intensely enjoyable as his full-length dramas. In fact, I want to begin by asking myself just why I *enjoy* them as much as I do, for 'enjoy' is surely the right word. At a first seeing or reading the sheer dramatic impetus of the situations portrayed carries one through in a long unbroken sweep. But in later readings Soyinka's works, and these three plays in particular, are comparable in some respects with those of Brecht, Miller, Pinter, N. F. Simpson, sometimes

Ionesco and others among modern playwrights by virtue of the specific kind of satisfaction they provide. In a context which is not primarily verbal, words here capture meanings and perceptions which one had never hoped to find epitomised in this way in a work of art, so that I want to stop and immediately read the page again, and wonder at it.

The words are set in such a way as constantly to catch the rhythm of human existence, so that one becomes aware of a character as a complete consciousness, and therefore of the complex relationships between different beings, beyond mere logic and analysis. A dramatist can hit a pitch which makes words vibrate simultaneously at different levels (an art of which Chekov is the past master). We sense sympathetically the quaint, the painful, the paradoxical pressures within and between individuals that prevent them from saying simply what they need to communicate. What is not said becomes as important as the spoken word, or even more important:[1]

> SUNMA: Who are you talking to, Eman?
> EMAN: Ifada. I am trying to persuade him to join the young maskers.
> SUNMA (*losing control*): What does he want here? Why is he hanging round us?
> EMAN (*amazed*): What. . .? I said Ifada. Ifada.
> SUNMA: Just tell him to go away. Let him go and play somewhere else!
> EMAN: What is this? Hasn't he always played here?
> SUNMA: I don't want him here. Get away idiot. Don't bring your foolish face here any more, do you hear? Go on, go away from here. . .
> EMAN: Control yourself Sunma. What on earth has got into you?
> SUNMA: He comes crawling round here like some horrible insect. I never want to lay my eyes on him again.
> EMAN: I don't understand. It is *Ifada* you know. Ifada! The unfortunate one who runs errands for you and doesn't hurt a soul.
> SUNMA: I cannot bear the sight of him.

Frequently our observation of the gap between what is uttered in conventionally grouped words and what is meant in the complexity of the human psyche provides an upper layer of gentle humour. This tier of meaning is not just a matter of the structures of separate sentences and speeches; it has more to do with the eddying movement of the human mind, circling round its private preoccupations while it is carried forward publicly by the continuous stream of a situation.

At the beginning of 'The Swamp Dwellers' the parents are waiting for the return of one of their sons who may give them news of their other son with whom they have completely lost touch. The mother inoculates herself against disaster by claiming to believe that the missing son has been drowned in the swamp: the father pooh-poohs this idea. It is clearly an old argument. They are actually bickering about it, releasing in this apparent callousness the unbearable uncertainties in their minds; they are peevish, perverse, anxious to score a point, each set in their own pattern of thought, yet fitfully trying to lend each other some mental protection – their long-tried, unsentimental affection revealing itself in wry humour, and sometimes finding itself involved in a warmer vein of memory. These and even subtler threads interweave across the opening dialogue, superficially banal as it is, till we see a whole married life unravelled before us, at once typical yet highly individual:

ALU: Can you see him?

MAKURI: See who?

ALU: My son. Igwezu. Who else?

MAKURI: I did not come to look for him. Came only to see if the rain looks like stopping.

ALU: Well, does it? (*Makuri grunts.*) It is time he was back. He went hours and hours ago.

MAKURI: He knows the way. He's a grown-up man, with a wife.

ALU (*flaring up with aged lack of heat*): If you had any good at all in you, you'd go and look for him.

MAKURI: And catch my death of cramp? Not likely... And anyway, (*getting warmer*) what's preventing you from going?

ALU: I want to be here when he gives me the news. I don't want to fall down dead out in the open.

MAKURI: The older you get, the more of a fraud you become. Every day for the past ten years, you've done nothing but swear that your son was dead in the marshes. And now you sit there like a crow and tell me that you're waiting for news about him.

ALU (*stubbornly*): I know he's dead.

MAKURI: Then what do you want Igwezu to tell you?

ALU: I only want to know if . . . I only want to ask him . . . I . . . I . . . He shouldn't have rushed off like that . . . dashing off like a madman before anyone could ask him a thing.

MAKURI: (*insistently*): Before anyone could ask him WHAT?

ALU (*flares up again*): You're always trying to make me a liar.

MAKURI: I don't have to make you one.

ALU: Bah! Frog-face! . . .

A comic relationship is similarly if less elaborately achieved in 'The Trials of Brother Jero' when Chume delivers his long-suffering wife at her destination by bicycle.

While Soyinka lets us enter into each character's private self-awareness, he succeeds at the same time in keeping us conscious of how they appear to the outside observer, to their society at large; we share twin view-points: subjective and objective. In such a situation we feel a spark of that outflowing towards humanity which any God worthy of man's awe must feel infinitely. A man matters to us in this context not simply because he is good, or because he does this or that or amuses us, but in himself, because he is himself. I think the kind of enjoyment I alluded to is related to this sense of being close to comprehending human activity at its source. A dramatist who works outwards from this intimacy of response to human beings does not need a 'plot' to keep us absorbed: he can simply unfold one of the patterns of the way people behave.

Because of this approach Soyinka can, incidentally, draw strangers very closely into his Nigerian world; however unfamiliar it may be, the setting is quickly brought to life. The scenes are essentially Nigerian – so much so that with a lesser playwright they might obscure the whole drama for the uninitiated. However, Soyinka is never writing *about* the Nigerian background in a sociological sense, but about human beings who happen to exist very fully in this particular time and place. So we see how the familiar human passions, failures, achievements, greatness or littleness of spirit, are manifested in a previously unfamiliar environment. We make contact with this society in the only meaningful way, from the inside, by means of what we already share in common with it. And this may prove to be as important from a viewpoint in another corner of Africa as from a position outside the continent. The oro sacrifice is 'incomprehensible' or 'primitive' if we simply consider it externally as a series of happenings. But if we are drawn in so that we see it through the sensibilities of those involved, it becomes an inevitable ritual enactment of the needs and fears within all of us, so complex that the sacrificers may not know how to escape the sense of guilt which they bring upon themselves:

> We did it for them. It was all for their own common good. What did it benefit me whether the man lived or died. But did you see them? One and all they looked up at the man and words died in their throats.

And the sacrificed may be exalted by an acceptance which cannot, however, be complete, cannot finally renounce the desire for life. Without any first-hand experience, we can partake of the existence of the swamp-dwellers with the same sort of ease as we can, say, of the life of a bewildered small-time family in a decadent, negative society in Arthur's Miller's *The Death of a Salesman*.

Soyinka is patently in the stream of international movements in twentieth-century drama, and has been influenced consciously or unconsciously by the contemporary scene. Only a small man tries desperately to assert his own individuality by deliberately shutting himself off from outside influence. A larger mind discovers itself opening out to everything within reach, building a unique world out of already existing components. It is the artist above all who resists mechanical pressures exerted by modern society to isolate the individual. No artist is an island, however hard critics may try to build coral reefs around him, or think they have scored a point by 'discovering' what 'influences' connect him to the mainland of humanity. There is a good deal of common dramatic ground between Soyinka and Brecht. The way that areas of the stage are used successively to conjure up different scenes in 'The Strong Breed', often centring their powerful visual actuality on carefully selected items of stage furniture and leaving the rest to the imagination, gets the best of many theatrical worlds with Brechtian inventiveness: an exact sense of place and an absolute mobility; rapid shifting of scene without loss of unity or continuity; a subjective precision of detail with an objective stylisation on a larger scale.

In the last chapter I discussed Ngugi's use of time-shifts in order to emphasise, amid the varied experience of his characters, patterns which would be obscured by a simple chronological portrayal of events. In drama Arthur Miller had already transformed the worn-out cinematic device of the 'flashback' into a method of annihilating time so as to raise vital issues concerning the relationship between the past and the present self. Soyinka does something comparable when he needs the same scope for his own different purposes, an achievement which Martin Esslin seems surprisingly not to have comprehended.[2] It is of no deep consequence whether Soyinka was aware of learning from Brecht or Miller or anyone else, though this may have some legitimate literary interest; and indeed Soyinka himself has commented revealingly on this point:[3]

I am not aware of any conscious influence on my work, but I can say that if I wanted to aim at any particular kind of theatre, I think, however subconsciously, I might aim at Brecht's kind of theatre which I admire tremendously, just his complete freedom with the medium of theatre.

Our essential concern, of course, is with what Soyinka himself made with the tools he found in his dramatic environment and which he adapted to his own ends.

With regard to language, the individuality of an artist resides in what he feels and how he feels it: and so whatever medium he chooses to clothe his ideas in belongs to him. Soyinka is never bothered by the need self-doubtingly to demonstrate his affinities. His drama is profoundly conscious of the earth, of place, of solidity; and so it follows from this at a second level that it possesses a spontaneous human solidarity and oneness:[4]

BEGGAR: Will I return with you to the city?

IGWEZU: No, friend. You like this soil. You love to scoop it up in your hands. You dream of cleaving ridges under the flood and making little balls of mud in which to wrap your seeds. Is that not so?

BEGGAR: Yes, master.

IGWEZU: And you have faith, have you not? Do you not still believe in what you sow? That it will sprout and see the harvest sun?

BEGGAR: It must. In my wanderings, I think that I have grown a healer's hand.

IGWEZU: Then stay. Stay here and take care of the farm. I must go away.

So the symbols cross boundaries through the very fact of being so firmly located. Though perhaps 'symbols' is a misleading term. The elements of Soyinka's drama do not stand for something other than themselves: they embody life.

In 'The Swamp Dwellers', the swamp itself, the waters, the drought, the crops, the blindness and mysticism of the wandering beggar, the complex family relationships, the waiting for the returning son, the fear of death, the ruthless destruction of brother by brother, the yearning religious response of the old folk and the corruption of the priesthood, all these things speak for themselves, and develop in significance in our minds as particular expressions of widely familiar experience. The ideas are dramatically projected with great simplicity but great force. The arrival of the gentle, prophetic beggar, fleeing from drought, dedicated to stay near water and serve the soil, just at the time when intense stage expectation of the other son's return has been built up; Igwezu, frustrated by hard dealing in the city, the failure of his crops at home, and the rottenness he sees around him, forcing the priest to listen to home truths at the blade of the modern sacrificial knife – the barber's razor: these are highly evocative stage moments. In finally stripping away illusions by exposing this false prophet, Igwezu is not, as Margaret Laurence suggests,[5] plunging deeper into confusion, but is in fact in the process of liberating himself, and potentially others, from bewilderment.

The characters in 'The Swamp Dwellers' fall into three groups: the parents, conservative, rooted in a sense of permanence; the corrupt priest and his followers; and the two positive individuals, Igwezu and the Beggar, moving, wandering, seeking, and then uncertain of what they have found. And yet there is a quiet sureness between them, even though the young man is too preoccupied with his own search to be able to focus the old man properly. There is little doubt that they have found something and that they trust each other.

The play is built upon a series of balances, counter-balances, contradictions, paradoxes. There is the juxtaposition of town and country. Both, if romantically falsified, offer disappointment and frustration; neither is idealised. There is no point in simply alternating between false hopes: 'Is it of any earthly use to change one slough for another?'[6] asks Igwezu – the city also is a swamp. And yet each must be faced; they offer challenge not refuge. Igwezu returns to his destiny in the town, and leaves the Beggar to his in the river delta. The background is flood and drought. Sun and rain both cheat man with false promises.

But human contradictions also betray us. Igwezu's girl-wife goes running when wealth just crooks its finger; while the dried-up ancients cannot face the fierce directness of youth: 'May earth reject the folly spoken by my son,' pleads the father. Makuri is more blind than the Beggar: to believe in the Serpent is an act of faith, a submission to an inner need to have something to worship; to believe in the Kadiye, the priest of the Serpent, is to submit wilfully to self-interest battening on superstition, a self-interest as ingrained as that of Awuchike, the son who has made good in the city. Faith is not to be found in the paunchy Kadiye, but in the searching, dedicated Beggar, who seems to subscribe to no dogma. Not only is he of a faith different from that of the swamp, he rejects his prescribed place in the established pattern of his own religion by resolutely inverting his bowl so as to refuse alms. The blind, the destitute, is the man committed to the earth, who will work, and cultivate, who will remain faithful. His words end the play. The old calls the young 'master'.

Yet Igwezu is also a man of vision, and perhaps accepts the Beggar's self-appointed role of bondsman in a different sense: there is a spiritual bond between them. Igwezu knows that if dotards stay in the village, so also do the innocent; and that if he does not deserve to be called the one, he cannot yet aspire to be the other. If there is still something of raw, even arrogant youthfulness in Igwezu's exaggerated sense of victory towards the end, yet he also possesses both an essential humility and a determined courage. He is willing to learn – 'I want to paddle as I go, like a little child.'

He shares this courage with the Beggar. Both have faced and dared their fates. The Beggar has set his back to drought by seeking fruitfulness at the end of the river's course. Igwezu has grasped mishandled power by the throat, has put it in its place, and let it go without seeking to take over from it.

Amid this complexity there are no answers and we cannot ask naively what the play is about. Such figures as the Beggar 'do not provide any formula for the future nor lead to a conciliation of opposing forces,' remarks Martin Tucker.[7] Igwezu realises that his outburst was in part an attempt to assert himself in the face of disappointment and frustration, a young man weighed down by the conservatism of the old and a load of conventional belief he cannot accept: 'was there something of a desire to prove myself worthy?'[8] Yet it is far from being an ignoble desire, to prove oneself worthy, even if one is not quite sure what one seeks to be worthy of.

The play ends without illusions but on a remarkably optimistic note. Like any work which without any hint of dishonesty can win hope out of despair, its final tone is exhilarating. Innocence is acknowledged as a positive; when Igwezu asserts that only the innocent and the dotards stay voluntarily in the swamp, the Beggar quietly replies with a question, which is at least half a statement: 'But you will return, master?' His own position is implied by the closing words, 'I shall be here to give account'; and we do not foresee Igwezu returning as a dotard. The Beggar's last speech, the last in the play, opens with the words, 'The swallows find their nest again when the cold is over.'

And so, as with all Soyinka's drama – notably *Kongi's Harvest*, while there is ambiguity, and the playwright has refrained from coming down simplistically on one side or the other of particular issues, these issues are not left where they were. The play raises the kind of question to which by definition there can be no easy answers, but it is in itself hopeful that there is something new to say.

Take the question of change, for instance: whether it is desirable, if so what sort of change is to be looked for, and who is qualified to bring it about. To say that neither the *status quo* of tradition nor the urban modernity that we know is desirable is not simply negative; to make this statement effectively forces us to identify, in both old and new, elements that might be placed together into a better whole. That there is something magnetic in the city is as obvious as that there is something worth preserving in the swamp. Surely any suggestion that the generations are irrevocably set against each other in the search is to be dismissed in terms of the mystic and experimental relationship between Igwezu and the Beggar. We may feel impatient because Igwezu, having seen through the exploiters who have a vested interest either in the serpent or in the cash nexus, defines no third way for us: but we are bound to realise that if he offered us a glib formula it would carry little conviction. At least he is searching, neither complacent nor cynical; and at least he recognises the Beggar as a fellow searcher whose blind eyes see in the same visionary direction. And the Beggar too can recognise in this bewildered young man a seeker after difficult truth. The fellow-feeling between them and the fact that they know confidently that they will meet again do not, of course, amount to a 'solution', but they dramatise a subtle and hopeful integrity of common endeavour.

'The Trials of Brother Jero', with – for Soyinka – its unusually simple linear structure, is at once the least complex and the most mannered of the three plays, its serious lightness showing Soyinka's great variety of mood and sure sense of style:

> Mind you, the beach is hardly worth having these days. The worshippers have dwindled to a mere trickle and we really have to fight for every new convert. They all prefer High Life to the rhythm of celestial hymns. And Television too is keeping our wealthier patrons at home. They used to come in the evening when they would not easily be recognised.

Jero's role has the sanction of a 'sign' in the long hair with which he was born. Just the same, he makes a very comfortable living out of being a prophet, and basks in the admiration of his converts. He is a stylish rogue who enjoys every minute of his own performance: he has blood-brothers in the pages of Ben Jonson. In him we see blind conventional faith being replaced by a more up-to-date cynicism. He can explode the rhetorical verbosity of the Old Prophet with his shrewd and wry realism:

> Actually that was a very cheap curse. He knew very well that I had one weakness – women. Not my fault, mind you. You must admit that I am rather good-looking . . . no, don't be misled, I am not at all vain. Nevertheless, I decided to be on my guard.

This is the story of a self-infatuated realist and what he finds he can get away with by playing upon the inner needs and desires of mankind, and their aspirations towards the extra-logical. It is characteristic of Soyinka that the gullibility of Jero's victims, which lays them open to our laughter and even our contempt, cannot be distinguished from their human vulnerability, their craving for divine visitation and support, which makes them pathetic and, in flashes, sublime in their folly.

Even at a first reading, the eternally bickering husband and wife, Chume and Amope, spring to life from the printed page, at once archetypes and sturdy individuals. The down-to-earth, greasy humour endears these characters to us even amid their assertiveness, their querulousness, their weakness, and their proud absurdity. The cringing self-pitying tone that Amope adopts to bully and henpeck her defiantly ineffectual spouse are in the vein of high comedy:

AMOPE: You didn't hear me complain. You did your best, but if my toes are to be broken one by one just because I have to monkey on your bicycle, you must admit it's a tough life for a woman.

CHUME: I did my . . .

AMOPE: Yes, you did your best. I know. Didn't I admit it? Please . . . give me that stool. . . You know yourself that I'm not the one to make much of a little thing like that, but I haven't been too well. If anyone knows that, it's you . . . I haven't been well, that's all, otherwise I wouldn't have said a thing.

The ending in which a 'Member' is first drawn into Jero's net by the prophetic promise of a ministry, and is then presumed to be about to have the disillusioned Chume, now rampaging after Jero, locked up as a lunatic – though in key with the stringent social satire of the whole piece – seems to me too contrived, and, in bordering on burlesque, to coarsen the vein of the play, though it may work robustiously enough on stage. The defeat of Chume is dramatically makeshift and opportunistic, and in terms of ideas does not appear to have been thought through. Jero has restrained Chume up till now from beating his wife since the intensity of his discipleship depends on his unsatisfied desires, a complex point made with nice comic control. However, though I do not wish to modify the qualifications I have made, Jero's last successful contrivance in which, at a stroke, he evades the harridan hounding him for debt and (reversing the situation between Subtle and Face in *The Alchemist*) defeats his presumptuous assistant-turned-rival, is certainly an ingenious *tour de force*. The ease with which Satan safeguards his own in a world so easily duped shades the end of the comedy with darker irony.

'The Strong Breed' follows to his death Eman, the solitary, self-sacrificing keeper of the clinic, the 'stranger' who saves an imbecile from death as scapegoat in an oro sacrifice by substituting himself. That, of course, is a completely inadequate summary of the tense, swift-moving drama which finds ample time within its complex structure to confront Eman, as he flees from his own self-appointed death, with his youthful past, and thus unfolds much of his psychological development from boyhood. Yet the more we appear superficially to know and understand, the deeper becomes the mystery of human nature. Why must man, in his alarming need to exorcise his fear of life and death, pursue his fellow man? Why should it be a stranger who offers himself in voluntary sacrifice for the transgressions of the past year which he has not himself committed? We are faced with the paradox of evil, and of goodness. 'I know they are evil and I am not,' says Sunma of her fellow villagers. 'From the oldest to the smallest child, they are nourished in evil and unwholesomeness in which I have no part.' It is true that she stands aside and that the other countryfolk appear in a violent enough context in the course of the play, but can we identify ourselves with the one rather than the others? Love is an elusive contradiction: 'Those who have much to give fulfil themselves only when they do so in total loneliness,' claims Eman.[9] 'Love comes to me more easily with strangers.' But how can one who feels for life so intensely be prepared to give it up? Does he offer himself in order to consummate an absolute love for 'a total stranger', springing neither from passion nor instinct? – or to complete the secret image of himself deriving from an inner compulsion to emulate his father? –

EMAN: I am unfitted for your work father. I wish to say no more. But I am totally unfitted for your call.
OLD MAN: It is only time you need son. Stay longer and you will answer the urge of your blood.

Like 'The Swamp-Dwellers' and later *The Road* and *Madmen and Specialists*, 'The Strong Breed' develops into a pattern of disturbing paradoxes, some of which we have already touched upon. The young child, the theoretically innocent little girl, is untouchable in her sickness, and this has made her heartless and self-obsessed. Sunma needs to get away from her home; Eman, the stranger, is impelled to stay. The injunction to return good for evil is reversed:

You think they love you? Do you think they care at all for what you – or I – do for them?

Commitment and cowardice are in conflict; Sunma flares up at Eman: 'You accuse me of losing my sense of mission, but you are afraid to put yours to the test.' This theme develops through the play. Yet eventually it is not the appointed victim but the pursuers who show 'cowardice' in the face of their own act, except for Jaguna and Oroge. Perhaps their final awed speechlessness is the beginning of wisdom. Eman, on the other hand, seeks peace and is promised cruelty.

Who then is polluted and who pure? The young Eman is horrified when his child-lover comes to contaminate him at the time of circumcision; but a moment later he is quitting the ritual precinct when he realises that his 'tutor' is an unsubtle old lecher, willing, like the Kadiye, to employ ritual convention for his own ends, in fact as a means of sexual blackmail. Is the young girl pure as she goes through the motions with her carrier, clinging with implacable self-absorption and self-interest to this image of man, created to heal and be destroyed like Eman? or the half-witted Ifada at whom she spits her poison? –

> You will hang it up and I will set fire to it. (*Then, with surprising venom*) But just because you are helping me, don't think it is going to cure you. I am the one who will get well by tomorrow, do you understand? It is my carrier and it is for me alone.

Has Eman's martyrdom indeed cleansed his destroyers in a symbolic sense they had not foreseen, as they stand dumbfounded at their action? The tables are turned and Jaguna's scornful words earlier come home unexpectedly: 'They are the ones who break first, these fools who think they were born to carry suffering like a hat.'

The claustrophobic opening of the play merges into Eman's haunted flight from those who seek to carry through his now unwilling sacrifice. As he flees he stumbles onto memories of his past which strike strange angles and perspectives across the apparently simple progression of life. His youthful self involved in the rites of passage, the man shattered by his long-patient wife's death in her first childbirth, the self that needs to be at one with the strong breed of his father, the man we first meet on his last confused and tortured day, are separated only artificially by time: in effect they form a single whole, and can thus be reunited by dramatic juxtaposition within the play's flexible structure. At length this concentrated medium shows us simultaneously the sacrifice of Eman and of his father, each in his own generation, offering themselves up and, equally, being offered up to death.

In Eman, then, we find much less equivocally than in Igwezu or the Beggar, or in the Professor of *The Road*, the characteristic Soyinka gesture, which Ngugi has characterised as 'an individual's lone act of courage'.[10] 'In this extremely dark play,' comments Oyin Ogumba,[11]

> Wole Soyinka explores the role of the spiritually elect in a human community. He seems to be anxious to make the point that there is apparently always a choice for the elect between escaping responsibility and taking it up squarely in spite of the prospect of doom. But the truly elect feels an inner compulsion, a tumultuous excitement to act his part. For him escape is impossible, an alternative course of action is unthinkable.

Ogumba's absorbing commentary overlooks, perhaps, the additional complexity that Eman, far from seeking a martyrdom which might be perversely interpreted as 'suicide while of unsound mind',[12] tries at the level of immediate action and consciousness to evade his chosen destiny by escaping. But there is no doubt that the general line of Ogumba's argument is sound; Soyinka himself agrees[13] that this play is 'very much mixed up with the whole element of sacrifice, so contrasting the idea of selfishness with willing self-sacrifice as opposed to the other general cannibalism of human beings'. The notion of collective guilt is central, but again in no simple sense. Which is the guilt that the carrier in fact expiates? – that, as the villagers by tradition assume, which the village has amassed during the past year, or is it the guilt of blood-lust in the act of hunting down the appointed victim, as they seem eventually to discover? Eldred Jones has no hesitation in identifying Eman as a Christ figure:[14]

> When the actual ordeal comes Eman's body flinches, but in the end, having offered himself in Ifada's place, he is sacrificed. Eman is represented in the play as a Christ-figure; the parallels are obvious: he is willing to die for a thankless people, at the end he flinches at the physical ordeal, and he dies lifted high on a tree.

In part, I would agree, the parallel is obvious; in part somewhat far-fetched: the suggestion is so strong that Soyinka's refusal to clinch it also seems plain, and it remains one more powerful overtone. Ogumba's summary appears to me less controversial:[15]

> The rest of humanity is either too sensible, like Sunma, to think that the sacrifice is worth it or too naive like Ifada to appreciate its significance. It is only the elect that have both the will and the temerity to make the plunge and consent to be the sacrificial victim.

Yet this, I think, defines questions rather than conclusions. If it is clear that society feels the need for sacrifice as a means of communal expiation and that there is an individual more or less willing to be sacrificed on their behalf, just what is being expiated and why the individual is willing to make the sacrifice remain as ill-determined as the problems of whom the sacrifice is being made to, and in what sense one allotment of human blood, willingly donated or not, could be thought to compensate for the acknowledged inadequacies of quite different persons. The Christ analogy does not account for the mystery of Eman; but it reminds us of the common ground existing between different sets of beliefs because of their faith in the positive value of sacrifice, which at subtler (and more paradoxical) levels becomes voluntary sacrifice.

And so Soyinka's drama echoes through our minds long after we have watched or read it, returning to us unawares at unexpected moments, when we find ourselves wrestling with its implications. As we perceive that the familiar psychological and religious dilemmas are being re-examined, we may be tempted into symbolic interpretations with fixed relationships between the items, but this is certainly to limit our dramatic experience, which should cut across formulas and categories. The patterns are compelling, endlessly suggestive and relevant, but neither fixed nor prescribed.

Though these short plays evade summary, they are tightly wrought. If we are to see the first phase of Soyinka's career in true perspective, we must certainly consider 'The Swamp-Dwellers' and 'The Strong Breed' together with the full-length plays: they are among his most telling works. Each presents two or more sides to specific questions while forcing us to judge the issues involved by refusing to make judgments for us. Such dual dramatic involvement, which at a crux withdraws into detachment, placing the onus of moral and social evaluation on the audience, is also central to *A Dance in the Forest* and *The Lion and the Jewel*. Likewise, by presenting a comparable balance, *Kongi's Harvest* was to insist that we ourselves should adjudicate between truth and hypocrisy, both ancient and modern. Furthermore, in 'The Swamp-Dwellers' and 'The Strong Breed' the nice ironies of *The Lion and the Jewel* have already deepened into profounder and more disturbing paradoxes, such as will lead to the desperate enigmas and the desperate honesty of *The Road* and later still of *Madmen and Specialists*.

NOTES

Quotations are from *T.P.* References below are given to *T.P.* first, followed by *C.P.* references in brackets. Differences in the text of quotations in *C.P.* are noted.

1 *T.P.*, p. 83 (*C.P.I*, p. 16); the following two quotations are from pp. 7–8 (81–2), and 117 (146).
2 Martin Esslin, 'Two Nigerian Playwrights', *Introduction to African Literature*, ed. Ulli Beier, Longmans, London, 1967, p. 262.
3 Wole Soyinka talking to Lewis Nkosi, August 1962: *African Writers Talking*, ed. Dennis Duerden and Cosmo Pieterse, H.E.B., 1972, p. 172.
4 *T.P.*, p. 41 (*C.P.I*, p. 111).
5 Margaret Laurence, *Long Drums and Cannons*, Macmillan, London, 1968, p.25: 'Igwezu's confusion is not presented as confusion but as some kind of liberation.'
6 *T.P.*, p. 41 (*C.P.I*, p. 111); the following two quotations are from pp. 40 (110) ('May earth reject . . .'), and 42 (112) ('I want to paddle . . .').
7 Martin Tucker, *Africa in Modern Literature*, Frederick Unger, New York, 1967, p. 116.
8 *T.P.*, p. 41 (*C.P.I*, p. 111, omitting the word 'worthy'); the following five quotations are from pp. 42 (112) ('But will you return . . .'), 48 (*C.P.II*, p. 146, with 'television' instead of 'Television'), 48–9 (*C.P.II*, p. 146), 50 (*C.P.II*, pp. 147–8), and 88 (*C.P.I*, p. 121) ('I know they are evil . . .').
9 *T.P.*, p. 94 (*C.P.I*, p. 125); the following five quotations are from pp. 104 (134), 88 (120), 89 (121) ('You accuse me . . .'), 87 (120 with 'at midnight' instead of 'by tomorrow'); 101 (131) ('They are the ones . . .').
10 Ngugi wa Thiong'o, *Homecoming*, H.E.B., 1972, p. 65.
11 Oyin Ogumba, 'Traditional Content of the Plays of Wole Soyinka', *African Literature Today* 4, 1970, p. 16.
12 As spaciously argued concerning Thomas Becket's martyrdom by the Fourth Knight in T. S. Eliot's *Murder in the Cathedral*, Faber, London, 1935, p. 68.
13 Wole Soyinka talking to Lewis Nkosi, *op. cit.*, p. 173.
14 Eldred D. Jones, 'The Essential Soyinka', *Introduction to Nigerian Literature*, ed. Bruce King, University of Lagos Press/Evans, 1971, pp. 127–8.
15 Oyin Ogbuna, *op. cit.*, p. 16.

CHAPTER 7

A Walk in the Sun

A study of Peter Palangyo's *Dying in the Sun*

> *I am thy father's spirit;*
> *Doom'd for a certain term to walk the night*
> *And for the day confined to fast in fires,*
> *Till the foul crimes done in my days of nature*
> *Are burnt and purg'd away.*
>
> *Have you a daughter?*
> *I have, my lord.*
> Let her not walk i' the sun. Conception is a blessing, but as your daughter may conceive, friend, look to 't.

(SHAKESPEARE, *Hamlet*, the first excerpt being the epigraph to Alex la Guma's *A Walk in the Night*.)

No literature, however long and firmly established, can hope to have added to it many unflawed masterpieces, or even major works of undoubted distinction, within a decade, though literatures with an extensive history may sometimes give a distorted impression in this respect because of the long shadows cast by past giants. If we are to give any extensive consideration to contemporary literature, we must widen our discussion to include works of uneven or ambiguous value, provided these stimulate serious reactions and would seem to merit more than a cursory first reading. Among the most useful services literary criticism has to offer are the evaluation of widely read books and participation in the process of identifying and appreciating with proper discrimination lights which are partly hidden under bushels. Older cultures are becoming increasingly aware of the critical importance of the current scene, if syllabuses in more progressive universities are anything to judge by. A new tradition of written literature, such as anglophone fiction from Africa, must diversify and spread its critical energy if it is both to give its readers an adequate spectrum of work to contemplate thoughtfully, and to stimulate writers themselves. It is in this context that I have set about the present study.

I return to Peter Palangyo's novel *Dying in the Sun* with a certain satisfaction since it is a work which I admire in many respects. Admittedly it is sometimes disappointing. Some of its philosophical generalisations are tenuous; some of the writing is confused; some of the metaphors are contrived. The very climax, the happy ending, so essential to the design, is hurried, while occasional sentences and phrases descend to mere sentimentality. Yet *Dying in the Sun* is a thoughtful and courageous work; if it attempts more than it can carry through to perfection, nevertheless it is powerfully conceived and essentially honest in execution. It concerns itself with dimensions of life in Africa which need to be explored. And it handles characters who are largely ignored by other writers except as background material or supporting cast: Ntanya is a primary school drop-out who has tried his luck as city houseboy and now shifts back uncertainly to country life in a family setting, without a missionary or a white man in sight. Teresa is a village prostitute.

Since articulate readers have found it easier to describe the novel's shortcomings than its strengths, it will be my primary concern to define the latter to explain why I think the novel transcends its weaknesses and survives as a valuable work. I shall not, of course, ignore its flaws; but I shall attempt to see these in perspective rather than emphasise them. Just as anyone who has been favourably impressed at a first reading may come back to *Dying in the Sun* and feel somewhat deflated, so, on the other hand, if one has been induced to return to it in a sceptical, even a derogatory, frame of mind, the book may surprise by its force and insights.

Ntanya, the protagonist, is in many ways a representative figure – deprived and aspiring, victim of the drift to the city and the conflicting desires and uncertainties it has created. Yet he is sensitive above the average; 'some people . . . are . . . isolated to carry a bigger and bitter cross of suffering,'[1] declares his grandmother. Ntanya's emotional crisis is seen as an experience which everyone has to go through: 'Everybody has got his night, the night when everything comes to a sharp point like a boil,' yet only 'some born with their eyes open keep vigil through the night to watch every move, every twitch of pain,' Ntanya among them. Because he is more sensitive than most, he is therefore more distracted by his bewildered inner life than the majority. He is disillusioned, but desperately and at length successfully seeks values by which he can lead a meaningful life. After travelling and seeing a wider world, he is involved in trying to re-absorb himself unpretentiously into the society from which he grew. His is a crucial African experiment, more generally significant even than the efforts of the educated man of two worlds to rediscover himself, but one which far less often finds a place in mature fiction.

The villagers are touched, and deeply touched, by the controversies and conflicts raging at a national level – as both James and the peasant who hangs himself know only too well. The book does not specifically refer to any 'back to the land' policy; but it observes that people who have lived a subordinate, but in many ways sophisticated, existence in a town some-times make their way back to the place where they were born, and in doing so find themselves confused by private inner conflicts which they scarcely themselves understand.

Unhappily Ntanya is at odds with his family as well as with social organisation, while needing and striving to come to terms with both. Above all, he is trying in this tangled world to make sense out of life, while being preoccupied with an awareness of death. His specific problems are compounded with inescapable human dilemmas. *Dying in the Sun* the book is called: death and sunshine are ever present. Peter Palangyo is one of those novelists whose work is an attempt firstly on behalf of themselves, secondly on behalf of their societies, and thirdly on behalf of all their readers, to face the fact that haunts all mankind: the fact of death. The transience of life is a key motif in tragedy and romantic poetry alike. The same awareness is at the root of the existentialist realisation that life is absurd, and that the trivial round of daily routine is meaningless: the key figure in Camus's play *Caligula* explains his abandonment of his old way of life by saying that he has discovered that men die and are not happy.[2] In *Dying in the Sun* the challenge of death presides over a Tanzanian village.

The novel opens with the protagonist on his way to his father's deathbed: it opens in desolation, 'a sadness verging on despair', and with an uncon-ditional curse upon God. The process leading up to the death of Ntanya's father is one of the main structural elements of the novel. It is a bizarre, bitterly ironical death of a man whom nobody has loved, whose alienation even at the last from his whole environment is epitomised by the village elder's abortive attempt to find something to praise in his life-history in order to make up his funeral oration: he can recall nothing admirable which is of real significance. Though he returns unquestioningly to his father's deathbed, Ntanya is torn by strange emotions:[3]

There was something in the old man's helpless posture that raised in Ntanya a mixed feeling of nausea, contempt, hatred, and pity. . . . Ntanya stared at this dying thing, his father who had so quickly turned into an object of embarrassment.

On arriving home Ntanya asks 'casually' whether or not his father is dead. This is not, as may appear on the surface, the casualness of indifference, but of over-involvement seeking to protect itself from scorn and pain: after all it is his filial relationship which has drawn Ntanya to abandon his job and return to the village. Yet this conventional and expected love for his father turns out to be akin to hatred.

Ntanya's mother was killed by her husband in drunken violence, though Ntanya's paternal grandmother insists that he had wrestled hard with the devil within him, even if in vain: 'Some strange spirit caught him. I've seen him cry, in between his drunkenness, trying desperately to wrench this strange weight off his soul.' It seems that Ntanya's father, like his son after him, also fought with despondency, but succumbed. Only after Ntanya has himself 'come through' can he weep for his father. At the time this death arouses no gentle feelings.

Ntanya's mood at the beginning is conditioned by his whole grotesque circumstances: 'a sadness so harrowing in its sensuality he could not even feel the blood trickling from the wound pierced through his torn trouser seat.' Though he is in an extreme state of exhaustion when the book opens, this is nevertheless a familiar, convincing, even everyday picture: 'broken people are alone . . . beyond pain or pleasure.' In spite of the intermittent upsurge of new strength he finds upon his return to Kachawanga, things will be yet worse for Ntanya in the penultimate stage of the novel when he listlessly passes 'like a ghost' through 'death-life'; Bunyan called it the 'slough of despond'; a character in one of T. S. Eliot's plays describes it as 'just ordinary hopelessness'.[4] When we first meet Ntanya, things have fallen apart at the centre of his consciousness. 'Some string had snapped in the very centre of his being,'[5] an image that is to link him with the broken-down old sex troubadour in Maria's bar.

Palangyo makes the whole experience intensely personal. Ntanya is fully realised as an individual going through all this. We observe the process within him. The image of death is reinforced at once by the key event in Ntanya's own childhood when, terrifyingly, he had unintentionally caused his sister's death in a fit of childish rage while he was being taunted. The image is made immediate by the vividness of the details, such as the child's-eye view of the grandmother's nostrils looming above him, 'big and dilated by the smell they had detected, the smell they knew so well, the terrible smell of death', at once unbearably actual, and yet generalised into a common experience. The medicine man had foreseen that 'before death there was a period of calm painlessness, a sort of ultimate relief'. And this childhood grandmother has also reached some sort of final acceptance 'beyond pity, understanding or pardon'.

Owls, the birds of death, flap their way through the book. The memory of the death of Ntanya's mother is recurrent, so that it becomes like something out of our own memory. There is the remarkable scene from Ntanya's childhood when he escapes in disgrace from a very hard primary school arithmetic lesson to go and sit by his mother's grave, and realises, in effect that school is absurd in the light of this death, and so he cannot go back to the classroom. One of the most alarming moments in the novel is when Ntanya wishes his mother were alive so that she could see her husband dying and savour her revenge. Time and again it is the old who are weeping for the young. At the lowest point of his 'death-life' Ntanya concludes that all human relations lead inevitably to mutual annihilation: 'Because we have this seed of destruction in us we spread it, much like a disease.' The bitterness, irony, meaninglessness are echoed in the father's inability to mutter more than, 'My, my, my . . .' as he lies dying, an unspecified possessiveness, it seems, a futile attempt to become attached to one's surroundings.

The idea of death is generalised in a significant passage when Ntanya renews contact with his boyhood friend James, who has become an administrator:

> Always somebody dying, always the fear of our own death. My mother
> is going to die soon too. We with jobs bury our minds in them, but you
> always face death and as a result you are not afraid. We bury our fear in
> these files . . . and these big houses, and drink, and yelling at houseboys.
> But deep down in the darkness when we are alone we are afraid of death.

The powerful image of the peasant who hangs himself is ever present in James's nightmares.

The dance in the bar is a sort of dance of death. 'From dust unto dust . . . from dust unto dust,' Ntanya recites to himself as the dust of the bar settles back into the calabashes of beer while bodies sway to the cracked gramophone record. Occasional strokes of irony link up with this negative pattern. The old man's bar-room philosophy, 'I always say that there are only two points where the whole of mankind meets, sex and death,' is greeted with a great gust of laughter. Relief, we are told, is an illusion. In the beer-shop during an interlude of frenzied happiness, Mugia asks, 'What would I do with intelligence here other than rot my gut and commit suicide? . . . Indeed what does anyone want intelligence for in a thoroughly unintelligent, even unintelligible, world?' Almost as an aside, it is scathingly remarked that the Catholic church will probably retrieve the mask from the old man's grave and turn it into a holy relic. When Ntanya's father is beyond speech but apparently attempts to make some signal, 'maybe', it is conjectured, 'he just wanted to move his head without reason, to prove that he could do so as a last gesture of revolt against God and death.'

Through this desolate world Ntanya is driven by his own strange spirit, lost and uncertain, but impelled. When his grandmother follows him to find out where he is going, she hears him repeating his dying father's apparently meaningless, broken words to himself, 'My, my, my . . .' He is tortured and twisted: in the bar he chokes back the bitter reality and denies that anyone is dying in his family, unable to expose his confused pain.

But through the book two other deaths run their course, which both parallel and yet in differing degrees contrast with that of Ntanya's father. The sex troubadour offers the closer comparison: his last jollification at Maria's is immediately juxtaposed structurally to Ntanya's second night vigil over his dying father, the night of his spiritual crisis. When Teresa contemplates claiming her earnings from Maria to buy a coffin for Ntanya's father, she suppresses her qualms with the thought 'that there is nothing wrong in mixing bitterness with bitterness'.[6] Yet in the case of the sex troubadour hopelessness is qualified. There is a sense of completion of a pattern, of fulfilment: 'I have settled my account in tears and I've nothing to regret.' When Maria asks cynically who wants to live long, it is the old man who declares, 'I do.' 'Yes,' he says of himself, 'you can say he spoke the truth at last. That he died a wise man.'

The death of Ntanya's grandmother is in more complete contrast to that of his father. Their failing powers are compared early on: 'It was not at all like the helplessness of Mama Ntanya. Hers was the helplessness of victory, the helplessness of an impala that has been shot with a rifle and falls down staring at the hunter.' Her death is at once expected and benign: it is not associated with sudden fear nor with any disillusionment about life itself: death is part of a design, a continuity:

Her death had not come as a shock to anybody and nobody mourned her since she had lived every bit of her life out till she had reached a point where there was nothing else to live. All over Kachawanga people had only sighed on hearing of her death saying that she was a lucky and sinless woman to have been able to wear out even her gums.

Dying in the Sun is thus aware of complexity and mystery: for all the open-eyed knowledge of death, there is no easy cynicism. The book harbours no illusions, so the positive conclusion appears valid and significant. The pathetic dance in Maria's bar is also triumphant. It may in a sense be a dance of death, but it is also a dance of delight, asserting the validity of these neglected and generally undervalued lives. Because these people have nothing to lose they are close to the reality of pain, but also to the reality of joy, which seems to be excluded from the bourgeois ideal of contentment. 'There was no mistaking it, these were happy people.'

The characters retain their own secrets: we do not know how Ntanya attempted suicide as a child: we do not know what he whispers into his brother's ear, for instance. The novel is concerned with 'the known-unknown darkness that had settled on their hearts' since 'the heart of a human being is a dark universe'. No easy cynicism; no easy optimism. Objects, we learn, cast good and bad shadows.

Ntanya has throughout a sense of quest. Early on this is identified as a need 'to reconfirm what deep down he believed in – his innocence'.[7] Later it is expressed in metaphor: 'He was looking for something, a lost seed on a wilderness of burnt grass. What was going to direct him?' There is no attempt to narrow down the quest by too specific a statement:

> Something was happening in him, he must see it through awake. In the meanwhile he must occupy himself, so as not to disturb what was going on inside him.

Through all this negative and bewildering experience, the quest continues, leading first to the night which has been referred to as representing a spiritual turning-point: 'Now was the night of the lone naked soul. After tonight all would be a summing up.' This night is a culmination, but it is not in fact a conclusion. James joins the quest towards the end of the novel and with the help of Teresa breaks the spiritual deadlock within Ntanya during which negative and positive forces appear to have reached a stalemate. Indeed both girls, Onya as well as Teresa, comprehend in some degree and in their different ways Ntanya's search for a meaning in life which could renew his will to live, and each participates in it as far as she can. From a few quotations this sounds rather cut and dried, but it is not so in the novel. 'For an experience has too many shadows or probabilities, the complexities of which were probably not meant to be deciphered by the human mind or heart' – and yet Ntanya is determined to try; if he does not in the end decipher them, at least he resolves them into a meaningful design. 'The deepest of our prayers,' we are told, 'are never really said to God or anybody in particular; they simply come as incoherently broken desires and hopes that can never be verbalised.' 'It's not my being a bastard or poor that has been bothering me. It's something much deeper,' Ntanya tells Teresa: in short, it is the human condition.

So within the total pattern of the book the looming negative mystery of death is counterbalanced by the positive mystery of love. We believe in the positive values which survive despair, because there is no false optimism. Kachawanga itself, when Ntanya first catches sight of it, is 'the only beautiful thing he had ever known in his wretched world'. We sense the strong family feeling which links the gathering of relatives – powerfully expressed in the group silence on Ntanya's first night at home. Onya's close attachment to Ntanya almost pains her: 'She would have chewed for him if that was possible.' The way they all treat the grandmother is a focus of these feelings:[8] 'His mother was now shaking like a leaf and he crouched down and held her in his arms tenderly, as tenderly as if she would melt or break to pieces.' When Ntanya sees his breakfast prepared for him as in the past, he thinks to himself, 'The poor old soul, the poor beautiful old soul.' And the intimate, teasing relationship between them is well realised.

And so there is a community in suffering. If living is 'the knitting of a necklace of scars,' this common experience holds the characters together. It is, indeed, almost the only link between Ntanya and his father: 'His only real claim on him was that he was a fellow sufferer. We suffer together and therefore we are relatives.'

The friendship between Ntanya and James is etched in economically. The original disappointment and distance between them avoids any over-simplification of the relationship. Ntanya, in his need for a friend, commits himself to James, and we find the emotional shift convincing: 'This time his hand was soft but not slimy; the government official had suddenly turned into a man.' Palangyo portrays the different faces of reality: we are saddened though sympathetic when Ntanya soon afterwards feels ashamed of his friendship with this representative of officialdom, in the bar. When later Ntanya finds James in tears, and when James makes his vital offer to help his friend's family, this silent, manly friendship is very much alive.

Teresa's first impulse towards Ntanya is simply described: 'Something had attracted her in Ntanya, something both sensual and deeper.' The relationship between the lovers explicitly takes up the celebration of happiness. Teresa's happiness tree is a bantering way of playing with the idea in light-hearted talk between them.

We have remarked on Palangyo's economy, and his acceptance of mystery without vagueness. Both are served by his ability to evoke images which impress themselves on our imaginations with a wealth of implication. Interestingly enough, Palangyo himself explicitly comments on the power of images when Teresa first implores Ntanya to let her go with him: 'There are certain images that although we see only once, we can never shake out of our memories, never until we die.' In *Dying in the Sun*, indeed, some of the most important images are recurrent, binding and emphasising the pattern of the novel: the dying man saying, 'My, my, my, . . . '; the hanging peasant; Ntanya at his father's bedside. Others are also clearly units in an articulated design: Ntanya and James playing in the mud as children; the family together in silence; Ntanya slumped on his stool unable to do anything; the old man in the bar. While others again stamp themselves vividly and precisely on our minds at a single stroke:

> he noticed his mother seated in the world cross-legged on the ground with a piece of calico tied round her waist and her other piece of calico . . . rippled in a mass on her lap.

At another moment Ntanya looks back on an incident in the city which summarises his suppressed and violent frustration and anger:[9]

> he had gone to bed with an ageing prostitute and, instead of paying her, had beaten her and burnt her clothes.

We might here mention a striking image of joy towards the end – the old blind woman with elephantiasis 'bubbling with happiness about how simply grand it was to be living.'

The texture of ideas and language is rich and intriguing, with vocabulary and variety of structures to support it. It is true that there are awkward-nesses in the phrasing which derive not so much from East African idiom as from personal idiosyncrasy or carelessness. The sentence I quoted a moment ago could be more happily composed: 'There are certain images that although we see only once, we can never shake out of our memories, never until we die.' But the freshness of the thinking usually carries us over these hitches in phrasing.

An author who adopts an only moderately articulate protagonist like Lawino or an anti-hero like Ntanya must outface certain technical problems. For my part I am not disturbed if, in employing the technique of the stream of consciousness, a writer expresses the character's introspection in terms beyond that character's vocabulary. This is a necessary part of fictional licence for which we can reasonably be expected to suspend disbelief, provided we are satisfied that the concepts and attitudes expressed are appropriate. With regard to direct speech readers find themselves more fastidious. Even if we allow that the people in *Dying in the Sun* are to be thought of as using the language that comes naturally to them, the English words that represent their speech do not always seem to convey a style which is apt. In the main Palangyo realises his characters faithfully and brings them to life, so we are surprised to hear Mugia in the bar holding forth about 'a thoroughly unintelligent, even unintelligible world'. The dying words of Ntanya's child-sister are precocious to say the least. We could accumulate sufficient examples to suggest that this is a significant flaw in the novel, even though a greater proportion of the dialogue flows naturally enough. On the other hand Palangyo uses bold but selective phrases in his own voice which are highly evocative: 'the intense purity of a child's anger'; the children when put through the motions of mourning are 'exhausted by the emptiness of their tears'.

Metaphors are of the very essence of the style. They lend it variety and richness; they extend the range of meaning and significance; they create a depth and resonance absent in more mundane and unimaginative prose. So given is Palangyo to a metaphorical mode of expression that at times it is in danger of developing into a mere stylistic habit, with the result that some of his comparisons are mechanical and contrived. The predictable appearance of yet another similitude pat in its place may irritate the reader, as it is also liable to do, for instance, in early works by Joseph Conrad such an *An Outcast of the Islands*. Unfortunately for the writer, the least successful images are likely to be the most obtrusive. The metaphors in *Dying in the Sun* are for the most part apt, and in key with the whole mode and setting, drawn from a familiar context, often from the animal life of the district. My quotations include a fair cross-section of such frequent and successful parallels.

But there is a smaller number which will not stand up to close examination, or which indeed may be patently meretricious even at a first reading.

The concept of Ntanya seeking the cube-root of his unsatisfied desires is extravagant: while this image patterns into the description of his becoming an outcast from school, yet since we have at this point, as so often, the sensation of participating in Ntanya's stream of consciousness, the idea may strike us as out of key with a man who baulked primary arithmetic. There are more glaring instances: 'He found himself suspended, between the night before and that evening, like a washing line between two posts' does not hold good even in the major term, while the overtones confuse rather than clarify the point at issue. (The washing line is functional *only* when suspended in this way; the two posts are specifically co-existent without any element of progression in time, and are linked to each other effectively only by the line, and so forth). This is an occasional but serious fault. But to notice only the minority of weak or clumsy comparisons would be lopsided criticism, for such ill-considered usages are the exception, not the rule.

At times Palangyo uses absolute emotional words with the same lack of inhibition that we find in D. H. Lawrence, though without the latter's rawness or self-conscious extremism: 'He had never hated anybody so much before. He did not even think this was possible.' And there are other moments when we seem to have to do with a less violent Lawrence: 'At times, even possibly most of the time, the flesh is much wiser than the spirit, just as children are at times so much wiser than adults.' Though, unlike Lawrence, Palangyo later uses the word 'happiness' as unequivocally as 'love' or 'hatred'.

Not infrequently in *Dying in the Sun* the voice of the author speaks directly to us, in the manner of nineteenth-century European novelists, generalising the ideas which the fiction illustrates:

> Have you wondered at times whether there is any difference between the love of a man for a woman and his love for God? They are both founded on weakness, the only human greatness, are they not?

The intrusions are not always very happy. Not only do they too often have the ring of pseudo-philosophical statements, either rather trite or inadequately supported, but they divert the writer's attention from the dramatisation of his theme and give him the sensation that experiences have been enacted – as they should be and as he does so often project them – when in fact they have only been asserted; indeed the abstraction does not always reflect the actual events in the book at all precisely, as in the second half of the following quotation:[10]

Everybody has got his night, the night when everything comes to a sharp point like a boil. After that night life reaches a climax, and the rest is just a summing-up, a going downhill through a road well known because it has been travelled before.

Equally disturbing is the use of the over-easy phrase in an emotional context, which tends to sentimentalise the situation rather than penetrate it. My quotations have not been able to avoid instances of this somewhat naive or self-consciously intense wording, which one feels to be the result of the withdrawal of self-criticism in a writer who so often conveys exact and subtle meaning: 'a sadness so harrowing in its sensuality . . .', 'the night of the lone naked soul', 'bubbling with happiness about how simply grand it was to be living'; examples could easily be multiplied, and several indeed lie ahead of us.

The novel's most serious structural fault – a lack of due proportion in the dénouement – is related to one of its greatest strengths, the tightness and economy of its patterning. The final statement of *Dying in the Sun* is positive. The hopefulness carries conviction because it is stripped of illusions. Palangyo attempts to show the change that takes place in Ntanya at the end of the book as a difficult progression, and to avoid glibness by leading us through his spiritual relapse after his father's death. I am convinced of the aesthetic propriety and the emotional integrity of the happy ending: it is carefully organised, an essential part of the whole design. But after the full statement of Ntanya's contradictory frame of mind at the beginning, the last transitions are too hurried to be altogether satisfying artistically or convincing as narrative. At a second reading I found this compression less troublesome since I was more aware of the inner structure of the story. Nevertheless I still have little doubt, after further readings, that the final ten or fifteen could be developed to at least twice their present length to the great advantage of the novel.

But let me return from these serious but secondary criticisms to the major positive features of the work. From the start Onya insists, 'You must be strong for us', and from the start Ntanya responds. 'Ntanya was going to count his fingers and wait for this silent self-birth of reorganisation in the dark forest of his soul.' Ntanya makes a discovery during the period of nursing his father: 'He had said before that with death nothing made any difference. But now he knew something did make a difference – awareness.' Teresa explains why she did not kill herself: it was a choice between absolutes: 'I remembered my mother's words that no matter how bad life is, it is always better than death.' Ntanya takes up Teresa's melody of hope:

'it's just as she was saying, Baranya; one should never close the hope door to happiness and love'. If one has been thinking of the book as being in some degree pessimistic, one may be surprised to realise how deeply these assertions are embedded in its very texture. Teresa becomes inextricably interwoven with Ntanya's quest: 'he persisted in trying to find a link between his search for what had gone wrong and his love for this woman.'

Above all there is the desire to gather disparate experience into a meaningful pattern:

> Could there be a link between this woman I have just said I will marry and my dying father – who may be isn't my father at all? Could this new-found ecstasy be but a reversal, a turning inside out of all my tribulation in this land, this world that has refused my handshake of friendship? Could this indeed be but asking the same question I asked at my mother's grave backwards, as I hear Arabs from the north write?

As Ntanya grapples with the negative paradoxes that bewilder him, they do not become less paradoxical, but the paradoxes and mysteries assume a positive aspect. As Teresa comes to new life away from Maria's hothouse,[11]

> Ntanya felt that he was somehow connected with this revival. His heart throbbed with victory and pleasure at this potency in him. He was still puzzled as to how one who had so little could bestow so much upon another.

As we contemplate various facets of the book, we may find that it too shifts from having one significance to implying the very opposite. The sex troubadour's grave, bedecked with his mask, appears a joke to passers-by. At first this may seem to us gloomily ironical, but on further consideration, does it not take the sting out of death, and convey appropriately the mood in which the old man both lived and died?

After the death of Ntanya's father, with the coming of the long rains, we are given a vivid picture of the natural upsurge of growth and fertility in which, ironically, as the aftermath of death, Ntanya's family may not join. Ntanya himself slips into a strange emotional limbo to balance his enforced idleness, which Teresa feels to be a return to the unreality of the bar-*cum*-brothel: 'Now it seems as if all I'm going to get is the death-life of Maria's house.' The mute disillusionment which Ntanya suffers has now to be exorcised. Teresa's attempt to break the spell by digging for the family does not succeed. Yet it is through her frontal attack that his negative mood is broken:

Why do you have to destroy yourself and us and blame other people for it? Your father died, many other people's fathers have died. You've lost a job, think you are a bastard, and so on and so on. All these things and more have happened to other people. They have not gone around destroying other people's lives because of it! . . . all you do is move around like a ghost.

In response Ntanya faces his despair (in a speech which, convincingly, Teresa does not understand) and outfaces it, and so they re-find life together.

'Most of all they laughed at their newly unearthed happiness, unearthed from so deep down in the mud of living.' They discover, in James's words, 'There is so much, so much to live for.' 'How much we have wasted of ourselves complaining incessantly about trivialities.' The twig on Ntanya's father's grave, which he had deliberately planted in such a way as to prevent its growing, sprouts nevertheless; Ntanya's newly-born son looks like Nterenya, his father. It seems that even the curse of Ntanya's father's life and death has been lifted.

Now falls the death of Ntanya's grandmother, a death which we are not allowed to regard as a negative event. The fear of death is behind us. Sex, love, and life are beautiful: 'It is beautiful, it is beautiful, it is beautiful,' exclaims Teresa. There is complete identification between her and Ntanya. 'Ntanya would then eat and drink to his satisfaction and always rest for a while in the sun after saying "Thank you mother." ' The book ends in an achieved happiness: 'every day Ntanya would water this seed with his joy, with this vigilance and care.' When he is assured that he is legitimate, Ntanya asks forgiveness of his father and completes the words that the older man had been stammering in death, 'My father, my, my . . . my own true father. Pardon me.'

The importance that Ntanya attaches to his technical Western-style legitimacy is perhaps exaggerated, and, on another level, weakens the conclusion in making the final resolution dependent on an external factor: would the emotional well-being of Ntanya and Teresa have been diminished at the end if Nterenya had not been Ntanya's progenitor? If so, this works against the general tendency of the novel which is to assert that men can control and determine their own emotional stability, by accepting the inherent contradictions in existence and seizing upon happiness in terms of human relationships wherever it offers itself, in spite of accompanying disillusionments. On the other hand, the importance of the re-establishment of the link with past generations through renewed rapport with his dead father is essential and positive at each level, in a way and to a degree that could not be true in a European novel.

Dying in the Sun resorts in a sense to a simple statement of the natural cycle: life – death – life. And yet it is not so simple since life has been honestly questioned. Hope and positive values have been won out of despair: there is no mere complacency. All these issues are mixed with the very soil of an East African village in *Dying in the Sun*. It is peasants, ex-houseboys, village outcasts who find these issues to be woven into the fabric of their existence and who resolve them in their own terms. The novel concerns itself with questions and truths inherent in contemporary African life. The furthest horizon of its characters lies within the borders of their own country. Both Teresa and Ntanya are the flotsam and jetsam of 'progress', bandied about between town and countryside, between settled tradition and the ruthless rat-race to stay alive. They, like their more favoured and sophisticated fellows, are torn between different sets of values and are subject to the most profound disillusionment which derives not from refined world-weariness but from bitter experience. *Dying in the Sun* not only lends some dignity to these broken people, but reminds us that however significant a figure the so-called man of two worlds may be, the Teresas and Ntanyas are just as much test-cases for this society. Their despair is a measure of a nation's spiritual confusion; their eventual achievement is a measure of its potential. That the resolution of their problems and tensions is hardwon, hammered out at grass-roots, is therefore most significant.

The book has unity; paradoxes are contained if not resolved; by an act of faith, the importance of human relations is reasserted and accepted as a mystery. The redeeming features of life are as universally inherent as the damning features. 'This mixture of joy and fear had also been in Ntanya's heart.' One must die in the sun as elsewhere; but there is no occasion to *submit* to death while the sun shines.

NOTES

1 *D.I.T.S.*, 2; the following quotation is from p. 48 ('Everybody has got his night . . .').

2 Albert Camus, *Caligula*, trans. Stuart Gilbert in *Caligula and Cross Purpose*, Penguin, 1965, p. 34; (this translation formerly published by Hamish Hamilton, 1948).

3 *D.I.T.S.*, p. 13; the following three quotations are from pp. 24 ('Some strange spirit . . .'), 1 ('a sadness so harrowing . . .'), and 1 ('broken people . . .').

4　T. S. Eliot, *The Family Reunion*, Faber, London, 1939, p. 55.

5　*D.I.T.S.*, p. 2; the following seven quotations are from pp. 3 ('before death . . .'), 4 ('beyond pity . . .'), 119 ('Because we have this seed . . .'), 20–1, 42 ('I always say . . .'), 37 ('What would I do . . .?'), and 54 ('he just wanted . . .').

6　*D.I.T.S.*, p. 91; the following seven quotations are from pp. 45 ('I have settled . . .'), 44 ('Yes, you can say . . .'), 13 ('It was not at all . . .'), 125, 41 ('There was no mistaking it . . .'), 21 ('the known-unknown darkness . . .'), and 41 ('The heart of a human being . . .').

7　*D.I.T.S.*, p. 11; the following eight quotations are from pp. 49 ('He was looking for . . .'), 15, 48 ('Now was the night . . .'), 49 ('For an experience . . .'), 53 ('The deepest of our prayers . . .'), 120 ('It's not my being . . .'), 5 ('the only beautiful thing . . .'), and 48 ('She would have chewed . . .').

8　*D.I.T.S.*, p. 9; the following seven quotations are from pp. 22 ('The poor old soul . . .'), 9 ('the knitting . . .'), 8 ('His only real claim . . .'), 21 ('This time his hand . . .'), 38 ('Something had attracted her . . .'), 65 ('There are certain images. . .'), and 23.

9　*D.I.T.S.*, p. 50; the following seven quotations are from pp. 122 ('bubbling with happiness . . .'), 2 ('the intense purity . . .'), 47 ('exhausted by the emptiness . . .'), 81 ('He found himself suspended . . .'), 98 ('He had never hated . . .'), 65 ('At times . . .'), and 72.

10　*D.I.T.S.*, p. 48; the following seven quotations are from pp. 12 ('You must be strong . . .'), 12 ('Ntanya was going to count . . .'), 54 ('He had said before . . .'), 77 ('I remembered . . .'), 78 ('it's just as she was saying . . .'), 81 ('he persisted . . .'), and 81–2.

11　*D.I.T.S.*, p. 104; the following eight quotations are from pp. 118 ('Now it seems . . .'), 118–19, 121 ('Most of all . . .'), 122 ('How much we have wasted . . .'), 127 ('Ntanya would then eat . . .'), 128 ('every day Ntanya . . .'), 128 ('My father . . .'), and 124 ('This mixture . . .').

CHAPTER 8

A Good Bad Heroine

A study of Cyprian Ekwensi's *Jagua Nana*

IT was G. K. Chesterton who coined the phrase 'good bad book' but George Orwell later made it peculiarly his own. Writing in 1946 on this favourite topic, Orwell turns from the consideration of what he himself calls 'escape' literature to another group of books altogether:[1]

> There is another kind of good bad book which is more seriously intended, and which tells us, I think, something about the nature of the novel and the reasons for its present decadence. During the last fifty years there has been a whole series of writers – some of them are still writing – whom it is quite impossible to call 'good' by any strictly literary standard, but who are natural novelists and who seem to attain sincerity partly because they are not inhibited by good taste. . . . Most of these have been prolific writers, and their output has naturally varied in quality. I am thinking in each case of one or two outstanding books. . . . In each of these books the author has been able to identify himself with his imagined characters, to feel with them and invite sympathy on their behalf, with a kind of abandonment that cleverer people would find it difficult to achieve. They bring out the fact that intellectual refinement can be a disadvantage to a story-teller, as it would be to a music-hall comedian. . . . Exhibitionism and self-pity are the bane of the novelist, and yet if he is too frightened of them his creative gift may suffer.
> The existence of good bad literature – the fact that one can be amused or excited or even moved by a book that one's intellect simply refuses to take seriously – is a reminder that art is not the same thing as cerebration.

This commentary seems remarkably apt in considering the work of Cyprian Ekwensi, that sprawling, journalistic, vital and popular writer who would well understand what Orwell is talking about in this passage, just as Orwell would have responded in the same spirit to Ekwensi's 'one or two outstanding books', one of which is *Jagua Nana*. To explore the positive and memorable qualities in this work without first frankly acknowledging its literary limitations would seem dishonest. I hope the authority of Orwell will allow me to do both without being dismissed as mere carping before I come to the real gist of my study.

Jagua Nana, like so many African works of fiction, is concerned with the clash between two cultures, but in the context of this novel the phrase takes on a quite different meaning from that which is normally understood by it. As is usual, the old confronts the new, but instead of one being essentially alien, we are presented with two different aspects of African society: the village and the city; the traditional and the ultra-sophisticated. It is true that Lagos itself may be described as Westernised, but in many ways this is a biased and unsatisfactory description: it would perhaps be more precise to say that it is modernised, and that the interplay between past and present has created a city life which, while sharing many common features with city life elsewhere, is also essentially African. White men do not play any key role either in the main action or behind the scenes: at most they are one of a number of groups who represent modern values, but not in any specially significant manner. Indeed, the typical remaining administrators from overseas as portrayed in the book do not seem to be 'with' swinging Lagos at all or to understand very clearly what is going on there: they find their proper place in modern African fiction as part of the background and setting.

In making the comparisons inherent in the contrast between the older, quieter ways in rural Nigeria, and the newer, brasher, more vivid life of the big city, *Jagua Nana* superficially conforms to conventional morality in praising the purity of village life and condemning the decadence of the urban rat-race. The author loses no opportunity to 'expose' the squalor and degradation of the new city culture. But it is clear in any frank appraisal of the novel that its real heart, the real source of its vitality, depends on viewing the city – and Jagua herself along with it – sympathetically. The writer shares her intoxication with the night-club, the bright lights, the glamour, which bespeaks a life lived intensely, a life which perpetually promises and quite often offers some form of excitement. In the process of becoming acquainted with the degradation that lies behind the flashy façade, the reader is in fact quite as likely to be attracted as repelled; but the attraction lies less in the familiar facts of the matter than in the zest with which this concentration of human life is comprehended.

After observing all the novel's manifold faults, this is one of the two main things that draws one back to this good bad book which impinges so boldly upon our imagination. Even for the puritanical reader, if such a one gets beyond the first few pages, the moralising must surely soon appear to be fairly obvious, and too familiar to support out vital interest. Without forgetting the down-and-out accounts of Nairobi life that have appeared more recently, I don't think any other novel from independent Africa so patently has the blood of the city in its veins: for a true parallel in this respect one must turn to South African writers. This blood is also, of course, Jagua's blood. And it is the creation of this character that makes *Jagua Nana* indubitably Ekwensi's most memorable novel – his 'outstanding' book as Orwell would term it. We shall return to a full consideration of her and her place in the narrative as the culmination of this short study.

Though nothing comes amiss to Ekwensi, and he will take up any topical theme that crosses his path, such themes do not shape and bind his books as they do those, say, by Achebe and Ngugi. In Ekwensi it is the central character who alone holds the whole structure together; the plot develops in a straight line, relating the experiences of the protagonist, with occasional minor flashbacks to sketch in earlier parts of the story. Of course some novels may be bound by both themes and personality – perhaps all readable novels must be so to some extent – but however broad a canvas *Jagua Nana* may fill, it is first and last an account of Jagua's life. All the other figures are cameos within her history. We barely get a glimpse of Freddie or Nancy in England. No part of the novel is ascribed to them. If the Freddie of the first part of the book comes to life, it is almost exclusively in terms of his relationship with Jagua, and not independently in his own right.

Indeed there is no great care to make the characters consistent and two cameos may be bracketed under the same name with scant probability. I cannot believe that the shy lover sitting on the edge of a chair in Jagua's room, is the same person as the Dennis Odoma who is the leader of a group of desperate and blasé thieves, though they both go under the same name. Freddie too changes beyond recognition; there is a sufficient time-lapse to enable us to argue that he has somehow been transformed by intermediate experience, but nothing is done to make the transition from the rather weak young man under Jagua's spell to the brash politician with a belligerent bodyguard at all convincing.

This form of novel has reappeared in many societies at different times, and in Europe has for long gone under the general classification of the 'picaresque': the very fact that English adopted a Spanish term for it suggests its international origins. The eighteenth-century British novelist who most aptly epitomises this tradition is perhaps Smollett, who speaks in his preface to *Roderick Random*[2] of 'that generous indignation which ought to animate the reader against the sordid and vicious disposition of the world'. The stimulation of such a response provides him with a broad journalistic brief to explore every colourful and dramatic aspect of human experience that capture his attention. Walter Allen says of Smollett that he 'exposes, crudely and brutally, a brutal and crude society'.[3] Allen sums up the picaresque tradition by saying that it[3]

> strung together a series of comic or farcical adventures, which together exposed the manners of society, given a unity by their happening to the same man, a rogue.

Ekwensi has in fact very little genius for satire, and not much more for farce. Some of the scenes in *Jagua Nana* would benefit very greatly from a greater measure of such talents, notably the whole episode with Chief Ofubara or the fights between the women. We catch a glimpse of the possibilities of this manner in the scene at the British Council lecture (perhaps the funniest in the book), and in Jagua's experiment in making political speeches. There is no doubt, however, that in other respects Allen's description of the picaresque novel easily embraces *Jagua Nana*. Jagua can certainly be described as a rogue, since she is not only a professional prostitute, but is also eager to sell goods for Dennis which she knows to have been stolen.

A further quotation from Walter Allen links *Jagua Nana* even more closely to the Smollett tradition:

> For him the novel was a branch of journalism, and nowhere in his fiction is the element of journalism, the simple aim of giving factual information, stronger than in *The Expedition of Humphrey Clinker*, his last novel.

Fiction and journalism, as I have already hinted, also come interestingly close in Ekwensi. The rather facile 'exposition' of social wrongs as a justification for describing in detail some of the more lurid aspects of life is reminiscent of the newspaper, as well as the considerable element of sheer reportage. For all the vivacity the adoption of this manner affords, we are bound also to notice the limitations of such an approach for the novelist.

The novel opens by addressing itself informatively to the non-African reader:[4] 'Jagua had just had a cold bath, and, in the manner of African women, she sat on a low stool. . . .' This rather pedestrian instructive manner distances the reader (especially the African reader) and hinders us from becoming involved in the action. And from the beginning we hear the

essentially journalistic tone of social protest, which in its indignant pronouncement of platitudes somewhat disappoints us in a context which has
geared us to expect a greater subtlety of insight, and a more personal
intimacy of contact:

> They and many others were practically strangers in a town where all
> came to make fast money by faster means, and greedily to seek positions
> that yielded even more money.

However, the whole movement of the novel naturally adopts the *Tropicana*, the prototype night-club, as its real centre, a place of heightened expectation, of temporary emotions, of movement, variety, a social crossroads.
It is in simple but neat and effective contrast with the pseudo-intellectuality
of the dull public lecture that precedes our first introduction to the *Tropicana*. We see Jagua in these rival situations, first honestly bored and then
vulgarly vital. We are treated to a good deal of raw cynicism: 'He should
know by now that in the *Tropicana*, money always claimed the first loyalty.'
Here begins a long series of shifts from one setting to another, one topic to
another, providing a cross-section of Lagos life, and crowding the novel
with a constant array of short-lived and loosely connected interests. The
snatches that we hear of the sincere, high-sounding speeches for Freddie's
planned departure reminds us of *No Longer at Ease*. The 'been-tos' are drawn
to our attention as another feature of the scheme:

> They were trumpet-blowers out to impress Jagua. 'Been-tos' who had
> been in England and acquired professional skills were regarded with great
> favour by the women.

The contrived pick-up of Jagua by Freddie and his friend serves to introduce
us to a typical posh suburb, Okoyi, and to allow a suitable discourse on the
contrasts between rich and poor districts.

Several times during the course of the book dreams are used as a more or
less unconcealed plot device, though (as so often in Ekwensi) when he
uses a hackneyed technique he does so with confident professional skill,
so that the dreams are in their way powerful passages. Perhaps the sentence
in the novel which most blatantly comes straight from a travelogue or
text-book is this, which appears on page 47:

> The plane's light winked – in colour too – from wingtip and nose and tail,
> as the plane pointed its nose at Kano, 800 miles away and even hotter
> but much less humid than Lagos.

If we might justify the description of the plane's landing-lights as a colourful visual image, we are left without comment on the geographical and meteorological data about Kano, a city which has nothing whatever to do with the novel and is not otherwise alluded to.

So now in turn we are carried to the farmlands and we are edified by uncomplicated praise of the country life:

> In Ogabu the people tilled the soil and drank river water and ate yams and went to church but came home to worship their own family oracles. They believed that in a village where every man has his own yam plots, there is much happiness in the hearts of the men and the women and the children.

Certainly Ekwensi is resourceful and fertile in ideas, and his mercurial manner brings off good strokes at each turn:

> this was a part of the world where Nature prevailed and nudism was no stranger; human bodies were not concealed with the art of non-concealment.

Yet undeniably the flow is jerky. The author feels free to drop his account of one aspect of life as soon as he loses interest in it, and to start another section or pick up another topic apparently quite arbitrarily, without any artistic necessity or structural control.

Some of the major scenes, for all that they are very dramatic, are also very contrived: an obvious example is the account of Nancy's capture, particularly in the sudden appearance of the band of young men to kidnap her, which is never explained. Such things can easily be presented plausibly, but it seems for all his desire to be realistic, Ekwensi's priorities are elsewhere. Immediate interest is everything. He will throw in a snippet on women's rights a few pages later rather than tidy up the fringes of the story:[5] 'She could see that he had never really experienced the sensation of African woman as equal.'

A fairly facile sentimentalism is ever near the surface. The characters are worked up into an emotional state quite easily and it is assumed that we will share their sudden sorrows, paroxysms and sentiments. The emotional climax of the reconciliation between the two island factions is related thus:

> Uncle Namme opened out his arms and the two men embraced. The tears came in a flood to Jagua's eyes as she watched the scene.

And so the travelogue moves on and we meet the Merchant Princesses, who are at length linked to the story through Jagua's final entry into their company at the conclusion, but for the moment we are introduced to them rather as an item on our itinerary than as an integral part of a close-knit narrative scheme:

> She owned a fleet of lorries which travelled north and east, distributing bicycles, soap, and cement. Jagua sat in her shed and listened almost mesmerised. She could find nothing at all unusual in this money-spinning woman who did not know how to write English.

Our picaresque journey takes us next into the underworld of thieves with Dennis Odoma. Needless to say, almost within minutes of Jagua's first visit to him she finds herself in the midst of a police raid. Characteristic of this inclusive and permissive structure is the introduction, as a lively vignette, of the screen dance performed in the *Tropicana*, and the tropical wrangle between traditional music and high-life which grows out of it.

One of the elements of melodrama is frequent coincidence even at key points in a narrative sequence. A particularly striking conjunction of this kind in *Jagua Nana* is the fortuitous grouping which determines not only that Uncle Taiwo and Freddie are fighting for the same seat in the elections, but that this also happens to be the area where Dennis Odoma lives, a chance proximity that allows all Jagua's points of interest to be strategically close together. So to the world of cut-throat elections. The clashes between thugs of rival parties also form an important element in Achebe's *A Man of The People*. Indeed it is already apparent that the plot of *Jagua Nana* would provide many a novelist with the basic material for at least six books. There is general and effective irony in the composition of Uncle Taiwo's election speech: the abuses that he enumerates we all know to exist; and we also know that far from wanting to cure these ills in actual fact, his one aim is to jump on the band-wagon and start taking his share of the profits. Clearly everything is grist to the mill of this novel, and yet there is a pleasant satiric stroke in this sequence which really has the air of coming from a different work altogether: the highly stylised concept of two rival parties being called O.P.1 and O.P.2.

The panorama is still not complete: there is a necessary element missing, and this is now supplied in the more detailed description of the final degradation of Rosa's slum. Even here Ekwensi finds scope to be chattily informative in telling us that the mattresses were stuffed with the kind of grass 'cut by prisoners at the racecourse'. All the characters are seen off the arena in turn in final flashes which outline their eventual fortunes. And as the pages run out, a sort of happy ending is contrived for Jagua as the result of her rather dubious piece of luck with the hidden windfall of stolen money.

I have heard undergraduates interestingly defending the banal sensationalism of much of the sexy phrasing as a proper and effective way to describe a brash and sensational society. We recall Walter Allen's assertion that Smollett 'exposes crudely and brutally, a brutal and crude society'. This raises important critical issues. There is no question as to the authenticity of such language. We recognise the phrasing to which the emancipated adolescent aspires: 'her breasts swelled into a sensuous arc', and which the group-conscious typist employs: 'They called her Jagua because of her good looks and stunning fashions.' The question is rather whether diction such as this can paint more than the predictable external picture of familiar subject matter: whether it can fulfil the real function of fiction and take us beneath the surface to new understanding and new sympathies. The same question arises with the all-too-recognisable brassy tones of juvenile revolt – sometimes for the sake of being in revolt – such as are heard in Charles Mangua's *Son of Woman*.

One of my own favourite instances in *Jagua Nana* forms part of the description of Sabina:[6] 'She turned her full back on Jagua. It was a back filled with lust.' The glib phrases are ready to hand when Freddie is first attracted to Nancy:

> He had never before felt the real difference between pure love such as was exalting him now, and the casual encounters with the *Tropicana* girls.

Freddie's situation is sensationalised without much real feeling:

> He was the glamorous young man in Jagua's life, the lover of the elderly beauty who must not press forward when those who paid for her luxuries were around.

We are inclined to respond by recalling that Freddie has chosen his bed and can quit it whenever he pleases, and so we are likely to react against his specious self-pity. Ekwensi paints for us the pathetic picture of the helpless prostitute in the clutch of circumstances who is taken up casually by a man with money to spare and is cast back onto the rubbish heap again when he has had his pleasure: 'In the cold streets she would once again revert to what she was, and who cared?' – but this scene is somewhat robbed of its pathos when we remember that this particular prostitute happens to have a sizable bank balance, and is certainly well enough off to carry quite a considerable share of the moral responsibility herself.

Ekwensi is impatient with his material. We are sometimes allowed to guess what is going to happen even when the effect of a particular scene depends on the sensation of narrative surprise. Suspense and build-up often go by default, but even when they are achieved the result may be anti-climax rather than tension. The precautions offered against swimming in the waters of Krinameh, for instance, are so patent a preparation for the dramatic outcome that we have anticipated the climax well before it takes place. Chief Ofubara's infatuation is too rapid and too naively lustful to carry any overtones of complex feeling. And Jagua's easy moralising after the event when she knew all along what the score was, does not affect us greatly:

> Why, why had she got her fortunes entwined with those of this dashing but tragic young man? She knew now. She knew that if a girl went to the *Tropicana* every day, that girl was a pawn; a pawn in the hands of criminals, Senior Service men, contractors, thieves, detectives, liars, cheats, the rabble, the scum of the country's grasping hands. . . .

But Jagua has been aware of this for years; and she seems herself to have avoided being a mere pawn very successfully. Our perspective on Sabina's acts of violence is that of a newspaper report; we are not on the inside of these events: we experience only the kind of shock we might feel on reading such an account in the press.

Sometimes it even seems that Ekwensi forgets what he has written in his own previous paragraph. 'Instinct told her that something suspicious was going on,' we read, and yet a few lines earlier Freddie has left the club suddenly, followed minutes later by his thugs, and then the waiter has reported that he thinks Freddie has been involved in an accident: it hardly needs much instinct to deduce that something is afoot.

The most improbable single item in the plot for me is the account of Jagua lugging Uncle Taiwo's bag around unopened. This is completely out of character, and has obviously been arranged for the sole purpose of providing a suitable dénouement with little concern for plausibility.

This catalogue of Ekwensi's limitations is made mainly to isolate more emphatically those features which nevertheless imprint this good bad novel on our attention very much more forcefully than many forgotten works which in comparison may have been more polished in many respects.

Apart from the sheer dash and bravado with which Ekwensi sweeps past all formal critical judgments to employ his style with slashing journalistic skill, there is an aspect of his handling of language which I particularly admire. This is the way that he employs pidgin English. I do not know of another West African novelist who can at one and the same time retain all the vigour and immediacy of pidgin while still making brief passages in it comprehensible to those who are unfamiliar with the lingo. This is not just facile local colour thrown defiantly in the faces of outsiders. It is to be seen as an essential and integral part of racy, detribalised town life:[7] 'but when she spoke to him she always used pidgin English, because living in Lagos City they did not want too many embarrassing reminders of clan or custom'. Pidgin is thus inseparable from the milieu of the novel and basic to its rhythm.

Ekwensi brings his characters to life in their own natural medium of expression without limiting his readership to West Africa. He does so with an unassuming ease which makes it appear a simple matter, yet reference to the works of those who have tried their hands at the same thing will convince us that it is not so. Other authors might do well to study this important feature of Ekwensi's writing – for which, oddly enough, he has been more often censured than praised – since the vitality and communicability he achieves might well be emulated in forms of speech prevalent elsewhere.

I discussed at the beginning of this essay the ambiguous, yet vivid and vital picture that the novel paints of city life in all its more dramatic aspects, and it is now time to link this picture to the portrayal of Jagua herself, since she is literally the life and soul of the work.

The book opens with Jagua squarely in the middle of the canvas in a well realised sketch. This is as it should be since she is to be our whole subject. The ageing prostitute is a recurrent picture in Ekwensi's fiction. From the start we are restrained from any sense of revulsion by a certain melancholy which lingers about her, and yet at the same time we are also prevented from feeling sad by our awareness of the courage, even the magnificence, which she so often displays: 'The sigh was a prayer to God to stay back the years and a challenge to herself to employ all the coquettish arts to help Him.' She is filled with a vague, restless aspiration, which keeps alive an untiring fire and a pathetic hope within her: 'Something will happen tonight, this night, she always told herself.' It is a truthful touch that it should be Nancy's taunt about childlessness that arouses her anger – partly anger and shame against herself, partly a fierce defiance, insisting that she should be allowed to be herself without criticism or interference.

The interlocking ironies involved in her relationship with Freddie are complex and powerful. He is boyishly dazzled; she is empassioned by his youth and innocence. She is at once both generous and selfish in paying his way: she seeks to help him, but she also seeks to keep him to herself. In accepting her financial backing he is understandably ambitious, and yet mean in that he does not intend to keep the stated or implied conditions. She hopes and fears: he pulls away. Whatever flaws one may notice in detailed presentation, this relationship is subtly comprehended and portrayed by Ekwensi; we are convinced, touched, irritated, confused in our emotions and moral reactions, even as we might be in real life, if, that is, we knew the full circumstances (which would be unlikely).

He has a genuine, reluctant passion for her: 'the torture of being held in sexual bondage by a woman very much older than he was, more cunning and more ambitious and infinitely more possessive.' The scene where Jagua creeps back to Freddie and calls to him through the door at night is touching and credible. Her need and her passion overcome her pride; his relenting is equally true to life. The neighbours recognise the grand scale on which Jagua establishes this relationship (certainly Freddie could not do so):

> There was a law about Jagua and Freddie which was too big for them to understand, and this was it – operating before their eyes.

In her absoluteness, we perceive even a touch of Cleopatra. When Freddie rejects her physically and holds out against her, she cries, ' "Kill me, make we two die together – now!" '; and Ekwensi adds, 'At that moment, she meant it.' The way she flashes from one mood to another is all of a piece with her character throughout; the next incident is equally true to her nature when she learns that her trump card has been devalued and Freddie has won his scholarship from public funds:[8] 'At this particular moment, if Freddie had confronted her, she would gladly have shot him.' Ekwensi knows Jagua well, in a way indeed in which he makes no attempt to get to know his other figures. But to know Jagua is enough for one novel: she fills the book. There is nothing elsewhere to compare with this full-length portrait of one of Lagos's night queens: she is seen without illusions, and without condemnation.

Rather later, as the incident on the island is developed, it is another true touch that after deliberately and calculatingly seducing Chief Ofubara, she herself begins to be won over by him: 'Now it was she, strangely enough, who was on the verge of losing her head over the Chief.'

What is above all intolerable to Jagua is boredom; and this is something which almost every reader can understand. We can sympathise with her lack of patience: she is a rebel against the humdrum, against dullness: life must constantly *be* something. Ekwensi clearly feels this too, and carries us along with him, and with her. And so she becomes, after the manner of many memorable characters in fiction, a rebel on our behalf. If she acts out our fears, she also acts out some of our dreams, above all our dreams of standing out against the monotonous tyranny of tame existence and refusing to be suborned by it.

Behind this craving for life lies a desperate reaction against trivial unfulfilment. Indeed perhaps the most successful attempt at serious patterning in the book is the relationship that is established by Jagua herself between the daredevilry of the thieves and her own feverish pursuit of excitement and fresh experience. Dennis Odoma attempts to sum up his own and his companions' attitude to life in these words:

> We just spen', to get anythin' we want. Anythin'. So why I worry? De day dat de policemen catch we, we go. Is all de same, whedder we live in cell or outside de cell.

Jagua realises that there is something in common between the bravura of these young men and her own bid for heightened existence:

> Somehow she felt that this young man's philosophy was intricately bound up with hers. He lived for the moment, intensely, desperately. He had no use for conventional methods of thinking. 'What you say is true,' she told him.

When she is with Chief Ofubara, Jagua at last realises that she is constitutionally incapable of settling down:

> Jagua sat quite still. She felt rotten, loose and awful. She knew that she could never really abandon her past life and settle down with someone like Chief Ofubara in a village like Krinameh. But the money would come in useful.

And so the scene in which she finally holds off from committing herself to Krinameh presents a strangely touching picture of self-integrity.

Thus, when we reach the point where her life is in ruins, with her brother standing as a symbolic figure of just accusation, we are sorry for Jagua: this is a remarkable and paradoxical achievement on the part of the author. The lurid atmosphere of Lagos night-life is a reality:

> That driving, voluptuous and lustful element which existed in the very air of Lagos, that something which awakened the sleeping sexual instincts in all men and women and turned them into animals always on heat.

Yet Jagua's involvement is not made to seem her own deliberate choice: this is the life that flows in her blood and she has no alternative. While the terms are nominally of disapproval, beneath the sermonising is a finer level of sympathy:

> Rosa had become – like many women who came to Lagos, like Jagua herself – imprisoned, entangled in the city, unable to extricate herself from its clutches. The lowest and most degraded standards of living were to her preferable to a quiet and dignified life in her own home where she would not be 'free'.

A text-book return to traditional attitudes and a conventional environment is possible only in a highly conventional happy ending – though Ekwensi is realistic enough to leave her as a prospective merchant princess rather than a prodigal daughter. Throughout the book, throughout her life, Jagua has known what she 'ought' to do. Like a great many prostitutes, she has always had a strong, even prudish, moral sense. But what she 'ought' to do has always appeared painfully irrelevant: such a way of life has never seemed possible or desirable to her. And so she is torn between the life that *is* possible and which we see in the novel, and the even more exotic, passionate dream within her.

If, then, Ekwensi is indifferent to certain criteria of excellence, a consideration of which might make this a better book by a 'strictly literary standard' (in Orwell's phrase), he has maintained the work in full vigour, and he may indeed 'seem to attain sincerity partly because [he is] not inhibited by good taste'. He certainly invites sympathy on Jagua's behalf. In doing so without special pleading, Ekwensi makes this a work of serious social, moral and creative significance, which leads us to ask difficult questions about our true values, and urges us to discount the pervading hypocrisy about human needs and aims which we recognise all around us – and perhaps in ourselves. A careful consideration of *Jagua Nana* will certainly confirm that 'art is not the same as cerebration', and will insistently remind us that in the present African context, even more than in that wherein George Orwell found himself, literary criticism is not living up to the demands which we should properly be making of it if it is satisfied to rest in 'intellectual refinement' alone.

NOTES

1 George Orwell, *Tribune*, 2 November 1945; *The Collected Essays, Journalism and Letters of George Orwell, Volume 4, In Front of Your Nose 1945–50*, Penguin, 1970, pp. 38–9.
2 Tobias Smollett, *Roderick Random*, 1748, quoted from Everyman edition, Dent, pp. 4–5.
3 Walter Allen, *The English Novel*, Phoenix House, 1954; quoted from Penguin ed., 1958, p. 68.
4 *J.N.* p. 1; the following five quotations are from pp. 1–2, 15 ('He should know by now . . .'), 31, 69, and 71.
5 *J.N.*, p. 101; the following five quotations are from pp. 96, 104, 165 ('cut by prisoners . . .'), 1 ('her breasts swelled . . .'), and 1 ('They called her Jagua . . .').
6 *J.N.*, p. 117; the following five quotations are from pp. 20, 32, 51 ('In the cold streets . . .'), 128, and 152 ('Instinct told her . . .').
7 *J.N.*, p. 1; the following five quotations are from pp. 12 ('The sigh was a prayer . . .'), 13 ('Something will happen tonight . . .'), 33 ('the torture of being held . . .'), 48, and 53 ('Kill me . . .').
8 *J.N.*, p. 56; the following six quotations are from pp. 101 ('Now it was she . . .'), 124, 124, 95, 180, and 165.

Angled Shots: Studies in the Art of Persuasion

CHAPTER 9

Literature: Closed Shop or Open Forum?

A Preamble to Part III

LITERATURE is all things to all men. In its own way it fathoms every facet of human experience. And so it is natural that specialists from various fields of study should take any outstanding writings which may prove relevant as basic material to illuminate their subjects. *Hamlet* is fertile ground for psychoanalysts; *Things Fall Apart* brings certain aspects of history to life. All the works we have discussed in this book are of serious interest in numerous ways to social scientists. What then is left for literary critics to do? Are they to restrict themselves to an examination of the aesthetics of good writing in isolation from its content? This would be for them to adopt Oscar Wilde's position that 'All art is completely useless.'[1]

Of course, Oscar Wilde is here also mocking those who have neither the wit nor the common sense to grasp the implications of his epigrammatic paradox. He is asserting that art is essentially a human as opposed to an animal practice. Only human beings can become absorbed in objects and activities which serve no external function in terms of material needs or instinctive drives. Art, like religion, is an act of faith; the basis for each lies outside the realm of objective demonstration. Wilde is insisting upon art – literature in particular – as a manifestation of man's spirit through the perception and expression of beauty. After grasping the complex and serious import of Wilde's ideas, most of us will still feel inclined to reject his extreme and defiant stance. But surely we shall equally want to avoid the opposite position of the unrepentant philistine who asks us to see literature as function only, and in effect to equate it with a set of textbooks which purvey information and calculated attitudes.

Most literary criticism that is long-remembered assumes a dual role for literature. It does not ask whether literature should give pleasure: it takes this for granted. It does not ask whether it is the task of literature to instruct its readers: this intention is assumed. The question is, then, nearly always one of balance, of emphasis: what is the relationship between the two demands that we make of literature? In this debate most critics who have outdistanced their own time have agreed with Dr Johnson, the self-appointed arbiter of the writer's moral responsibilities, that precedence must be given to gripping the reader's attention: 'to instruct by pleasing'.[2] If pleasure is in this context often to be seen as a means to an end, yet it may also be allowed its own rights: 'he who pleases many must have some species of merit', just as 'That book is good in vain, which the reader throws away.' 'Poetry,' declares T. S. Eliot in a later age,[3] 'is a superior form of amusement,' clearly assuming that its readers are capable of being entertained in a variety of ways.

'Literature' has thus always been held to embrace the whole art of communication through words, and literary criticism to be an exploration of the artistic interplay between form and content as they fuse to create delight and understanding. If we survey the established canon of English literature we shall find such a breadth of interpretation implicit in the range of accepted masterpieces. Alongside prose fiction, drama and poetry, we will observe a very wide spectrum of other forms with unquestioned holdings – sermons, letters, historical works, political speeches, pamphlets, and journalism, as well as weighty discourses upon education, art and society, and so forth. The judgment of time seems to have determined the literary status of such works, quite a number of which continue to give us immense satisfaction as classics of rhetoric even when their specific topics are otherwise forgotten.

On the contemporary scene, as ever, there is no authority but individual judgment which gradually accumulates into a consensus of opinion as time passes. Established educational structures have been slow to admit contemporary works into the hallowed conservatism of syllabuses (even when their literary form is beyond debate). Similarly, the literary world, while being more eclectic in time so far as the principal genres are concerned, hesitates for at least a couple of generations before admitting additions to the category of *belles lettres*, not knowing yet whose judgment to rely on.

Africa has been comparatively progressive, not only in acknowledging the importance of literature to society, but also in seeing that a new literature cannot afford to be as pedantically exclusive on its critical and educational fronts as one which has centuries of material to draw upon. This situation need not, and in the main does not, lead to lack of discrimination. It has been perceived that a training in the arts is above all a training in judgment in a wide variety of spheres. A training in literature is, in particular, a training in the validity of words, arguments, and the patterns by means of which experience is effectively communicated. A further logical step would be to broaden our attitude towards the literary value of contemporary non-fiction at its best. The burning importance of novels, drama and poetry lies in the immediacy and force with which they convey our world to us, its dilemmas and possibilities. We come to understand life around us more fully through the compelling interest with which literature communicates it to us. The same may be true of writings which can conjure word-magic in non-fictional forms. A refusal to open our minds in new ways to such works would be a betrayal of literary criticism as a vital social and educational force.

It is a false compartmentalisation of our experience to divide up our thinking about books so as to regard novels, plays and poetry as forms worthy of serious critical consideration and non-fiction as ephemeral and trivial. Many works of fiction succeed in diverting us for a while, thus justifying themselves and fulfilling their proper function, without our wanting to read them again, or to give serious thought or discussion to their content; and without their making any serious impression on our emotions or our awareness of other human beings. Other books, while having no evident literary aspirations, may produce a lasting impact on us through what they have to say, though we may not stop to consider that what makes this statement memorable and effective is the art with which the facts and opinions have been put before us. It is seldom enough to have something important to say in order to reach a wide audience: it is essential as a rule to speak with eloquence. Topics which have been blurred by familiarity demand our attention only when a master of words reilluminates them – witness Swift's and Orwell's writings, James Baldwin's *The Fire Next Time* or Lewis Nkosi's *Home and Exile*. The fact that three, at least, of the four books we are to discuss in this section have seldom been honoured with literary critical evaluation tells us more about our conventional view of 'literature' than it does about the works themselves.

Okello Oculi's imaginative writing creates a picture of 'the prostitute' and her milieu, just as Fanon summons up for us the world of 'the native' or Achebe the whole social setting of 'the man of two worlds' in *No Longer at Ease*. If we set *Prostitute* beside *Jagua Nana* we shall realise that these two complement each other, and we cannot do without either. Our consciousness of the life-style of a night-queen is enlarged and modified as much by Okello's work as by Ekwensi's. The latter tells a story very much more specifically than the former, but I think it is an open question which of the two most exercises our imagination – if pressed, I would say it is Okello.

In taking a closer look at *Prostitute*, an East African salvo of protest, we shall at the same time be considering a volume which does not pander to any formal desire to classify writings. It has verse passages within its predominantly prose structure. It is certainly not a novel in any conventional sense, and yet it creates recognisable characters in the same way as fiction, and seems by general agreement to fall more readily within the boundaries of that vague conception 'creative writing' than does, say, *Home and Exile*. Yet, if *Dying in the Sun* takes advantage of the licence of fiction to depict the bewildered soul of Ntanya in depth as he tries to make sense out of his world, so our mental picture of the South African scene comes to life as we watch the 'character' Lewis Nkosi living there in *Home and Exile*. On the other hand, if *Prostitute* and *Home and Exile* offer protest and human challenge, so do *No Longer at Ease* and 'The Strong Breed'. If Fanon and Kenyatta force questions on the literate young African of today, so supremely do Ngugi and Achebe. The arts and skills of persuasion are not restricted to the world of pamphlets and public speeches – any more than mastery of style is the prerogative of the novelist. Dickens is only one of many campaigners who saw the novel as (among other things) a form ideally suited to firing people with ideas and ensuring that protest would be heard; just as Baldwin and Fanon have deployed the skills of literary and rhetorical art in works of non-fiction to stamp their ideas on the consciousness of a generation. If *Things Fall Apart* makes us cast a long look back over our shoulders to see what terrain lies behind and what we should learn from it, so also does *Facing Mount Kenya*.

These comparisons are superficial, perhaps; but they remind us that our concern in trying to plumb beneath the surface of literature is not to set up categories for the sake of doing so; nor to exclude for the sake of excluding; (any more than it is to produce another set of mere synopses.) We must look at works and evaluate them; comprehend them more fully; get more out of them. We shall not want to limit ourselves to the attested masterpieces of fiction, though these are inexhaustible, and constantly provide us with new points of departure. We shall want also to winnow grain from chaff in works of mixed quality – there is too little grain in our world for us to reject supplies simply because they need separating from husks. And we shall also want to explore neglected sources which have been overlooked because their yield can be used and classified in other ways as well.

True critical insight extends horizons; it does not narrow them. Insight is our criterion. We shall embrace all works which employ words so that truth may be 'carried alive into the heart by passion'.[4] Given insight, certain works which we might have assumed to be flat and lifeless when only their surfaces were considered, take on new literary dimensions; while in re-reading and contemplating major works, we shall be induced not simply to pay them lip-service, but constantly to discover fresh and important perspectives within them.

NOTES

1 Oscar Wilde, *The Picture of Dorian Gray*, Ward, Lock & Co., London, 1891, The Preface.

2 Dr Samuel Johnson, 'The Preface to Shakespeare', 1765, *Johnson on Shakespeare* ed. Walter Raleigh, Oxford University Press, London, 1908, p. 16; the following two quotations from Johnson are from *The Lives of the Poets* (1779–81), the life of Pomfret, last sentence; and the life of Dryden, Bohn's Standard Library, ed. Mrs Alexander Napier, George Bell, London, 1908, I, p. 469.

3 Also quoted by R. P. Blackmur as the concluding quotation to his essay 'In the Hope of Straightening Things Out' in *The Lion and the Honeycomb*, Harcourt, Brace, New York, 1955, p. 175.

4 William Wordsworth, Preface to the *Lyrical Ballads* (added in 1802), *Wordsworth's Literary Criticism*, ed. N. C. Smith, Frowde, London, 1905, p. 25.

CHAPTER 10

Legitimate Protest

On Okello Oculi's *Prostitute*

IF, in the light of what has been said in the previous chapter, we are prepared to abandon the over-simple distinction which is too often assumed to
exist between literature and non-fiction, then the criteria normally applied
to classic authors may well also be relevant to certain imaginative and compelling rhetorical works of our own time. I have chosen to discuss Okello
Oculi's *Prostitute* first in this section because traditional critical classification
may be more attuned to granting literary status to a work of such ambivalent
form than to the writings we shall consider in the remaining chapters. And
so *Prostitute* can serve as a bridge between the second and third parts of this
book.

The evident difficulty in determining sharp boundaries between what is
and what is not 'literature' may help to remind us how arbitrary and unhelpful mechanically determined categories are if they encourage us to
exclude from literary discussion works which are readily susceptible to
literary critical analysis and appreciation. At the same time, a work such as
Prostitute clearly needs, at least in part, to be judged on its own terms,
regardless of preconceived formulae. Indeed, those who have no fixed points
of departure will be better able to ask what this prose-poem apparently sets
out to do, and how successful it is. If in the process we find ourselves re-
assessing literary critical assumptions, this is to our advantage.

In *Prostitute* we are confronted with permanent and universal abuses and
social dilemmas, presented as burning issues in their contemporary and
indigenous forms; they are set before our attention in very considerable
detail, with powers of close observation. This is Uganda here and now,
however similar parallels elsewhere may appear to be. While discussing
Prostitute in a broadcast, Okello Oculi himself referred to another of his
works to help explain his impulse in writing:[1]

The trouble with slum conditions is that people often turn their eyes away from what is obviously rotten and what is obviously very unpleasant. In *Orphan* there is a little sentence which says: 'In the village the problem of unnoticing is not there.' In town what I call the problem of unnoticing can start creeping into people's consciousness till eventually what they don't like begins to form like a sediment, as it were; and once this sort of sediment forms in the social environment, people start getting less and less shocked, and this to me is very frightening. I think if one is very concerned about change in society, about reform, about positive policies being adopted in order to help people, one cannot afford to stop getting shocked by what one sees.

Prostitute, then, aspires to be an antidote to complacency. Though, in the same broadcast, Okello very naturally and properly denied that he had any particular audience in view when he was actually composing the book, since he felt himself to be saying what he had to say to whomever would listen, rather than to be striking contrived attitudes for the benefit of a set group; yet looking back – and forwards – he attempted to define the kind of people he would like the work to reach:

> At best one hopes that at least people who make policies, the leaders of this country and leaders maybe even in Eastern Africa, may find the book carries a message which is important for the sort of social policies they have in mind. That is one's best hope, at least it is my best hope: that this book can be of use.

There we have very ably and directly expressed the very opposite of the creed of 'art for art's sake', couched in terms which are far from philistinic or wilful: this is art that is to be useful. The functional nature of the work does not minimise the importance of its literary achievement since the one will depend on the other. Literature and the art of persuasion, far from being in conflict, overlap. It will be to our purpose to investigate how Okello's aspirations are embodied, and how far *Prostitute* achieves its aims.

The author's comments already quoted may help us to look at the work fairly and squarely, without complaining of its apparent failure to do one thing while overlooking the fact that it has succeeded in something very different – the kind of critical blind alley down which the assessment of literature according to categories can so easily lead us. Dickens himself might well have subscribed to the concept of 'unnoticing', and have agreed that an attempt to reverse the process might be a hopeful means of opening people's eyes to what they look past every day. It might be observed that Dickens' attack was often more rousing in principle than applicable in detail; yet there is in his novels a specifically reforming spirit which by implication, amid the windings of the complex plots and particularly in the light of the happy endings, is optimistic; and which in terms of human conduct, presents the reader not only with starkly delineated negatives but also with romantically coloured positives.

The same is not true of *Prostitute*, which, for all its wit and ingenuity, is relentless. Okello is fully preoccupied with an awareness that facing the unsavoury facts of our environment is a prerequisite of any serious consideration of reform. You cannot improve what you will not contemplate. The shock tactics that Okello Oculi employs have therefore certain immediate aims. He hopes to undermine administrative self-righteousness and hypocrisy by demonstrating incontestably that all is certainly not right with the world. From this admission he wishes us to proceed to the recognition of the fact that squalor is not necessarily the product of degeneracy:[2] 'People at home . . . used to add that one should never laugh at weeds because they did not choose to be the unwanted.' We are reminded of Bernard Shaw's insistence that poverty is a crime – society's crime. The corollary to this realisation is that true degeneracy is to be found in its most blatant and inexcusable forms not among the outcasts, the misfits and the unfortunates who have gravitated to the slums largely because they have no choice, but among the callous bourgeoisie, the upright citizens and moralistic administrators who take part, as unobtrusively as they can, in the life they publicly condemn. A simplistic reformer who looks to *Prostitute* for a handbook of vices and virtues will be disappointed, for he will find them inextricably interwoven, and confused by conventional attitudes, so that the only way forward, as in real life, is to attempt a more sophisticated and difficult analysis in untwining causes from effects.

Okello Oculi's fearless honesty in 'noticing' results in a vision which is original. He says and observes things which others do not choose to observe or to say. While the prostitute is seen as a victim – indeed the appalling slum conditions and sexual commerce among which she lives are the core of the book, and while contrasts are drawn between the life she is leading and the life in the village from which she is cut off – such juxtapositions are frequent and deliberately patterned as in the opening section or the passages of verse. Yet there is no attempt to draw an idyllic picture of the countryside any more than of the solid and respectable middle-class.

Nor is the prostitute herself sentimentalised. All sections of society are viewed with a severely critical eye, and their abuses are seen to augment each other. If the prostitute is presented as a victim, she is so not only at the hands of the big man in his shiny black car and his set, but in the first instance she is also deliberately offered up as a sacrifice by the kowtowing village community which, in its sycophancy, abandons the young girl to a situation which is predictably beyond her control. Later the uncompromising village father is adamant in his rejection of this Mary Magdalene.

On balance it is clear that the village lives by more positive values than the city. The image for the unspoilt country girl is the natural murram road in contrast to the prostituted tarmac highway. In the town the crime of unnoticing is complemented by the imminent spectre of fear: 'all this fear started here in the town', where Bisi, the fearless, is brutally eliminated. But in *Prostitute*, as also in *Orphan*, village life, though it may be more elemental and natural, is also shown to be riddled with physical miseries and petty jealousies:

> All over the expanse of the homestead their pain-stricken faces, bare, hardened faces that have been left exposed since the departure of the grasses they once nurtured with their own insides, stare one in the face with blank looks of thirst in mid-sunshine.

There is no defence against natural disaster, nor any end to false attitudinising: the child is killed by the snake, and the community is never out of sight of empty gesturing by converts to an imported religion.

Rebecca, the prostitute's girlhood friend in the countryside, who is an important figure at the end of the book after she has apparently ended up in a conventional village marriage, is earlier on a wild and far from angelic figure. The scene of the Minister's visit and the journey in the provincial bus are sadly realistic. No more than token resistance is offered by the mother to deter her husband and the village elite from cynically sacrificing her daughter to known dangers: 'She had tried to protest but [the wife of the chief] had shut her up.' And if the chauffeur who presides over the girl's abduction 'stood there like irony' as a symbolic city lackey to the big man, he is in effect no more than an accomplice of her own family. The stylised passages in the book throw into even stronger relief the grim actuality of much of its reportage of things as they are; while (a piece of structural sophistication) the scene of the final rejection of the fallen daughter is intensified by being focused through her bitter memories during the seedy ride back to the city afterwards.

On the other hand, the car-owning, more affluent clientele of the night-queens is constantly exposed as being mean, heartless and degradedly sensual. We are to meet the disappointed suitor who has Bisi killed off, cynically, almost casually; and the old man who bites the prostitute's face and nearly breaks her tooth. In the dialogue between the Man and the Lady in Chapter 9, petty snobbery is apostrophised. In contrast with *Jagua Nana*, *Prostitute* finds no facet of society immune; no single romantic backwater of the social scene is left unscathed. Even Bisi, the one man who has a genuine passion for the protagonist, however limited it may be, is not to be pitied as having been stunted by lack of opportunity; he is a professional waster who has squandered his chances of education and has turned his back on a ready-made career.

The prostitute herself is both prey and predator. Like Jagua Nana, she has her heroic qualities, reflected in the way she makes the best of the life she is flung into; and we are led to perceive that she discovers islands of sensual exhilaration, even exaltation, in this sea of filth. Yet she utterly alienates our sympathy when we see her taunting Bisi, who in his own way is devoted to her, with a catalogue of her commercial loves. At best we regard her as being caught in a self-destructive, psychopathic trap from which she cannot escape. There are moments when we can pity her only as an incurably twisted case, not as an individual.

Once we are conversant with the horrors of this environment, Okello can continue to make his message bite only by sustaining our interest through constantly varying his approach, and by dealing in extremes, which still retain shock value after our senses are in danger of becoming numbed. At moments the writer is dry and sardonic:[3] 'Slum flats are one of the few things people share a lot in towns.' With Orwellian restraint, he will force us to react by his own impassive understatement of the unacceptable: 'Children remained behind always. There are a few of them who cough very badly these days.' One character speaks scathingly of his own sub-mission to corruption: the father gives an assurance that he will step up the scale of his dissimulation if those who call the tune are not satisfied with his present performance: 'if you want bigger lies you will certainly get them in abundance.' In her grim arabesque monologue about bed-bugs, the prosti-tute laments that they are the only creatures with whom she shares any real relationship: 'who misses me, who glows at my presence except them?' And in the dialogue, in particular, it is as if Okello Oculi determines from the start to outface our revulsion:

'You have disease!'
'You too, your big thing is rotten.'
'As for you even the urine in your bladder starts stinking. . . .'

And so we proceed to the total inversion of recognised norms: 'Stench is our aesthetics.' The very water in the slum district can itself never be clean. The simplest necessities of life become a nightmare version of pollution and corruption. The twig from a tree swilled down the gutter in this running filth is made the image of the tortured human body. The rotting refuse is depicted in careful detail. Festering and decay are the inescapable conditions of existence. The text is crowded with incongruous juxtapositions and paradoxes: the purity of water at its source is in stark contrast with this garbage culture; neon lights are reflected in pools of scummy bilge; the section of the book which describes the world in which cars dominate is entitled 'the graveyard'.

The epitome of waste and destruction – abortion – is the characteristic act of this submerged society and is seen as an ultimate image of its nihilism:[4]

> They can all see me throwing the luggage into the pit if they want to. Why should I keep somebody's child in my stomach and bother with it for nine months when the depositer is free and loose and running around enjoying himself!

The grotesque reversal of all standards stops nowhere, till abortion itself becomes a bizarre force, a sport: the abnormal becomes the normal:

> After all who cares about abortion these days. People wash their hands with it. I hear the school girls organise competitions in it to see who will be the first and also who will have the greatest number of abortions.

Readers enticed to pick up the book by its provocative title will find here little opportunity for sexual titillation. The danger is that we shall become disgusted with sex rather than enthralled. Chapter 5, which comprises a series of ancedotes from the lives of the sisterhood, builds up a whirl of non-relationships, a spiral of negative emotion, a frenzy of hate and violence:

> Nurses suck people as ticks suck the blood of cattle. When they are full and the skin walls of their stomachs are stretched out hard as the skin on the surface of drums after a lot of heat in the sun, then they fall off at will if they want to.

The 'kiss' at the opening of Chapter 7 inspires nothing but profound horror in the reader, till there is a deadening of all sensibility:

I will hardly talk with any qualms about offending you because you are no longer capable of recognising what is offensive anyway.

The climax of anaesthetising emotion is reached in the scene of the two men fighting over a twelve-year-old girl:

And the poor girl will probably get two shillings. 'Man and woman, go ye forth and multiply thy kind!' What a curse. Let her get her first lessons.

The rats which infest the whole environment are seen as taking the place of children. Okello is relentless in his mission. He spares us nothing:[5]

You wouldn't recognise a coy, shy, girl with peasant smooth face, tough firm original native hair, relaxed and loose fatty bottom and strong bulging breasts, if you saw her only a week later. Follow her up a month later into this place and if you are the slow type she will even impose things on you, if you are not careful.

Perhaps these quotations crowded together will lead anyone who has not yet read *Prostitute* to wonder if it is not itself a sick book, indulging perversely in degradation for its own sake. However, though it is true that there is a deep strain of pessimism in this work: 'In the end we all lose'; yet the author contrives to stand clear of direct involvement in despair. The chief character appears to be finally disillusioned rather than the writer: 'Even grasses on lawns get mowed down and uprooted. It is all so transitory and irreversible'. In the Prologue, Okello asserts that 'sorrowing concern' may be 'a passionate cry for Life'. Beyond the statement of the facts, there is a level of restless questioning: 'Should the teachers fight too like the way he says they fought the white people? Must people who are outside always fight against those inside?' While there is certainly no easy optimism at any point, the implication is that something could be done about these conditions which degrade human beings. In reconsidering *Prostitute* I find myself constantly recalling the passage in which George Orwell asserts:[6]

It seemed to me then – it sometimes seems to me now, for that matter – that economic injustice will stop the moment we want it to stop, and no sooner, and if we genuinely want it to stop the method adopted hardly matters.

One particular character who appears in the course of *Prostitute* presents a sort of paradigm for the relationship between the author and his society and, more specifically, his readership, though I doubt whether this parallel occurred to Okello Oculi himself: I refer to the role of the old woman who will not silence her protest when the big man comes to the village, but insists on breaking into the fatuous formalities which are being exchanged with queries and demands relating to the realities of the people's plight:[7]

> The men had tried to drown out her voice but she had insisted, 'Child, we here . . . our eyes are dying . . . have you brought any medicine . . . or some blankets for this killing cold!'

Okello Oculi also insists: he likewise will not allow his voice to be drowned out. But these are voices of conscience rather than of despair. The words of the old woman and of the author are directed towards each member of their respective audiences individually. This is not a general frontal attack upon specific policies nor an appeal for administrative measures alone. Those with means are being asked what particular actions they are taking in a particular situation, and at the same time we are reminded that no public measures are possible until we stop lying to ourselves about the painful reality around us. This applies to smug administrators and degraded victims alike: the prostitute is 'A woman in search of truth! What doesn't she know! She sees it in the mirror every day.' You can inherit the earth only if you are willing to look at it and know it first.

In Okello's book, characters, in the ordinary fictional sense of the word, are supplemented by certain ever-present images which epitomise this society and its life. These images mirror the human condition dynamically because Okello has a rare power to infuse them with a life of their own which we enter into, whether it be bed-bugs, tarmac and murram, or derelict cars in the scrapyard. When mechanics of the junk-heap break up the wrecks, 'it looks so wasteful and the broken pieces look so deserted, so alone and unwanted and useless.' We ourselves are present in the slum village, which has an immediate physical, tactile presence; the smell of human flesh, of urine, of putrefaction is in our nostrils and enters the pores of our skin. 'Your car key you wave at me to unlock my body which unlocks the tiny door to my dungeon in the slum.' Insofar as we identify with the work itself, it does not leave us wishing to pontificate, to moralise self-righteously, but to cleanse – not just to scrub and to sprinkle DDT, but to set about and root out the pollution which is harboured in the very fabric of society. The book thus seeks to rouse us to active and effective anger.

And through these compelling images, the shadow of the city falls also across the village scene. The barbarity of abortion is brought home to us with ghastly force in the picture of the hen savaging its own egg: '. . . The wall of shell cracked with a crude noise. The raw innocent liquid inside was exposed' while the old woman sits unnoticing:[8]

> Everything, the whole existence around, had witnessed that homicide and just looked on; refusing to intervene against that gouging and desecration. Indifference is a very blunt cruelty.

The prostitute's fearful return to her childhood home is invested with a sense of tragic inevitability since the very shrubs on her route anticipate the reception she is to receive: 'Even on the path that led to my father's homestead the bushes were so damned reserved, so silent, so proud and aloof.'

There are, as I shall suggest in a moment, certain hindrances to the text always evincing the direct reaction that it seeks to provoke, but I do not think that these obstacles are inherent in the author's vision, which is compelling, nor to the sordidness of his material, which is cast in a way calculated to arouse positive indignation rather than mere sensuality or disgust.

The constant parallels between human and inanimate existence are not just clever games with words. They aim to reactivate our awareness of an actuality which we prefer to ignore: as a rule the facts of degradation in the slums 'shout to cellophane and plastic ears'. The contrast between the unspoilt and natural village girl and the tarnished, blasé town prostitute is so familiar as to evoke little response when baldly stated. The extended metaphor of the murram road and the tarmac road, on the other hand, grows into a kind of parable which we must – and readily do – interpret for ourselves. The author seeks to re-alert dulled responses. The actual details of slum existence are woven into our awareness in a manner beyond objective horror and disapproval. You know nothing about bed-bugs until you can conceive of taking them wearily for granted.

Prostitute is not wholly successful, but its methods of persuasion are intense and imaginative and, if they reach us at all, are likely to make a lasting impact whether or not we have any critical reservations about the way they are expressed. Whenever bed-bugs are brought to our attention again, we shall probably remember the satirical dimension of Okello's description of these vermin:

they bug at the risk of their very vulnerable lives just to satisfy and dissipate the emotional fire in them. And the hunger rises and bothers them every day in utter inconsideration. Sometimes I wonder what the meaning of such bother is. And why inject it into such tiny little things – why make them so dependent, and so anxious to have it all out of themselves. Putting so powerful a force into and against so tiny a thing seems most mad.

Their shyness and fear of light irritates me. Each time I come in and light the lamp they all scramble away, as if they can run. If they want me why can't they stand firm and face me? Why be ashamed? Seeing little bugs looking ashamed is so silly. Me these days I just wag and wiggle boldly. Why not? I envy bitches. They are so open and frank. I also throw myself out at them these days. I can't stand hiding. Why not just excavate it all and scoop that damned thing called privacy out.

The multiple levels of meaning are self-evident. There are moments, indeed, when we may with only slight exaggeration compare the basic technique with that employed by Swift in Lilliput and elsewhere: the bedbugs are miniature portraits of the prostitute's customers. We too find ourselves dreaming the fantastic nightmares of this environment – for instance the grotesque vision of garbage engulfing the cars in the street at the end of Chapter 3.

Amid the dirt and crudity we are made aware over and over again of wonder and joy. The beauty of the human body and the positive excitement of virility survive in the most tortured surroundings, in themselves unpolluted by their setting:

> At those moments being human is so durably beautiful and you feel that you exist and everything else and everybody else knows that you exist and have a right to be here and breathe freely.

The conflicting pattern of energy and violence is potentially creative as well as destructive, and exists variously not only in human beings, but also in motor cars.

Obviously the manner of this book is very different from the traditional novel formula. There is no plot in the ordinary sense. It is made up of a series of meditations by the prostitute herself; in snatches here and there the framework of her life is built up. The whole approach to the subject-matter is impressionistic – an intense, imaged mode which is more familiar in poetry. Sections of the work could be regarded as tone poems, to borrow a musical term. But it would be wrong to go beyond this and suggest that the style is specifically poetic (a comment which is too often made vaguely about colourful prose). There is a compulsive identification with physical objects, and a special understanding of the relationships between things and men. Just as inanimate substances take on a life of their own, so animate beings are depersonalised and blend into a common intermediate element. The 'mechanic' is not an individual but a figure. Objects possess an impulsive energy and a fearful destructiveness, qualities which by implication are even more strongly developed in human beings.

Many readers find it hard to accept the text as a convincing representation of a prostitute's thoughts and attitudes. They think she expresses herself in too thoughtfully argued and sophisticated a manner. But, as I pointed out in discussing Ntanya in *Dying in the Sun*, when an author aspires to get inside a character's stream of consciousness, we do not necessarily expect the ideas and feelings which that character is experiencing privately to be expressed in the style and phrasing which they would actually use in direct speech. The issue is not whether we can imagine this individual saying or writing these words, but whether they express convincingly what we can take to be their mode of being, thinking and reacting to their environment. According to this principle, Okello has, arguably, succeeded in large measure, for a prostitute may well be aware of, and may strongly resent the hypocritical double-standards that critics of her profession often adopt. It may be that deliberately or not, Okello endows her with more than sufficient intelligence to render her personally culpable and responsible, as well as society. For Okello Oculi is not concerned to make out a 'case' for this particular night-queen. He does not expect us to like her very much nor to feel sorry for her sentimentally; and he himself is certainly critical of her own part in the debasement of society, just as he is of virtually everyone else's. His point is not that she continues to be an innocent victim, but that *all* share the guilt for a society that harbours prostitution; it is not the prostitute alone who is guilty. That the imaginative perceptiveness of her own plight makes her more blameworthy than stupid harlots may therefore be seen as an aspect of the author's 'sorrowing concern'.

Apart from the prostitute herself, only two other personalities emerge from the background, Bisi and Rebecca. In Rebecca there burns the same wild, impulsive spirit as in the cars, the tarmac, and the prostitute.

We sense that the whole process of prostitution is echoed in many aspects of life. Society prostitutes itself. In his radio discussion the author has indeed encouraged us to go further and relate the life of the prostitute after whom the book is named to the recent history of the African continent – a viewpoint which in particular illuminates the final verse section in Chapter 10. If we enter into this mode of thought, it can make us powerfully aware of the nature of society and of individual experience. We live the prostitute's life with her from the opening paragraph, and this is no small achievement on the writer's part.

It is difficult to guess the range of the possible audience for this kind of writing, but I suspect that it is much wider than conservative commentators may assume. *Prostitute* is intrinsically a passionate work, and has at the same time an external sensational attraction which can draw in a very varied public; readers who then become excited by the pulse of the writing and the ideas will not refer their reactions to any formal criteria. If the book holds their attention, it does so, and that's all there is to be said about it. If we read the book to the end, it will make its effect upon us without our having to formulate any explicit response. At the very least, for most of us the book is likely to increase our awareness of prostitutes as people, and of slums as places where people are living.

During our broadcast together I discussed with Okello Oculi my misgivings about the unevenness of the style of the book, which I find makes it more difficult to read than it need be in ways which are unrelated to any difficulties in the approach or content. Sentences are allowed to pass muster which are pointlessly convoluted, clumsy or hard to follow:[9]

> First of all putting on the plasters of make-up takes washing up; then trying on that oil, then the other powder on top and then the other one.

> When they talk fast and loud, excitement rides out so firmly on the backs of the streams of their let-outs.

> This was when they wanted a repeat of a prolongation of the music through whose walls they had found the ecstasies of their bodies.

> . . . stinking away with alcohol like a pregnant crocodile.

Okello offered three responses to my doubts. He declared,[10]

> I was trying to write a novel as I imagined, supposing one of those old observers in the countryside, those bald-headed grey-haired old men had written, what sort of novel would he write? This was definitely my concern in trying to invent a form of style which was – you know – which was very African.

This conscious purpose seems to me to have influenced the form and the style positively in the main. Any characteristically coherent village elder has indeed a great imaginative power over words in his own language.

In fact I am not at all sure that the weaker stretches of phrasing (such as the sentences I have just quoted) do proper justice to such an elder. These stutterings and stumblings are not relevant to the principle that Okello was so constructively pursuing. It may well be true, as he himself has suggested,[11] that it is natural for Okello Oculi to 'think in images' which are 'independent of language and of audience', but this does not relieve an author of the need to express these images clearly when the time comes to translate them into whatever language he chooses as a medium. Such sentences as I have singled out, and they are quite frequent in the text, act as a deterrent, which is particularly likely to influence the less committed reader, whom the writer most needs to attract and hold.

The author has also suggested that such wording was meant to reflect the uneven coherence of characters themselves in real life:[12]

> it does seem to me that there are moments when people's heads get blocked, people think in stop-gaps; and there are other moments when people are very lucid . . . if a drunkard if confused, I think it is a fact that the drunkard should sound confused.

Responding to these comments in the same broadcast, Austin Bukenya took a different view:

> I think even if you are describing the thoughts of a drunk man, you, as an artist, are bound to express this muddle clearly, so that it is communicated to the reader clearly.

Certainly, the question involved is one of communication. It is not easy to see that there is any useful scope for prose which deliberately and faithfully sets out to reconstruct moments of non-communication for their own sake.

Thirdly, Okello said, 'I think every writer has the freedom to be poor in parts, because, after all . . . a writer is somebody who has talked in ink instead of just talking: he's written it down.' The question of freedom is not really in dispute: the writer is free to write badly and the reader to put the book down when he is bored. It is more a question of holding the reader's attention and maintaining communication. The writer who is interesting enough to carry us over dull or rough patches has survived a hazard to which every author is liable; but he might have been still more interesting and have held more readers if there were no shoddy passages. Okello Oculi might well ensure that more readers stay with him to the end, and grasp more of what he has to say, if his structures presented less of an obstacle race. This does not refer to imaginative experiments in style which any reader worthy of consideration will be prepared to respond to, even if this means some mental exertion. But a work of protest is a work with a message which seeks to recruit as many readers as possible who are in principle ready to listen, a task made much harder by irrelevant obscurity.

The experiment of mixing prose and verse in this work is bold, and there seems no reason why it should not work, particularly in a book which is forging a new form out of elements which are familiar taken separately. However, I know few who have read and admired *Prostitute* who feel that the verse passages add very greatly to the whole. Much of the poetry is very difficult, and attempts to elucidate it do not seem particularly rewarding, though the success of *Orphan* makes one willing to try. The less difficult parts of Chapter 8 are probably the most effective of the not very extensive verse passages.

However, in spite of these criticisms, *Prostitute* remains a powerful inducement to increase our awareness of aspects of society that need ministering to. The work plainly implies positive values and norms; and even expresses nostalgia for a healthy life in its last pages, and elsewhere. By contrast we are made aware that the unhealthy life we are shown is a perpetual battle against forces which ought to be on our side but are not:[13] 'I chose to die while I was still running and kicking and fighting it out against them all as a man should.' Objects and people alike have an ill-defined but violent need to react. 'There is a yearning inside for revenge; for a chance to assert oneself.' If this urge is not given a constructive outlet, there is every danger that such energy will become part of a negative downward spiral. A new kind of stand needs to be made; *Prostitute* convinces us of the need for such a stand and gives us a clearer picture of what it would involve than any vague good intentions of our own are likely to do. The passage of verse in the final section of the book includes a line that might indeed be the motto for the whole work: 'Protest glows from the edge of life.'

NOTES

1 David Cook, *In Black and White*, East African Literature Bureau, Nairobi, 1976, 161–2; the following quotation is from p. 168.

2 *Pros.*, p. 125; the following four quotations are from pp. 25 ('all this fear...'), 19 ('All over the expanse...'), 16 ('She had tried to protest...'), and 21 ('stood there...').

3 *Pros.*, p. 10 (two: 'Slum flats...', 'Children remained...'); the follow-

ing four quotations are from pp. 14 ('If you want bigger lies . . .'), 23 ('who misses me . . .'), 25, and 27 ('Stench is our aesthetics').

4   *Pros.*, p. 59; the following four quotations are from pp. 60, 76, 80, and 81.

5   *Pros.*, p. 98; the following four quotations are from pp. 99 (two: 'In the end . . .', 'Even grasses . . .'), 7 ('sorrowing concern . . .'), and 21 ('Should teachers fight too . . .').

6   George Orwell, *The Road to Wigan Pier*, Gollancz, London, 1937; Penguin, London, 1962, p. 130.

7   *Pros.*, p. 16; the following four quotations are from pp. 91 ('A woman . . .'), 34 ('it looks so wasteful . . .'), 28 ('Your car key . . .'), and 51 ('The wall of shell . . .').

8   *Pros.*, p. 52; the following four quotations are from pp. 49 ('Even on the path . . .'), 30 ('shout to cellophane . . .'), 24–5, and 38.

9   *Pros.*, pp. 10, 38, 75, 93.

10   David Cook, *op. cit.*, p. 168.

11   *African Writers on African Writing*, ed. G. D. Killam, H.E.B., 1973, an interview with Okello Oculi by Marti Mueller and Laura Tanner, 128.

12   David Cook., *op. cit.*, p. 167.

13   *Pros.*, 69; the following two quotations are from pp. 44 ('There is a yearning . . .'), and 128 ('Protest glows . . .').

CHAPTER 11

Facing the Facts

On Jomo Kenyatta's *Facing Mount Kenya*

Facing Mount Kenya by Jomo Kenyatta, though it sold only 517 copies when first published in 1938,[1] achieved a certain prestige even then, and over the following forty years has won a place in the forefront of East African consciousness. Literate East Africans know and respect the work and are always ready to discuss it; Ngugi describes it as 'powerful';[2] it remains available in paperback and is studied in schools. It is hard to think of another work from Eastern Africa which has made a comparable impact inside and outside the area for such a significant period.

Facing Mount Kenya is presented as if it were essentially a work of analytical scholarship, and is organised within the logical framework and argumentative design of an academic thesis. Indeed it grew from seminar papers presented when its author was working in a university environment in the London School of Economics.[3] Yet for all that the accuracy of the description of social mores is well attested, Kenyatta does not follow up each point rigorously with scholarly details and references when this might divert the reader from other unstated purposes. Our interest is deliberately maintained by the employment of considerable variety in method and manner to a degree seldom found in more narrowly scholarly works; throughout we are conscious of the personal approach of the writer, which comes to us in a pleasant, direct, highly readable style. Malinowski testifies to the book's scholarly standing, yet this is much more than a research dissertation in ethnography which happened to be published through a sequence of special circumstances; and it is not to be supposed that Kenyatta ever thought of it as that and no more. 'Taken by themselves,' says Jeremy Murray-Brown,[4] his unofficial biographer, 'the factual and descriptive parts of his book were a contribution to his chosen science, but *Facing Mount Kenya* as a whole was a masterly propaganda document.'

Kenyatta's treatise has the inner purpose of asserting the human rights of the Gikuyu, and through them of all African societies, in spite of certain aspects of the dominant colonial policy and assumptions, in particular the self-righteous adoption of the role of civilising agents, which subsumed the colonisers' divine mission as disseminators and upholders of Christianity. It turns out, of course, that a plain organised statement of the facts of the Gikuyu social system in their theoretically ideal form, which forms the main body of the book, provided a far better basis for arguments deploring the undermining and uprooting of traditional patterns than any mere vague and angry emotionalism could have done. And so throughout this work of 'disinterested' scholarship the academically conventional aims of providing fresh knowledge, and of regrouping available information more significantly are pursued; but behind these purposes lie the hope and intention that this increased understanding would have a direct and immediate influence upon attitudes, and therefore upon policies in the administrative and political spheres.

Furthermore, it was also intended, surely, that the Gikuyu themselves would realise that their way of life could be presented to their self-appointed overlords coherently and with dignity, and that, with the consequent increase in self-confidence and the will to protest intelligently, every educated African politician would have his hand strengthened in attempts to influence current theories of colonial rule.

As the book has become for us partly distanced in time, we can survey it with some significant degree of objectivity, observing the methods that Kenyatta employed at a time when an African intellectual needed the aid of every kind of finesse to get any hearing at all. On the other hand, the content and the message are sufficiently close to present concerns to stir our own feelings, and give us food for thought as to how men really influence each other through words when they have no other weapons available and an enormous weight of prejudice to overcome.

The argument which forms the backbone of *Facing Mount Kenya* is powerfully and meaningfully shaped. Society is analysed and its separate elements are described in a clear and orderly fashion, a process which at length invites us to put these parts together again in a new synthesis. We see that the society of the Gikuyu forms an articulated and unified pattern which must ultimately be studied, comprehended, and assessed as a whole. Perhaps even more importantly, it is shown to those who were eager to interpret their partial knowledge of the facts as a complete picture, that ignorance of one part of the system is in a very real sense ignorance of the whole.

This determination to present the Gikuyu social ethos in its entirety reminds us of Achebe's comparable urge in *Things Fall Apart*. And like *Things Fall Apart*, *Facing Mount Kenya* provides an incentive and a basis for the enquiring mind a generation or more later to ask what traditional values could be and should be reasserted today in the very different milieu of a decade which has undergone detribalisation and urbanisation and which yearns towards the technological age. Individuals who have by circumstance or choice become alienated from traditional society stand in as much need, it could be argued, to contemplate past life-patterns in the round as former colonial administrators or 'pretenders to philanthropy',[5] though for different reasons. To recall one's heritage piecemeal encourages the tendency to dismiss it item by item; but to see it as a complete way of life is to be reminded of its compelling positive features and their possible durability even in changed conditions.

Facing Mount Kenya, then, shows how the kinship system underlies the whole Gikuyu conception of land tenure, and the land tenure system binds the overall economic structure. Thus education is presented as an appropriate training for this kind of life; and initiation is understood as an essential bond, committing the individual to this integrated society. Attitudes to sex are found to be at once healthy, moral and liberal in the best sense of the word: there is neither a brooding sense of guilt engendered by repression, nor licence bred of indifference.

Marriage is construed as a genuine part of human responsibility within this social design, essential to the maintenance of the whole framework, within which everybody has a necessary place; and polygamy is regarded as an indispensable factor in this pattern of life if a reasonable social balance is to be achieved. Government among the Gikuyu is soberly discussed as being not only excellent in its parts, but also as giving the whole structure roots in the past and stability in the present: the task of administration is described as a solemn interlocking of responsibilities.

The author has judiciously withheld discussion of the most controversial aspect of Gikuyu society from an international point of view – religion and ethics – till an advanced stage of his argument. As a result he is able to discuss this important subject in perspective, and can hope to offset within the context of his whole analysis some of the biased assumptions likely to have affected his white readers, and, indeed, any African converts among his audience. Gikuyu religion can now be seen as similar to other religions in so far as it rests on a set of extra-logical beliefs and acts of faith which provide a moral rationale for the conduct of the entire social complex. Within this setting, so-called 'magic' is in effect a means of containing and coping with both mystery and disaster which trouble all men, as well as being for a few a generally disapproved means for expressing personal deviation from social norms.

The study is closely supported at every stage by evidence from either the personal experience or the personal knowledge of the writer. Reference to formalised sources are scanty by the standards of pure scholarship, but this is inherent in the very nature of the material, which – as is clearly implied – has not been previously studied with adequate care or in full detail. Thus facts supported from direct evidence in the field must properly take the place of data gleaned from documents and libraries. This is indeed a fortunate circumstance for Kenyatta as a would-be reformer, since live experience provides a more dynamic medium for communication than second-hand data. The quotations from Gikuyu, all quoted in the original and in English translation, bind the text to the reality of the society.

Malinowski, whose reputation in the field of anthropology was and remains incontestable, bluntly asserts:[6]

> [*Facing Mount Kenya*] is one of the first really competent and instructive contributions to African ethnography by a scholar of pure African parentage.

The careful construction of the argument from the introductory general statement, to detailed description, to conclusions, is all along emphasised, and the transitions are signposted, for instance by his favourite formula: 'With these few remarks we will proceed to describe how a hut is built.' This presentation is fundamentally different from the structure of fiction, yet it proves to be in many ways an equally cogent framework for making[7] 'a personal statement of the new outlook of a progressive African' in its 'aggressive assertion of the primary role of culture in a people's discovery of their identity'.

In his introduction, Malinowski approves of Kenyatta's proper admission of bias, which, he reminds us, must exist, but which once stated can be taken into account by the reader, and to some extent controlled by the author.

> In the present work I have tried my best to record facts as I know them, mainly through a lifetime of personal experience, and have kept under

very considerable restraint the sense of political grievances which no
progressive African can fail to experience,

Kenyatta tells us.[8] And Malinowski adds, 'He presents the facts objectively,
and to a large extent without any passion or feeling:'[9] he clearly saw Kenyatta
using scholarship with patent integrity but nevertheless in the service of a
larger aim.

Malinowski welcomes the particular weighting that Kenyatta gives to
his conclusions, since he has not tampered with the facts: 'Any African bias
contained in them is all to the good.' Aware of the unique nature of this
testament in its time, Malinowski goes further than most of his contemporaries would have done in adding that there is 'perhaps a little too much
in some of the passages of European bias.' Here he points out the danger of
Kenyatta's weakening his case by using European terms for African in-
stitutions; but he also observes that this is a marginal limitation in this text.
Indeed while Malinowski's criticism is just, so is his care to confine his
reservations, since Kenyatta is more frequently precise in the terms that he
employs or dismisses. For instance, he specifically rejects the phrase, still
too commonly used, 'ancestor worship' – which John Mbiti has had to
campaign against three decades later – and explains his reasons clearly:[10]

> their atittude towards them is not at all to be compared with their attitude
> to the deity who is truly worshipped. To clarify this point I shall therefore
> use the term 'communion with ancestors'.

The author somewhat disingenuously claims,

> My chief object is not to enter into controversial discussion with those who
> have attempted, or are attempting, to describe the same things from
> outside observation, but to let the truth speak for itself.

Although the last clause can be said to beg the question, and attempts rather
too obviously to knock the ground from beneath the feet of any opponents,
this assertion can be justified. Kenyatta does argue his case from carefully
collated field data, which is more rather than less valid because much of it
is lodged in his own memory (like Achebe's). Furthermore, he does in the
main keep the two aspects of the book distinct: the collection of data, and
deduction from assembled facts. It is also in a sense true that he does not
intend to 'enter into controversial discussion', since he hopes that in supporting with full evidence his own statement of the facts, he will have proved

those who are attempting 'the same things from outside observation' to be wrong, thus obviating all need for further debate. Disingenuous the claim may be, but it demonstrates Kenyatta's awareness of his own rhetorical intention in seeming to eschew controversy, and his rhetorical skill in handling this technique. He seeks to win a victory not (as he points out) by fighting, but by leaving the enemy totally demoralised in his rear.

Most of the specific dismissal of colonial assumptions is argued from the evidence he adduces. He is sweetly reasonable in pointing out such errors of judgment:

> after they have cleaned off the dust which they got from the fields, they look, in all respects, as though they have been enjoying themselves the whole day. This is why most of the Europeans have erred by making general remarks that 'the African is a lazy being and likes to bask in the sun, while his wife or wives work for him.'

Or again in explaining the real causes of overcrowding:

> Nowadays the system of having two huts for a man with only one wife is dying out, owing to the heavy burden of hut taxes imposed on the people by the British Government. The result has been congestion, whole families being crowded in one hut.

This deliberate attempt to put the record straight can develop at certain points into a clear and calmly stated summary of certain recognisable expatriate states of mind:

> the more the European tries to influence his pupils in the direction of new habits, standards of life and general Europeanisation, the more he comes up against social background which he does not understand and . . . the teacher is disappointed. Thus sooner or later he becomes either disillusioned or cynical, feeling that these people are too stupid and obstinate to learn anything else.

And so 'the European' becomes a dramatically generalised 'character' as does 'the other' in *The Wretched of the Earth* – a method of argument which we shall have reason to investigate more closely in the next chapter. On the other hand, this device could also be compared with the creation of fictional stereotypes in *No Longer at Ease*. Similarly we could set beside Fanon's 'native' Kenyatta's rhetorical personifications of 'the boy', 'the girl', 'the father', 'the mother', 'the husband', 'the wife', who help to give life and colour, as well as the impression of personal conviction, to the theoretical description of society, especially when they are brought to life in model dialogues.

Many East African readers will find themselves in a good position to judge Kenyatta's powers of persuasion when he comes to the extremely important subject of circumcision. Peoples who do not themselves practise circumcision often have attitudes about it that, without being identical in detail, are as deeply entrenched and as sceptical as those of its European opponents. Most of those, on the other hand, who share Kenyatta's views on this question will have been confronted on a number of occasions with African antagonists who deplore the practice. In either case there is a special opportunity both to determine whether the arguments in the book are couched in a form likely to change the opinions of those who hold almost opposite views, and to compare their effectiveness with the more tangential force of fiction in *The River Between*. Ngugi and Kenyatta both emphasise the psychological rather than the physical significance of this socially bind-ing rite though their methods of doing so are altogether dissimilar:[11] 'The real argument lies not in the defence of the surgical operation or its details, but in the understanding of a very important fact in the tribal psychology of the Gikuyu – namely, that this operation is still regarded as the essence of an institution which has enormous educational, social, moral, and religious implications'; 'I want to be a woman made beautiful in the manner of the tribe.'

Sometimes the factual commentary attempts a direct comparison with circumstances in Europe:[12]

It is of these lands that the early European travellers reported that they had seen huge lands 'undeveloped' and unoccupied'. To them it may have seemed so, but to the Gikuyu every inch of their territory was useful in some way or another. To the Gikuyu these lands were no more un-occupied than moorlands in England.

Indeed this approach leads to a patterned contrast between the two cultures as known to the author; this contrast is sometimes drawn dispassionately, sometimes defensively, sometimes emotionally. On iron-working we are told:

This method may seem primitive in the eyes of the western world, but nevertheless the system fulfilled the needs of the community.

The Gikuyu and European systems of education are compared, to the distinct disadvantage of the latter; the lack of formal classroom instruction in ancestral Africa is expounded as a favourable circumstance, in line with some modern Western educational theory, if not practice:

> the child is not handicapped by attending school and listening to formal instruction which is for the most part unrelated to his interests and needs.

The negative effects of such classroom constraint are vividly dramatised through Ntanya in *Dying in the Sun*.

This method expands further into some interesting but very sweeping generalisations which deserve renewed consideration in our own time. The issues which Jomo Kenyatta perceived in the late 1930s as involving distinctions between East Africa and Europe are, as education spreads, becoming increasingly the internal problems within African boundaries and have provided some of the most fundamental and searching themes for African novelists in the '50s and '60s:

> For [according to European values] freedom of personality is the highest good, and co-ordination with other people and especially mutual sub-ordination are on the contrary something accidental.

> We may sum it up by saying that to the Europeans 'Individuality is the ideal of life,' to the Africans the ideal is the right relations with, and behaviour to, other people.

> The European educational system looks forward to social groupings which are largely determined by economic, professional and religious associations. . . . The ties of family and kinship, sex and age-grouping, as we have seen, form the basis of the whole structure of indigenous education.

A fine balance is achieved in this dialectic, which recalls our discussion in Chapter 1. In our present study it is not necessarily criticism to observe that these arguments cannot be regarded as an extension of the scholarly process of building statements on careful factual detail:[13]

> No doubt educational philosophy can make a higher synthesis in which these two great truths are one, but the fact remains that while the Europeans place the emphasis on one side the Africans place it on the other.

The critical analyst of *Facing Mount Kenya* may at first be led to believe that every now and then the author is carried beyond his own purpose and intention into an open emotional outburst. On more careful consideration, however, it may appear that such sequences are deliberately calculated and placed so as to make use of scholarly dissertation as a basis for political protest and influence. Sometimes such passages are defined by the non-objective tone with which facts are reported:

> The Gikuyu, in their natural generosity and hospitality, welcomed the wanderers and felt pity for them. . . . These early Empire builders, knowing what they were after, played on the ignorance and sincere hospitable nature of the people.

This manner readily leads to passages of passionate commentary, cliché-ridden it is true, but so skilfully placed in the body of the work as a whole that even the clichés take on a new validity from contact with the controlled, objective discourse leading up to them. Such harnessing of precise and stereotyped forms of expression to achieve rhetorical impact characterises the way in which this work employs a formal structure of ideas to present a personal standpoint on political issues:

> the people were put under the ruthless domination of European imperialism through the insidious trickery of hypocritical treaties.

At a first reading we are unlikely to observe consciously that Kenyatta has shifted his position from that of the disinterested researchist to that of the unabashed preacher: 'The European should realise that there is something to learn from the African and a great deal about him to understand.'

Kenyatta anticipates the creative writers of decades to come in elaborating the predicament of the man of two worlds:

> The new civilisation he is supposed to acquire neither prepares him for the proper functions of a European mode of life nor for African life; he is left floundering between the two social forces.

We might be reading about Obi Okonkwo in *No Longer at Ease*. This inner aspect of *Facing Mount Kenya*, which is not explicitly admitted to exist, reaches its climax at certain points in savage rhetorical anger and irony; for instance in the catalogue of 'recompenses' received for Africa's bloody participation in the European quarrel of 1914–18:[14]

> The reward for this was taking away the best lands from the Africans, the introduction of *kipande* with its diabolical system of fingerprints as though the Africans were criminals, imposition of heavy taxation and denial

of freedom of speech, of the Press, and of forming political or social organisations. This is what 'democratic Britain' did in recognition of the services rendered by the Kenyan Africans in 1914–18.

Kenyatta's language is generally sonorous and calmly authoritative. He employs fairly long and elaborately constructed sentences which support the logic of his arguments by their carefully balanced proportions and their clear sequence of ideas. The structures are varied but quite easy to follow, the periods being built from a well-judged selection of the most familiar forms. These features produce a style which, without being difficult or pompous, is weighty, judicious, suggesting an unaffected wisdom:

> The land being the foundation rock on which the Gikuyu tribal economy stands, and the only effective mode of production that the people have, the result is that there is a great desire in the heart of every Gikuyu man to own a piece of land on which he can build his home, and from which he and his family can get the means of livelihood.

For all his apparent straightforwardness, Kenyatta employs a surprisingly high proportion of polysyllabic words (except where he is aiming at special effects). Most of these longer words are nevertheless in familiar, everyday use or are the exact words proper in a particular social or cultural context, for which there are no obvious alternatives; any heaviness is thus offset while the rhythm, the dignity, the reasonableness of a style with measured vocabulary remains. However, many sentences do contain one or two less usual words, quite often those to which our attention is particularly drawn. Since Kenyatta is not given to flowery writing, these literary words are used precisely to fine down an exact meaning. So on the one hand there is little verbosity, and yet there is a rhetorical richness, there is depth and subtlety of meaning, and we hear a quiet yet respected elder speaking with modulated deliberation.

These features are illustrated by two characteristic sentences near the opening of the first chapter:

> This knits together distant relatives and facilitates the feeling of rendering mutual support in all important matters in the interest and the welfare of the *moherega*. In perpetuation of this feeling, representatives of a *moherega* generally meet on occasions of big events, such as marriage ceremonies and initiation or circumcision ceremonies.

Half the words are polysyllables and a third are of three syllables or more;

yet only 'facilitates' and 'perpetuation' – and perhaps 'mutual' – are at all unusual and none is merely showy. These erudite words are counterbalanced by the near-colloquial register of 'big events'. The sentence structures are neither elementary nor obscure; the most familiar correct wording for the subject is used, without jargon, sounding knowledgeable but unpretentious. Only when there is no English equivalent is a Gikuyu word introduced.

When in the same manner the author says of the members of an age-group, 'They act as one body in all tribal matters and have a very strong bond of brotherhood and sisterhood among themselves,' he can leave us to grasp the positive values thus imputed to Gikuyu society without having to press his point. He does not tell us how to react, but we react as he intends. Europeans who have never experienced this cross-weave of social bonding may feel a touch of envy and be likely to respect this system; detribalised Gikuyu (whether in 1938 or the 1970s) may feel drawn back towards their heritage; those who are still strong in the tradition will feel pride and satisfaction. Kenyatta commands these various levels of persuasion simultaneously while remaining the calm, unbiased observer at the centre.

By these means, Kenyatta achieves that mixture of impressions which is one of the chief aims of the rhetorician: he persuades us that his evidence and arguments are incontrovertible while avoiding any suggestion of pressurising us to agree with one-sided or prejudiced views. This manner is calculated to impress the impressionable without alienating the more sophisticated and sceptical.

He needs to add only a little extra colour to produce the strong tones of controlled protest, as in the sentence from which I have quoted elsewhere:

> The Gikuyu lost most of their lands through their magnanimity, for the Gikuyu country was never wholly conquered by force of arms, but the people were put under the ruthless domination of European imperialism through the insidious trickery of hypocritical treaties.

If we have followed Kenyatta step by step up to this point, we may be unconsciously tempted to accept the highly emotive epithets 'ruthless', 'insidious' and 'hypocritical' almost as if they were objective.

At another moment, Kenyatta can, by a slightly different twist to the same style, employ it ironically to capture the high-sounding rationalisations of Mr Elephant in the fable:

> As the hurricane had gained access owing to the unoccupied space in the

hut, I considered it necessary, in my friend's own interests, to turn the undeveloped space to a more economic use by sitting in it myself; a duty which any of you would undoubtedly have performed with equal readiness in similar circumstances.

Here the absurdity of the parody is supported by exaggerations in the style which are elsewhere kept under careful control: the precise phrases turn into the slogans of glib self-justification in the form of technical jargon: 'undeveloped space', 'economic use'; while word-choice is now deliberately self-important and verbose: 'gained access', 'with equal readiness'. The repudiation of specious colonial arguments is left implicit. We are provoked into spontaneous outcry. Kenyatta remains unruffled. His purpose is achieved.

Alternative language patterns are available to Kenyatta for purposes of contrast. Most of the fable outside the court-scenes is less polysyllabic, recalling the more direct eloquence of the village story-teller. And, interestingly, in the first chapter the Mogai (the Divider of the Universe) is given a more spare and austere manner than Kenyatta allows himself in his own voice:[15]

> Go and take one lamb and one kid from your flock. Kill them under the big fig tree (*mokoyo*) near your homestead. Pour the blood and the fat of the two animals on the trunk of the tree. Then you and your family make a big fire under the tree and burn the meat as a sacrifice to me, your benefactor. . . .

Only the last couple of phrases echo the patterns which dominate elsewhere.

In attempting to maintain as his characteristic manner a fairly stern scholarly style, Kenyatta occasionally drops into a self-consciously pedantic tone which smacks of bombast: 'the behaviour and status of every individual in the Gikuyu society is determined by the governing principles which we will categorically enumerate here'; but in the main the language is well disciplined.

The most significant sections are those that lead up to direct emotional statements and appeals. At such moments we may be challenged by a series of rhetorical questions and affected by the use of imagery, as at the culmination of 'System of Education': 'But how can he discover the exact flavour of the old vintage, and where is the cellar to be seen?'

The development of polemic may account for the occasional neglect of scholarly method, even in the calm collection of facts. These lapses are fortunately rare, or they might have impaired the work not only as an ethnographic study, but also as a framework for his carefully directed rhetoric. Instances of minor omissions may be found when the legend of the origin of iron is left without any more factual alternative; or when the usually sharp and precise descriptions are replaced by a woolly account of how the Gikuyu shield is made. To compare a cattle raid in pastoral Africa with a smash-and-grab raid in metropolitan London is so inaccurate as to work against the impression the writer intends to give. To compare tribal conflicts with the Spanish civil war is to raise issues amid which the original subject matter is likely to be lost. On a number of occasions we would like to be told more than is set down; for instance we are curious to learn what demands are made of actual invalids in the rituals connected with an epidemic; in a feast made to placate ancestors for earlier neglect, one would like to know how the arbitrating elder determines 'the character and the mood of the spirits which join the feast'. And we must agree with Malinowski that while there may be some substance in the idea that tele-pathy plays a major role in certain magic effects, this part of the argument is not, disappointingly, expressed in a sufficiently scholarly fashion:

> In this form the magician's suggestions are easily transmitted by means of vibration to the brain, and thence to the mind.

The methods of presentation in *Facing Mount Kenya*, as we have seen, are much more varied than the author claims, ranging from the careful objective reportage of facts to highly emotional rhetoric, with many inter-mediate stages. The prophecy of Mogo wa Kebiro is reported straight-forwardly, so that while contributing to the general impression of objectivity, this description implies an acceptance of the prophetic truth being recorded. The same is true of the passage already alluded to on the history of the introduction of iron. In at least two instances the colonial regime is left to condemn itself by direct quotation. On page 46 and the next page extracts from Lugard's *The Rise of Our E. African Empire* are employed with trenchant and controlled irony, a form of scholarly anger:[16]

> Kikuyu promised to be the most progressive station between the coast and the lake. The natives were very friendly, and even enlisted as porters to go to the coast, but these good relations received a disastrous check. Owing largely to want of discipline in the passing caravans, whose men robbed the crops and otherwise made themselves troublesome, the people became

> estranged, and presently murdered several porters.... [Soon after the above
> incident, we are told that the Gikuyu were] taught a lesson, [they were
> compelled to make] the payment of fifty goats daily and the free work of
> three hundred men to build the fort they had destroyed.

It is no accident that it is immediately after this passage in which Kenyatta
allows the aliens to condemn themselves out of their own mouths, that he
permits himself to flare up in a brief but violently emotional piece of rhetoric,
from which I have already quoted.

On page 270 Kenyatta quotes from a book with which he found himself in much greater sympathy, Daniel Thwaite's *Seething African Pot*,
beginning with the sentences,[17] 'It was deemed unnecessary for white men
to have any special training before dealing with and being put in charge of
natives. It was a common assumption that work on the colonies required
men of less education than work at home, so the colonies became a sort of
clearing-house for failures and worse'; and Kenyatta neatly supports
Thwaite's argument by quoting in a footnote from the *Report on Higher
Education in East Africa* for September 1937. Kenyatta clearly feels that this
quoted evidence is an appropriate basis for another highly sardonic section
of commentary:[18]

> On this evidence the African asked for further enlightenment from his
> missionary teacher [with regard to the practice of polygamy in the Old
> Testament], but the missionary ignored all these queries, with the assump-
> tion that the African was only suited to receive what was chosen for his
> simple mind, and not ask questions.

One wonders whether Mr Kenyatta had ever come across Bernard Shaw's
The Black Girl in Search of God, which he would no doubt have appreciated.

The sequence of which the previous example forms part is worth further
consideration: the exposition of factual data, leading to the straight-faced
quotations from Lugard, on to high rhetoric, and finally – to conclude the
chapter – one of the most memorable parts of the book, the satiric fable of
Mr Elephant and his house. This is a unique passage, but one which rever-
berates throughout the whole work, being handled apparently unassum-
ingly but with a complex power which briefly reminds us of Orwell's
Animal Farm, written some years later. The fable permits the paradoxical
combination of a high degree of objectivity (since the figures are representative) with considerable subjectivity (since the animals are personalised to
the point of becoming individual characters in their own right).

Within the telling of the story the manner constantly shifts. There is the detailed, narrative style of the skilled tale-teller:

'My dear good friend, your skin is harder than mine, and as there is not room for both of us, you can afford to remain in the rain while I am protecting my delicate skin from the hailstorm.'

This switches to the wry use of actual historic terminology:

'I command my ministers to appoint a Commission of Enquiry to go thoroughly into this matter and report accordingly.'

As the bantering fable mirrors more and more closely the paradoxes of actual events, it cuts dramatically to the core of the writer's and reader's bitterness, but with a lightness of touch which makes it clear that the sufferer is more sophisticated than his oppressor:

'My good man, please confine yourself to the relevant issues. We have already heard the circumstances from various unbiased sources; all we wish you to tell us is whether the undeveloped space in your hut was occupied by anyone else before Mr. Elephant assumed his position.'

And so the author creates a ludicrous parody of the situation he has so far been engaged in defining factually. It must then, as now, have been almost impossible to forget the tone of this fable once one had read it in any future consideration of the subject. Arrogant European self-righteousness has been debunked. The techniques of story-telling have been admirably employed, since at all levels we like to see the underdog winning wittily. The happy ending to the fable is no deviation from the whole complex purpose: it allows us to contemplate what would in the real world be an apt allotment of retribution and reward. There is, therefore, an implied incitement to resist oppression, since it is made to appear that such resistance might be effective. And yet this incitement could be neither prevented nor punished, since even to have acknowledged that it existed would have been to assume the validity of the fable point by point when applied to the existing situation in Kenya. It requires special rhetorical skills to be able to outface a powerful regime without fear of reprisal.

When the subject of belief in spirits is first raised, it is in terms of impersonal reportage. The author wisely does not commit himself, since an early statement of his position would allow the scoffing reader to dismiss the whole work before a sufficient weight of evidence has been brought forward to make this impossible. The writer's own acceptance of certain traditional beliefs, as in love-magic and rain-magic, are therefore reserved for later chapters. There is a continued subtle blend of fact and irony. The use of proverbs in evidence creates a complex blend of effects, combining ancestral wisdom with everyday intercourse – a duality which Achebe and other novelists were later to exploit very fully. What is at first introduced almost as an apologia may turn out to be positive assertion: as in the discussion of European educational attitudes. The fact that Gikuyu practices are in line with *avant-garde* European thinking is held back till the final summary which then clinches the matter by reference to Montessori. Likewise, the suggestion, difficult to controvert, that Gikuyu attitudes to sex are compatible with the most up-to-date 1930s liberal, moral thinking on the subject is reserved as a last stroke when the tide of argument is at length running entirely in the author's direction (under his careful guidance). The only way for doubters to react is to express open disbelief as to the sexual restraint which it is claimed the Gikuyu exercise: but Kenyatta has already satisfactorily presented his credentials as a reporter of facts.

On the one hand the continuity of African values is asserted; on the other the ineffectualness of European methods is demonstrated. The replacing of traditional oaths and ordeals by swearing on the Bible is shown to lead not to rehabilitation but to a breakdown of the social structure. The hollowness of vaunted European justice is authenticated by first-hand report:

> It would not be an exaggeration to say that in most cases judgment depends entirely on who pays most. I speak here with experience in both European and *kiama* courts, where bribery and corruption are prevalent.

This line of argument builds up into a direct appeal in terms of prevailing policies:

> The above remark is strictly directed to the chiefs who are appointed over the heads of the majority of the people, and who, like their masters, want to get rich quick at the expense of the poor Africans who have no voice at all in the administration of their country.

We are again conscious of looking forward to Achebe and other novelists when we are given an account of the unChristian demands that the Christion religion makes on colonised villagers. Trenchant comment is given on missionary morality in insisting that converts should abandon all but one wife and all the children of any other wives:[11]

> the African could not understand how he could drive away his wives and children, especially in a community where motherhood is looked upon as a religious duty.

The book is, however, significantly incomplete in its account and defence of Gikuyu life. The emphasis seems to be too exclusively on an essentially functional life-cycle. It is true that many values are implied and briefly and partially outlined, in the discussion of education for instance, or in a passage such as the following:

> In the old order of the African society, with all the evils that are supposed to be connected with it, a man was a man, and as such he had the rights of a man and liberty to exercise his will and thought in a direction which suited his purposes as well as those of his fellow men.

And yet the Gikuyu 'good life' as a philosophical concept is neither detailed nor emphasised. We are told how a new generation can be reproduced in the old image, and how efficient a social unit this would be, but the idea of this effective continuity as a positive moral process is left to the reader. Culture which is not immediately functional is hardly discussed at all, apart from scattered and rather perfunctory references to the entertainment value of music and dance. Joy in design, joy in words as public speech, the aesthetics of village life are, at best, taken for granted. Recreation and fellowship are not specifically considered.

It is not easy to be sure why these facets are overlooked. Was it because they did not fit into a factual research scheme? These limits, as we have seen, are not allowed to restrict the work in other respects. Was the shape of the author's vision determined by scholarship on the one hand and by practical political protest on the other? He is more selective in the aspects of Gikuyu life which he describes than might at first be realised, and this limitation also affects the strength of his argument and appeal.

It would be grudging to over-emphasise these omissions, since *Facing Mount Kenya* was in its time such a remarkably forward-looking book and remains an important record of a society and the beginnings of effective protest within it. The rhetorical outbursts are judiciously limited in length and scope, until the last pages – still very economically – gather together all the threads of the author's larger purposes. The conclusion follows a well-calculated summary of all the important points that have been made. With these reiterated, already demonstrated facts reassembled for us, Kenyatta ends with two pages of controlled, fully justified outcry and appeal. Having thoughtfully prepared his case, founded on careful and unshakable data, he is now ready for this climax towards which he has been working and planning:

> There certainly are some progressive ideas among the Europeans. . . . But so far the Europeans who visit Africa have not been conspicuously zealous in imparting these parts of their inheritance to Africans. . . .

> Along with his land they rob him of his government, condemn his religious ideas, and ignore his fundamental conceptions of justice and morals, all in the name of civilization and progress. . . .

> As it is, by driving him off his ancestral lands, the Europeans have robbed him of the material foundations of his culture, and reduced him to a state of serfdom incompatible with human happiness.

Jomo Kenyatta's pioneering work raises significant issues concerning the relationship between scholarship and popular impact. It demonstrates that the methodical researchist may, if his study is combined with vision, have an effective role which leaves far behind the outdated concept of ivory towers. It reminds us that research in the humanities and social sciences has an importance which can stretch far beyond the limits of a university campus. It is rare that the range of effects achieved by *Facing Mount Kenya* can be encompassed within a single book. Such scope is dependent on historic opportunity and on the appearance of a man who can combine scholarly methodology with social passion and harnessed eloquence. Nevertheless this work offers a challenge to all academics to enlarge their vision without losing sight of their vocation to pursue truth in painstaking detail; and it reminds all scholars that the opportunity sometimes exists to make the jump from minute analysis to public implication. It is clear that scholarship must, if it is to attain its potential effectiveness, regard responsible rhetoric not as an enemy but as an ally.

NOTES

1 Jeremy Murray-Brown, *Kenyatta*, George Allen and Unwin, London, 1972; quotations are from the Collins/Fontana edition, 1974; p. 195.
2 Ngugi wa Thiong'o, *Homecoming*, H.E.B., 1972, p. 7.

3 Jeremy Murray-Brown, *op. cit.*, p. 200: 'Dinah Stock first helped him put the scattered essays from his seminars into the order in which they appeared in *Facing Mount Kenya*, correcting where necessary his English and his spelling.

4 *Ibid.*, p. 191.

5 *F.M.K.*, p. xviii.

6 B. Malinowski, Introduction to *F.M.K.*, p. xiii.

7 *Ibid.*, p. xiv; Ngugi wa Thiong'o, *op. cit.*, p. 7.

8 *F.M.K.*, p. xvii.

9 B. Malinowski, *op. cit.*, p. x; two further quotations from the Introduction are both from p. xi.

10 *F.M.K.*, p. 265; the four following quotations are from pp. xvii–xviii, 60, 77, and 125–7.

11 *F.M.K.*, p. 133; *R.B.*, p. 51.

12 *F.M.K.*, p. 37; the following five quotations are from pp. 73, 105, 121–2, and 122 (two).

13 *F.M.K.*, p. 122; the following four quotations are from pp. 44–5, 47, 124 ('The European should realise. . .'), and 124–5.

14 *F.M.K.*, p. 212; the following five quotations are from pp. 55, 2, 2 ('They act as one . . .'), 47, and 50.

15 *F.M.K.*, p. 4; the following quotations are from pp. 1 ('the behaviour and status . . .'), 128 ('But how can he discover . . .'), 87 ('is made of buffalo hide . . .'), 268 ('the character and the mood . . .'), and 290.

16 Lord Lugard, *The Rise of Our East African Empire*, Blackwood, 1893, II, p. 535; quoted in *F.M.K.*, p. 46 – the interpolations are Kenyatta's.

17 Daniel Thwaite, *The Seething African Pot: A Study of Black Nationalism, 1882–1935*, Constable, London, 1936, p. 3; quoted in *F.M.K.*, p. 270.

18 *F.M.K.*, p. 271; the following five quotations are from pp. 48 (two), 50, 225, and 226.

19 *F.M.K.*, p. 272; the following four quotations are from pp. 212–13, 317–18, and 318 (two).

CHAPTER 12

Actions and Reactions

On Frantz Fanon's *Les Damnés de la Terre*,
translated as *The Wretched of the Earth*

'I DO not trust fervour,' declared Frantz Fanon in the Introduction to *Black Skin White Masks* (1952).[1]

> Every time it has burst out somewhere, it has brought fire, famine, misery. . . And contempt for man. Fervour is the weapon of choice of the impotent. Of those who heat the iron in order to shape it at once. I should prefer to warm man's body and leave him. We might reach this result: mankind retaining this fire through self-combustion.

This is an important statement to bear in mind in approaching *The Wretched of the Earth*, which Sartre described as a classic of anti-colonialism, which is referred to in dust-cover jargon as a manifesto of the Third World, and which is perhaps too often regarded as simply an endorsement of violence in a revolutionary situation. For all the boldness of his approach, any tendency to over-simplify Fanon's theses is bound to misrepresent them.

In fact Fanon is concerned with propounding a theory of history, perceiving a repetitive pattern in events in perspective, which one may then attempt to project into the future. It is therefore inevitable that his approach should be altogether different from the methodical collection of data in *Facing Mount Kenya*, or the essay manner interlarded with episodes which characterises *Home and Exile*. We are to learn lessons through *The Wretched of the Earth* from the past, especially the immediate past, to be applied to the present, which is unfolding into the future. If this is to be the end result, Fanon must formulate convincing patterns out of the confused mass of conflicting experience: he must simplify his vision without falsifying it.

One of his major means towards achieving this purpose is the creation of mythical figures, types, generalised personae. He does not give these figures specific names: he is not writing fiction, nor epic, nor satire. But he does want us at least intermittently to identify ourselves and others whom we know with these prototypes. If this terminology is to be adopted, we should be sure what we mean by myths. They do not exist, and yet they are not misrepresentations. We are aware that Everyman, the man in the street, the common man, the American, the Communist, the Englishman, the African, are creations of the intellect – but not figments of the imagination. These cardboard personifications can, of course, be easily employed as part of the machinery of slogan-making, or of conditioning a society through propaganda – the semi-hysterical use of the bogey term 'Communist' in America in certain situations is an obvious example.

On the other hand, if we reject any possibility of using these concepts intelligently, we may find that we are unable to discuss certain social movements and realities clearly at all, even though they represent actual experience. 'History repeats itself' is both true and untrue; if we refuse to abstract from conflicting details the level at which this statement has meaning, we shall be losers not gainers. Fanon's 'native' does not exist specifically any more than Everyman does, but through this concept the writer is able to focus widespread experience and behaviour: we could not think certain useful thoughts without this generalised figure:[2]

> The native knows all this, and laughs to himself every time he spots an allusion to the animal world in the other's words. For he knows that he is not an animal; and it is precisely at the moment he realizes his humanity that he begins to sharpen the weapons with which he will secure its victory.

Once this method has been consciously observed, it will be seen to be all-pervasive. 'The peasant who stays put defends his traditions stubbornly, and in a colonized society stands for the disciplined element whose interests lie in maintaining the social structure'; while 'the more the intellectual imbibes the atmosphere of the people, the more completely he abandons the habits of calculation, of unwonted silence, of mental reservations, and shakes off the spirit of concealment.'

Such an approach can be employed with intellectual honesty only on a large scale. To adopt it in brief utterances, where its generalising techniques cannot be seen in perspective, all too easily leads to speciousness and verbal trickery. Fanon exposes himself and his ideas fully; he builds up an ambitious testimony which can be apprehended and criticised precisely. This is tantamount to asserting that, however closely we shall still want to examine his arguments, there is in essence no intellectual dishonesty in Fanon's manner. By these means Fanon conveys to us particular moral and political interpretations of history:

> Each generation must, out of relative obscurity, discover its mission, fulfil it, or betray it.

This interpretation at once assumes not only that a generation has a coherent identity, but also that it has a mission. Having taken this abstraction as a given entity, he can in these terms go on to prescribe for the present:

> As for us who have decided to break the back of colonialism, our historic mission is to sanction all revolts, all desperate actions, all those abortive attempts drowned in rivers of blood.

Further to this all-embracing 'mission', we are given to understand that each section of society has a definable 'role' to play. These parts having been allocated, it can then be reasoned that the bourgeoisie, to take a particular case, has fulfilled its role in Europe, but that its counterpart in Africa has not. It would be easy to misrepresent this method of argument, which is in fact by no means vague. While Fanon feels free to use such terms as part of the shorthand of debate once they have been established (though he does not necessarily define them on their first appearance in a work), there is a cogent body of thought illuminating and supporting them. In *Black Skin White Masks* he has set out one important definition in a formal fashion:[3]

> What I call middle-class society is any society that becomes rigidified in predetermined forms, forbidding all evolution, all gains, all progress, all discovery. I call middle-class a closed society in which life has no taste, in which the air is tainted, in which ideas and men are corrupt. And I think that a man who takes a stand against this death is in a sense a revolutionary.

For all this he is quite ready to give the devil his due, and can by analogy describe the failure, as he sees it, of the modern African middle-class by comparison with the achievement of its counterpart elsewhere:[4]

> The bourgeois phase in underdeveloped countries can only justify itself in so far as the national bourgeoisie has sufficient economic and technical strength to build up a bourgeois society, to create the conditions necessary for the development of a large-scale proletariat, to mechanize agriculture

and finally to make possible the existence of an authentic national culture. . . .
[In Europe] such a bourgeoisie, dynamic, educated and secular, has fully
succeeded in its undertaking of the accumulation of capital and has given
to the nation a minimum of prosperity.

So Fanon's classification of society into groups, and by means of type-
figures, leads not to slogan-making but to careful critical analysis. This
same method is found operating in many different areas: for instance in
insisting on the fable-teller's function in edging society forward from tribal
to national consciousness:

> The storyteller replies to the expectant people by successive approxima-
> tions, and makes his way, apparently alone but in fact helped on by his
> public, towards the seeking out of new patterns, that is to say national
> patterns.

The framework of argument in *The Wretched of the Earth* leads one to
regard it as developing in a single line of thought, but in fact it handles
overlapping material, complementary aspects of its subject, and sometimes
different phases of development in a revolutionary situation which, when
placed side by side, seem to present us with contradictions. But if on further
consideration we see these for what they are, stages in a progression, or
alternatives which need not both be appplicable to one specific situation,
we realise that in spite of the fact that all these aspects could not be simultaneously true in a given place, they are nevertheless not presented illogically.
For instance, Fanon states very definitely that his natives present an implacable front to colonial wiles and tricks; and yet on page 113 he expresses
misgivings about their being taken in by colonial blandishments:

> It must be clearly explained to the rebel that he must on no account be
> blindfolded by the enemy's concessions.

Or again, it is made very clear that the bourgeois elite come to dominate
government by a familiar and recognised process; yet on page 124 the
government is presented as the saviour of the peasant-farmer in the face
of the landed bourgeoisie:

> In the districts where this is the case, the only efforts made to better things
> are due to the government; it orders them, encourages them and finances
> them.

It will be seen that in either of these instances the same society may enter each phase at a different time; and that the two situations may also exist concurrently in different places.

Fanon's method is cumulative and massive. On the other hand he is extremely emphatic. The former quality makes him all-embracing and inclusive; the latter impels him to formulate each piece of his argument without qualification, in absolute terms. If this duality were to lead to prevarication or to a clouding of the issues, it would be reprehensible. But it does not: Fanon exposes his ideas frankly and fearlessly for critical consideration. And so he may be allowed to set forth alternative situations without diminishing his emphasis at any point.

It is true that this method of argument is full of pitfalls for both writer and reader. But if these pitfalls are avoided, it provides an opportunity for the essential points to be highlighted in a memorable fashion. The impact of Fanon's work is largely determined by its firm and bold lines. The fact that it has stood up to much hostile appraisal suggests that the author does not abuse his chosen mode of argument.

If Fanon generalises a great deal, it is also true that he knows a great deal. He uses his real and widespread knowledge of the African scene as a basis for generalisation:[5]

> Believe me, the zombies are more terrifying than the settlers; and in consequence the problem is no longer that of keeping oneself right with the colonial world and its barbed-wire entanglements, but of considering three times before urinating, spitting or going out into the night.

Though in terms of any particular locality it may be necessary to suggest qualifications and modifications in detail, the point Fanon is making is as a rule widely applicable in principle. Fanon generalises the African situation with a purpose, in order to interpret it. If we follow his line of thought as a whole, and then, after recognising that he has made a case, feel impelled to offer our own adjustments and applications, this is in keeping with Fanon's purpose: he seeks not to be an authority but to stimulate reaction.

Of course it is Algeria that Fanon really knows well and from Algerian experience that he develops his arguments. It is at once clear that this leads him into sweeping statements which may disregard the fact that different circumstances in various places produce different conditions. 'The starving peasant . . . is the first among the exploited to discover that only violence pays. For him there is no compromise, no possible coming to terms.' Yet it is not everywhere that the peasants are, or were, starving. '. . . The native peasantry lives against a background of tradition, where the traditional structure of society has remained intact.' What, then, of areas dominated by extremist Christian converts, such as the *balokole* in Uganda? Fanon sees one of the most important effects of the revolutionary situation in Algeria as lying in the breakdown of rigid and frustrating conventions of authority within the family:

> The most important point of this modification, it seems to us, is that the family, from being homogeneous and virtually monolithic, has broken up into several elements. Each member of this family has gained in individuality what it has lost in its belonging to a world of more or less confused values. . . . The old stultifying attachment to the father melts in the sun of the Revolution.

This passage from *A Dying Colonialism*,[6] in which Fanon refers the shift from solidarity to individualism which we have discussed in earlier chapters specifically to Algeria, serves to remind us of significant differences. The Arab family situation was not identical with that in traditional sub-Saharan Africa. Even so the same effects may be produced by very different causes; yet it is far from clear that this social transformation will be universally welcomed, even by African radicals. Again, in the *Wretched of the Earth* Fanon asserts,[7]

> the dreams . . . in the villages are not those of money or of getting through their exams like the children of the towns, but dreams of identification with some rebel or another, the story of whose heroic death still today moves them to tears.

In 1961, when this work was first published in French, examination fever was rapidly catching on in many parts of rural Africa like an epidemic.

Some readers may have been deterred from applying Fanon's ideas to their own environment by the apparent anomalies which this may involve. Fanon forcefully argues that the elitist government normally chooses to maintain the policy of having no policy:

> The only worth-while dogma, it was repeatedly stated, is the union of the nation against colonialism . . . the militants asked whether the wind of history couldn't be a little more clearly analysed.

This is all very well, but on the other hand a theoretically meaningful policy can be evolved on paper when it is already too late to hope that it will be implemented. The author sees clearly that a co-operative movement is liable to corruption; and provides a solution:

> If the government wants to bring the country out of its stagnation and set it well on the road towards development and progress, it must first and foremost nationalize the middleman's trading sector. . . . If you want to progress, you must decide in the first few hours to nationalize this sector.

Quite apart from the controversial nature of these arguments, Fanon might be seen as preaching despair in a situation where time has run past and his advice has not been taken. The colonial policy of trying to force a favoured party into command at independence is well illustrated by the case of Kenya; yet the colonial initiative failed and nevertheless some of the effects that Fanon forecast were, it could still be argued, apparent.

But after all this has been said by way of qualification, it is still clear that Fanon's method of generalisation is a significant means, in his hands, towards a fundamental analysis: he says things which radicals, militants, and revolutionary thinkers have found valid in widely separated areas:

> But it is a commonplace to observe and to say that in the majority of cases, for ninety-five per cent of the population of underdeveloped countries, independence brings no immediate change.

In disagreeing with certain white theories in *Black Skin White Masks*, Fanon makes no claim to be disinterested, but frankly insists upon his own position:[8]

> I sincerely believe that a subjective experience can be understood by others; and it would give me no pleasure to announce that the black problem is my problem and mine alone and that it is up to me to study it. But it does seem to me that M. Mannoni has not tried to feel himself into the despair of the man of colour confronting the white man. In this work I have made it a point to convey the misery of the black man. Physically and affectively. I have not wished to be objective. Besides, that would be dishonest: it is not possible for me to be objective.

For all our awareness that things vary locally, there is a valuable attempt in *The Wretched of the Earth* to perceive a predictable pattern in events by synthesising past experience. The very fact that we are aware of variations as variations may make us more willing to acknowledge the validity of the generalised pattern. After reading Fanon, we are no longer thinking, or planning, in an infinite area of disconnected and unreadable facts.

This work, then, has the same claim to consideration in a literary critical context as any eloquent and stylish statement of particular views on matters of public concern. The kind of challenge and delight it offers is similar to that which I derive in reacting to Matthew Arnold's *Culture and Anarchy*, Bernard Shaw's prefaces to, say, *Major Barbara* or *The Apple Cart*, and George Orwell's *Homage to Catalonia*. The argument is shapely, yet cast in a form to emphasise intellectual and moral tensions. Here we find stimulating ideas projected with an intensity that enables them to take root, grow and bear fruit in one's mind. We are engaged excitedly, imaginatively, in grappling with profound thoughts couched in provocative rhetoric:

> If the building of a bridge does not enrich the awareness of those who work on it, then that bridge ought not to be built and the citizens can go on swimming across the river or going by boat. The bridge should not be 'parachuted down' from above; it should not be imposed by a *deus ex machina* upon the social scene; on the contrary it should come from the muscles and the brains of the citizens . . . so that the bridge in whole and in part can be taken up and conceived, and the responsibility for it assumed by the citizen. In this way, and in this way only, everything is possible.

And, like Kenyatta in a different fashion, Fanon can probe and illuminate topics which also concern the novelist. It is often hard to remember that the book was written in 1961 because it seems to be coolly surveying in retrospect events which have in fact taken place since. Consider, for instance, Fanon's analysis of one of Ngugi's motifs in *A Grain of Wheat*:

> The big farmers have, as soon as independence was proclaimed, demanded the nationalisation of agricultural production. Through manifold scheming practices they manage to make a clean sweep of the farms formerly owned by settlers, thus reinforcing their hold on the district. But they do not try to introduce new agricultural methods, nor to farm more intensively, nor to integrate their farming systems into a genuinely national economy.

The stock-in-trade of Fanon's style is the very emphatic statement: 'In the period of decolonization, the colonized masses mock at these very values, insult them, and vomit them up.' Fanon is pithy and uncompromising: 'He is overpowered but not tamed; he is treated as an inferior but is not convinced of his inferiority.' This is at once epigrammatic and confidently self-assertive. The trenchancy of his thought enables Fanon to combine qualities not usually associated; to be at the same time blunt and complex – he says of the black middle-class that 'It is already senile before it has come to know the petulance, the fearlessness or the will to succeed of youth.' And thus, while this liking for brilliant aphorism may be linked with his tendency to generalise, there is nothing to suggest that this is in any way naive writing:[10]

> Without pity, they use today's national distress as a means of getting on through scheming and legal robbery, by import-export combines, limited liability companies gambling on the stock-exchange, or unfair promotion.

The detail of his subject matter is clearly grasped, and the gist of his thinking is well argued.

Yet Fanon is not averse to the use of forceful slogans: 'for his minimum demands are simply that the last shall be first'; nor to revolutionary simplifications: 'In this colonial context there is no truthful behaviour: and the good is quite simply that which is evil for "them".' On page 40 he summarises 'the dreams of the natives' in what must be taken as a rhetorical manner rather than as attested evidence. And so Fanon's style is paradoxical. Although he has the advantages of apparent simplicity – directness and wide appeal – he is far from being as simple as he seems. Apart from the employment of balanced and sophisticated constructions, he uses complex images and concepts:

> That impulse to take the settler's place implies a tonicity of muscles the whole time; and in fact we know that in certain emotional conditions the presence of an obstacle accentuates the tendency towards motion.

He draws a most useful parallel between the breach that exists in industrial societies separating the leader and the rank-and-file in a trade union with that which exists between similar groups in a newly independent state. And he feels free to enter into some degree of technicality:[11]

> In these regions, with the exception of certain spectacular advances, the different countries show the same absence of infra-structure.

> The spectacular flight of capital is one of the most constant phenomena of decolonization.

Sometimes, though rarely in this work (except in the final case studies) compared to some other of his writings, we remember that Fanon is a psychiatrist:

Here on the level of communal organisations we clearly discern the well-known behaviour patterns of avoidance.

This magical superstructure which permeates native society fulfils certain well-defined functions in the dynamism of the libido.

Without carrying these technicalities to excess, the author, in introducing those such as I have quoted, assumes that his readers are as intelligent and well-informed as he is himself.

Paradox is indeed an appropriate device to employ in attempting to analyse a situation which evidently demands a total reversal of the *status quo*:[12] 'In fact, as always, the settler has shown him the way he should take if he is to become free.' If he sees the intellectual as being too solemn, excessively methodical when caught up in 'the terrible stone crusher', Fanon himself is well aware of the extralogical elements in the conflict, and he seeks 'a national *morale* which comforts the heart of man'.

Fanon's arguments are spiced with wit and sharpened with irony. These are not decorations, but essential aspects of his positivism on the one hand and his controlled bitterness on the other: 'As far as doctrine is concerned, they proclaim the pressing necessity of nationalizing the robbery of the nation.' He solaces himself at times with dry under-statement: 'Blown-up bridges, ravaged farms, repressions and fighting harshly disrupt the economy.' And he handles his antagonists, both white and black, with sardonic contempt: 'For in fact they are not at all convinced that this impatient violence of the masses is the most efficient means of defending their own interests.' He loves to expose the contradictions inherent in the expedient assertions of racialists, who naturally change their tune as circumstances alter:[13]

So they say that the natives want to go too quickly. Now, let us never forget that only a very short time ago they complained of their slowness, their laziness and their fatalism.

And (as we found Kenyatta doing earlier) he leaves those he opposes to condemn themselves out of their own mouths whenever opportunity offers, himself maintaining a dead-pan expression:

[M. Mba, President of Gabon, states] in all seriousness on his arrival in Paris for an official visit: 'Gabon is independent, but between Gabon and France nothing has changed; everything goes on as before.' In fact, the only change is that Monsieur Mba is president of the Gabonese Republic and that he is received by the president of the French Republic.

The art of turning the tables accords nicely with Fanon's wish to be at once both emphatic and balanced. For instance, he hits out at both the ex-colonialists and the black elite in a fine pattern of irony:

> The Third World often gives the impression that it rejoices in sensation and that it must have its weekly dose of crises. These men at the head of empty countries, who talk too loud, are most irritating. You'd like to shut them up. But, on the contrary, they are in great demand. They are given bouquets; they are invited to dinner. In fact, we quarrel over who shall have them. And this is neutralism.

Although Fanon displays a remarkable lightness of touch which enables him to face even the distasteful parts of his subject without flinching, yet he is, of course, just beneath the surface, in deadly earnest and he intends us to realise this:

> Now it must be said that the masses show themselves totally incapable of appreciating the long way they have come. The peasant who goes on scratching out a living from the soil, and the unemployed man who never finds employment do not manage, in spite of public holidays and flags, new and brightly-coloured though they may be, to convince themselves that anything has really changed in their lives. The bourgeoisie who are in power vainly increase the number of processions; the masses have no illusions. They are hungry; and the police officers, though they are now Africans, do not serve to reassure them particularly.

Any reader of *The Wretched of the Earth* will be convinced that Fanon is propounding clear revolutionary theses; but he does not repeat or summarise these with the same pedagogic thoroughness that we find, say, in Kenyatta's *Facing Mount Kenya*. He insists on some points more than others; one may ask whether the exact emphasis is systematic or deliberate. In looking more closely into Fanon's methods as a persuader, we will want to question the efficiency of his planning. It might at first seem that the layout is casual, even accidental, since for all the vehemence and conviction that he expresses, he avoids the kind of formality that would make us feel that we were deliberately being worked upon. He convinces us, rather, that we are being left free to make up our own minds. But Fanon is a good debater; unobtrusively yet firmly he is guiding the direction of our thoughts. Even so, it is to be doubted whether five different readers each summarising Fanon's thoughts would produce such similar results as if they were giving a digest of *Facing Mount Kenya*. It may be of interest if I give my own outline, which falls under seven headings, for others to compare with their own.

First comes the cluster of ideas relating to the peasantry's attitude to revolutionary ideas. Fanon sees the peasants as the core of the movement:[14] 'in the colonial countries the peasants alone are revolutionary.' He describes them in almost romantic terms, and yet his picture is exact: 'in their spontaneous movements the country people as a whole remain disciplined and altruistic.' 'The peasant's cloak will wrap [the militant nationalist] around with a gentleness and firmness that he never suspected.' He has a true understanding of the political sophistication of peasant populations, who are not to be considered as easy dupes just because they do not embrace martyrdom. Though the people may speak panegyrics in the presence of officials, 'in the street when evening comes, away from the village . . . the bitter disappointment of the people, their despair but also their unceasing anger makes itself heard.' Fanon insists that the people at large are eager to learn and fully capable of understanding things often deemed beyond their intellectual powers: 'they like having things explained to them.' 'Experience proves that the masses understand perfectly the most complicated problems,' provided, of course, that language is used to expound meaning, rather than to obscure it from the uninitiated:[15] 'Everything can be explained to the people, on the single condition that you really want them to understand.' It thus follows that 'the political education of the masses proposes not to treat the masses as children but to make adults of them.'

His second thesis is that 'violence . . . will only yield when confronted with greater violence.' By a characteristic paradox he sees the past situation being reversed once more in this respect: 'by an ironic turning of the tables it is the native who now affirms that the colonialist understands nothing but force.' Fanon takes no delight in violence but sees it as a grim necessity; but to understand his arguments we must also realise that he sees it also as creating a social melting-pot in which old shibboleths dissolve and new assumptions take their place:[16]

> Violence alone, violence committed by the people, violence organised and educated by its leaders, makes it possible for the masses to understand social truths and gives the key to them.

Indeed, I would place this as the third tenet, that violence properly understood and directed can be positive and purifying:

> At the level of individuals, violence is a cleansing force. It frees the native from his inferiority complex and from his despair and inaction; it makes him fearless and restores his self-respect.

Fourthly, Fanon insists that the transformation of society can be effected constructively only if one is working to a formulated ideology with a coherent itinerary:

> You do not turn any society, however primitive it may be, upside-down with such a programme if you are not decided from the very beginning, that is to say from the actual formulation of that programme, to overcome all the obstacles that you will come across in doing so.
>
> The task of bringing the people to maturity will be made easier by the thoroughness of the organisation and the high intellectual level of its leaders.

And fifthly, one of the cornerstones of this programme must be to take the revolution back to grass-roots in the countryside. The centre of government should be moved out of the largest city; and the party network should be based in the rural districts: 'The party should be decentralised in the extreme. It is the only way to bring life to regions which are dead, those regions which are not yet awakened to life.' Moreover, the abuse of the party concept is often related to a refusal to move away from the sophisticated and already privileged commercial centres. Fanon is, still further, against an *imposed* one-party system, though the implications of those italics may be significant in many situations.

Sixth I would place the need to give emphasis to nationalism at the stage of social evolution under consideration. On the one hand this means moving away from tribalism by every possible means wherever and whenever this adopts a chauvinistic or separatist stance. On the other it suggests the need to move in stages towards internationalism, which means building up a national consciousness first – in itself a complex enough task – before being concerned with 'African unity'. Fanon is, as ever, fearless in putting forward ideas which are controversial even among those most likely to support him in general.

Lastly I would include the demand that tradition be seen as dynamic and as having immediate reference to the present: it is to be respected, and at the same time more willingly adapted to modern circumstances than extreme conservatives might allow:[17]

> When a people undertakes an armed struggle or even a political struggle against a relentless colonialism, the significance of tradition changes. . . .
>
> the native intellectual who wishes to create an authentic work of art must realise that the truths of a nation are in the first place its realities. He must

go on until he has found the seething pot out of which the learning of the future will emerge.

Fanon displays no false modesty in willingly adopting the role of a prophet. The scope to which he aspires is revealed in the scale that his style asserts. His love of rhetorical balance is demonstrated in the largest terms: 'To the saying "All natives are the same" the colonised person replies "All settlers are the same".' Or again,

> From now on, it is *we* who pursue *him*; in spite of all his technical advantages and his superior artillery power the enemy gives the impression that he is floundering and getting bogged down. As for us, we sing, we go on singing.

And if we wish to confirm Fanon's sense of rhetorical climax, we might reread the dramatic culmination of his description of the corrupted new elite. This is one of a number of highlights within a pattern of cool, large argument. Fanon has set out upon a fundamental rethinking of major issues of his time, and he intends that we shall be aware of this and accompany him in his flights. He solemnly rejects the policies of the first phase of black self-government in uncompromising terms:

> Let us be frank: we do not believe that the colossal effort which the under-developed peoples are called upon to make by their leaders will give the desired results.

A prophet cannot be apologetic or timid; and Fanon by implication accepts the responsibilities of the prophet's role, and is vindicated when he is felt to achieve prophetic vision. Indeed, as I noted earlier, he observed things which later became commonplaces ahead of most other people. Like almost all prophets he presents us with a warning, which is also in effect a declaration of policy, a policy to which the only alternative offered is disaster on a classic dimension: 'The Cold War must be ended, for it leads nowhere.' How do we view the forebodings of a prophet in the light of later history? It may be presumptuous to ask this question a mere fifteen years or so ahead. Yet it is not implausible to attribute current problems primarily to failures in the areas he identified.

Yet Fanon is not in the main a prophet of doom. He is remarkably and most encouragingly optimistic. His theme seems constantly to be 'We shall overcome.' In *Black Skin White Masks* he declares:[18]

The future should be an edifice supported by living men. This structure is connected to the present to the extent that I consider the present in terms of something to be exceeded.

He is vividly confident, especially through his conviction of the educability and positive assertiveness of the peasant:[19]

For this same people, poverty-stricken yet independent, comes quickly to possess a social conscience in the African and international context of today; and this the petty individualists will quickly learn.

His time structures inspire the reader with the sense that his hopes are in the process of being realised even at the moment of writing: 'The groups recognize each other and the future nation is already indivisible.'

The whole of the brief 'Conclusion' to The Wretched of the Earth is in the vein of rhetorical exhortation: it is a confident call:

But if we want humanity to advance a step further, if we want to bring it up to a different level than that which Europe has shown it, then we must invent and we must make discoveries.

There is no complacency in Fanon's optimism. He is a seasoned arguer who constantly makes us aware that the tasks he is outlining are difficult; but he insists at the same time that everything is possible. He convinces his audience of the need for action and then encourages them to act.

However, for all his buoyancy, many African readers find Fanon disturbingly assertive both in his style and in his policies which, it is sometimes suggested, are like his social analyses in that they are carried over too indiscriminately from a particular situation to general application. And yet Fanon shows a strain of genuine humility which has no ring of verbal trickery. He puts forward his fiery positivism in Black Skin White Masks, for instance, with a diffidence which is surely sincere:[20] I will say, however, that every criticism of that which is implies a solution, if indeed one can propose a solution to one's fellow – to a free being.'

Ultimately, Fanon is a socialist and a humanist in the very widest sense of the terms. He treats anti-colonialism as a base to be taken for granted – so much so that it is unnecessary even to discuss the pros and cons of the matter in The Wretched of the Earth. Working from this base, he takes as his immediate target the first African elite, and he comments that it is embarrassingly evident at once that no simple division can be made in any situation on the assumption of good and bad being identified with black and white respectively, or even with African and colonialist (as he explicitly discovers both here and in *A Dying Colonialism*). His humanism is fiercely honest and unqualified:

> I said in my introduction that man is a *yes*. I will never stop reiterating that. *Yes* to life. *Yes* to love. *Yes* to generosity. But man is also a *no*. *No* to scorn of man. *No* to degradation of man. *No* to exploitation of man. *No* to the butchery of what is most human in man: freedom.

And he constantly demands that policies shall be spelt out in these terms:[21]

> The problem is to get to know the place that [black politicians] mean to give their people, the kind of social relations that they decide to set up and the conception that they have of the future of humanity.

His internationalism is simply another facet of his humanism:[22] 'There is no Negro mission; there is no white burden. . . . I find myself suddenly in the world and I recognise I have one right alone: that of demanding human behaviour from the other.' But for all the largeness of his conception, he is determinedly practical. He sees internationalism as meaningless if presented as an immediate goal, since it can grow up intelligibly only as a natural consequence of true nationalism:[23]

> Far from keeping aloof from other nations, therefore, it is national libera-tion which leads the nation to play its part on the stage of history. It is at the heart of national consciousness that international consciousness lives and grows. And this two-fold emerging is ultimately the source of all culture.

Whether or not the individual reader finds Fanon too strong a meat to stomach, his sincerity can hardly be in question, and we must be moved and influenced by his passionate expression of ideas. For his emphatic style is not, in effect, self-assertive, but rather it is committed to asserting those ideas:[24] 'What matters is not to know the world but to change it.'

NOTES

1 *B.S.W.M.*, p. 8.
2 *W.O.T.E.*, p. 33; the following four quotations are from pp. 88 ('The peasant who stays put . . .'), 37 ('the more the intellectual imbibes . . .'), and 166 (two).
3 *B.S.W.M.*, p. 160.
4 *W.O.T.E.*, pp. 140–1; the following quotation is from p. 194.

5   *W.O.T.E.*, p. 43; the following two quotations are from pp. 47 ('The starving peasant . . .'), and 88 ('The native peasantry . . .').

6   Frantz Fanon, *L'An Cinq de la Révolution Algérienne*, Maspéro, Paris, 1959, trans. Haakon Chevalier as *A Dying Colonialism*, Penguin, London, 1970, pp. 81, 83. Fanon expresses a different view of the comparable change outside the family group in *W.O.T.E.*, p. 36: 'Individualism is the first to disappear. The native intellectual had learnt from his masters that the individual ought to express himself fully. The colonialist bourgeoisie had hammered into the native's head the idea of a society of individuals where each person shuts himself up in his own subjectivity, and whose only wealth is individual thought. Now the native who has the opportunity to return to the people during the struggle for freedom will discover the falseness of this theory.'

7   *W.O.T.E.*, p. 91; the following three quotations are from pp. 137, 144, and 59.

8   *B.S.W.M.*, p. 61.

9   *W.O.T.E.*, p. 162; the following four quotations are from pp. 124, 34 ('In the period . . .'), 41 ('He is overpowered . . .'), and 123 ('It is already senile . . .').

10   *W.O.T.E.*, p. 37; the following three quotations are from pp. 35 ('for his minimum demands . . .'), 39 ('In this colonial context . . .'), and 41.

11   *W.O.T.E.*, p. 76; the following three quotations are from pp. 82, 42, and 43.

12   *W.O.T.E.*, p. 66; the following five quotations are from pp. 39 ('the terrible stone crusher'), 79 ('a national *morale* . . .'), 37–8 ('As far as doctrine . . .'), 48 ('Blown-up bridges . . .'), and 49 ('For in fact . . .').

13   *W.O.T.E.*, p. 59; the following three quotations are from pp. 52, 65, and 136.

14   *W.O.T.E.*, p. 47; the following five quotations are from pp. 89 ('in their spontaneous . . .'), 100 ('The peasant's cloak . . .'), 147 ('in the street . . .'), 38 ('they like having . . .'), and 151 ('experience proves . . .').

15   *W.O.T.E.*, p. 152; the following three quotations are from pp. 146 ('the political education . . .'), 48 ('Violence . . .'), and 66 ('by an ironic turning . . .').

16   *W.O.T.E.*, p. 118; the following four quotations are from pp. 74, 28–9, 117, and 149 ('The party should be . . .').

17   *W.O.T.E.*, p. 180; the following four quotations are from pp. 181, 72 (To the saying . . .'), 108, and 79.

18   *B.S.W.M.*, p. 11.

19   *W.O.T.E.*, p. 38; the following two quotations are from pp. 73 ('The groups recognise . . .'), and 254.

20   *B.S.W.M.*, p. 45; the following quotation is from p. 158.

21   *W.O.T.E.*, p. 189.

22   *B.S.W.M.*, p. 163.

23   *W.O.T.E.*, p. 199.

24   *B.S.W.M.*, p. 13.

CHAPTER 13

In His Own Country

On Lewis Nkosi's *Home and Exile*

THE South African scene in our time presents as painful, indeed as tragic a picture as any peacetime milieu in the twentieth century. It has given rise to some fine and moving literary documents, which break through the wall of apathy, born of familiarity, with which the rest of the world in the main faces the South African disaster, more powerfully and memorably than any other form of statement or protest has been able to do. Yet it may occasion some surprise, not that works like *A Walk in the Night* and *Tell Freedom* have taken us inside the actuality of living from day to day in a police state, but that, given the length of time that the situation has endured and the dynamism of the people suffering, there are not more writings that have achieved distinction in depicting this scene which is at once tense and casual, dramatic and commonplace.

But if one considers more closely the problems facing the South African writer, the fact that only a handful of works emanating from this background have lodged themselves permanently in our consciousness is less surprising. It is in a sense almost impertinent to attempt simply to mirror this long-drawn-out, legalised oppression; and yet it must appear irrelevant from inside the situation to let another protest from these extreme circumstances fall on the dulled ears of outsiders:[1] 'how does one begin to write about apartheid in a way that would be meaningful to people who have not experienced it? I don't know,' admits Nkosi. When one is dealing with absolutes of bigotry and repression, what is there to report on the matter to one's fellows who are enduring the campaign? 'I have often thought many times afterwards how difficult it must be to try and reclaim some of this bitter reality for imaginative literature. Words seem to break under the strain.' In any case, it is doubtful whether one will have the chance to be heard on this subject. And yet how can one write about anything else? The position has continued long enough and is so intractable as to be beyond expression. Indeed, after some contemplation one is filled with even greater admiration for those writers who have impelled their sentences to raise an echo in this vacuum.

In asking questions about the art of verbal persuasion in Africa we are bound to contemplate once again the South African scene and the writings it has fostered. One work from this context which I think we should not allow to slip out of our memories and thus should not see go out of print without protest is Lewis Nkosi's *Home and Exile*. Apartheid and its many evil corollaries have been with us for many years. We have observed that it must be a hard task to convey something of the essence of living in South Africa to strangers, or to say something which is not banal to those who are there; it may be even harder to say things again which have already been said. So we would not necessarily be wise to insist on studying only the latest writings on the subject. It is true that matters have worsened in many respects as time has gone on; but this may make literary statement increasingly difficult. Things for which words could be found some years ago may now force all but the most inspired into a tight-lipped silence. In these circumstances it does not seem to me that the resonances of *Home and Exile* have ceased to vibrate.

It is clear, further, within the framework of the present critical study that *Home and Exile* employs completely different methods of persuasion from *Facing Mount Kenya* or *The Wretched of the Earth*, both of which adopt systematic approaches to their subjects, which would be unhelpful in dealing with the stark South African situation where the facts are not in question, but the nature of the experience which those facts dictate is too easily glossed over both because of its extremity and its familiarity. In its skilful and unusual blend of classical essay structure and brisk narrative manner, *Home and Exile* can readily complement our analysis of these other works with their more obviously formalised rhetorical organisation.

If we are not to pervert Nkosi's vivid representation we must, of course, constantly bear in mind that in *Home and Exile* he is writing of the South Africa of two decades past and more. He constantly reminds us that even by the time he was working on the book things had become much worse. To reread his words, which by most standards represent an intolerable enough situation, and to remember that what he is depicting would be liberal beyond imagination within current circumstances, cuts deep into the sheer incomprehension of those of us who attempt inadequately to imagine South Africa at a remove. However, we are called back by Nkosi's vigorous anecdotes from the temptation to over-dramatise, and instead we are reminded, as Athol Fugard puts it, that 'people are living there'; that these are day-to-day events, week after week, month after month, year after year, only becoming worse by constant, almost imperceptible, stages. If we bear all these things in mind, then Lewis Nkosi's account is one of the most immediate and intimate realisations of life within South Africa that an outsider can encounter.

The total contrast between the material that Nkosi is presenting and Jomo Kenyatta's subject-matter in *Facing Mount Kenya* is, naturally, closely related to their total difference in method. Kenyatta is describing a coherent society which he wishes to elevate in the minds of previously uninformed readers, and so he follows the process of closely argued analysis. Nkosi is describing a society in fundamental moral and human chaos, and for this purpose he finds the anecdotal style of informally related memoirs controlled within a traditional essay framework appropriate on various levels. In fact he uses this scrap-book method with great but apparently casual skill to build up for us the experience of existing inside a generally confused life-pattern – not just that of a confused individual life but of a confused society. In the resultant design it is obviously impossible to distinguish between stylistic instinct and deliberate organisation; but we can nevertheless see quite a long way into his literary techniques. Like his colleagues on *Drum*, he writes up the South African scene in 'cool sober prose in which they permitted themselves the luxury of a laugh'.[2]

The mode of writing that Nkosi adopts in retelling actual incidents can indeed be strung together quite easily after a fashion, and for this very reason it is all the more difficult to write really well or significantly in this manner: it is because Nkosi has succeeded in doing so that *Home and Exile* seems to me to deserve the kind of attention that this essay is giving it. Nkosi is, of course, fully aware of what he has set out to do:

> instead of writing a political essay, I thought I would simply set down some of the experiences that I and my contemporaries have been through in South Africa. I don't think there is any need to strive for effect; the situation is surrealistic enough as it is.

He says this near the beginning of Section 2; but he has already put this method into practice throughout the first section. It will already be apparent to anyone familiar with the book that I am primarily concerned with the 'Home' part and secondarily with the sub-division entitled 'Exile'. Styles adopted in the 'Literary' half of the book are significantly different, though I shall hope in the following analysis to establish certain links, especially with regard to content. One could interestingly compare the use of language in Chapter 7, 'Black Power or Souls of Black Writers', with that in the first half of the book.

In the chapters with which we are mainly concerned, Nkosi infuses his episodes with the very kind of narrative life that he later complains is missing from Richard Rive's fiction. We are captivated by brief, sharp characterisations in brilliant cameos:

> Ezekiel Mphahlele, the Fiction Editor, magisterial and 'concerned' – more with the profounder issues of life and literature than with DRUM's sleazier prose, one imagined.

Indeed Nkosi has contributed much to ensuring that the remarkable group of *Drum* figures has remained a lasting tradition and a continuous presence in the sphere of African writing. Several sections of the early part of the book are centred on his first day with the *Drum* team – from which he flashes forward and backwards at will. These incidents give a racy impression, but are complex in phrasing, and factual in content, their success being in the main determined by the true writer's skill in selection:

> Under the cloak of darkness, groups of us, without obtaining police permits for white members of our convoys, drove into the sealed-off African township, dodging police patrols, assisting young white girls over fences in badly lit township alleyways, outraging, in the process, the happy calm of black citizens who were most astonished to see pink faces materialise, unbesought, in the protected centres of their unstable lives. They were shocked and scandalized; they worried about the danger and enmity they were going to earn from the disapproving authorities.

This sentence has something of the ease and relaxation of a loose-jointed colloquial manner, but the structures are linked in a sophisticated pattern, and the choice and arrangement of words is literary in the best sense of being exact, interesting, fresh and alive: 'the protected centres of their unstable lives'. This style can even absorb a word like 'unbesought' without self-consciousness, even at a first reading.

The author uses himself as a first-person character with wry, self-revealing humour, exposing first his innocent Puritanism and later his self-confident sowing of his wild oats. He effectively creates an attractive swashbuckling personality for himself in these escapades; and in deprecating manner presents himself in a role which he seems in fact to feel is rather winning in its ingenuous bravado:

> I was young enough and really too eager not to be flattered by any woman who had the time to listen to my dreams. I was also vain in the most secretive manner; I actually thought that the world ought to care what I wanted to do; and as far as I was concerned the world consisted mainly of beautiful women.

But even if he does admire the image of himself climbing through the white actress's window, the honesty is real enough for all that. We feel the writer's force as a personality in the anecdotes he relates. The vital, well-judged, but unpretentious style contributes much through its variety and vividness to bringing his own and others' characters to life. The same disarming honesty pervades also his critical writing later in the book – notably in the chapter 'Fiction by Black South Africans'.

This is the inside story. This vein of uninhibited narrative convinces us that he really knows the scene. The writing has the zest and immediacy of journalism without its relative carelessness or impersonality. He can be deliberately objective when he chooses, though. With calculated casualness he depicts how close to the surface social neuroses bring violence in the incident of the young man who suddenly finds himself slashing his knife at anyone and everyone. The way the author slightly distances himself at this point makes us terrifyingly aware that this incident is of a kind familiar on the everyday South African scene and simply has to be accepted by anyone who is to survive in this society. Likewise, having convincingly presented his credentials as a reporter, he persuades us that he is making a simple statement of the facts when he describes citizens who are passionate adherents of apartheid sending off their wives in order to have affairs with their maids, or the Boer preacher enjoying the servant-girl in the garage while his wife cooks the dinner in the kitchen. If Nkosi is to carry us inside a world where these contradictions are taken as a matter of course, he must not raise his own voice in recording these scenes. Thus it is important that he has established his reputation as a faithful camera trained upon his surroundings. Nkosi is able to bring home to us many telling details of squalor on the one hand and perverse racism on the other by introducing them exactly where they belong in a more comprehensive description of action. We do not feel that this knowledge is being forced upon us, nor that our emotions are being played upon unwarrantably.

Nkosi communicates to us his great zest for life and experience; his exuberance has been unquenched by the South African circumstance; and he thus becomes in himself a proponent of the African resilience of which he talks. This is epitomised in his love for the city:

> For me the city was nevertheless warm and exciting, vibrant with an undiscovered life. . . . In Johannesburg I loved the city noises, the home-bound crowd, the chaotic traffic.

The irrepressible feel for the city as a city is reflected again later in his reluctant acceptance of New York. In Johannesburg we feel in spite of everything the warmth and humanity of the great press of people. The humanistic positivism of which Nkosi also speaks in general terms is ever present when he is depicting the life of this sprawling conurbation with all its contradictions and inequalities.

How can a writer cram black South African experience into his pages without overwhelming readers with such an unanswerable demand for emotional response that they will flinch away and put the book down to escape the barrage of feeling? There can surely be only one answer to this question, which Nkosi provides for us as clearly as any South African novelist. It must rest in the absolute refusal to over-dramatise suffering or the human condition; which means, as a corollary, that while an opportunity may be provided for readers to acquire sympathetic knowledge of what is going on, there must be no hint of an appeal for pity. Self-pity inflicts perhaps the most damaging spiritual wounds that human beings can force upon themselves; a whisper of it will alienate us more quickly than any other quality, since it excludes all spontaneous reaction by others. In this respect not only does Nkosi express the *Drum* credo very well, he has clearly learnt the lesson very thoroughly himself:[3]

> even in one's personal life one was supposed to exhibit a unique intellectual style; usually urbane, ironic, morally tough and detached: one's education was to be a pure form of realism which would eliminate the thinnest traces of self-pity, especially in reporting the uncertainties of urban African life in face of rigorous apartheid laws, as well as in reporting the wanton gaiety, lust and bravery of this life.

'I have to be wary,' Nkosi confesses, 'not to get too intense about these things.'

As we have seen already, Nkosi takes us into his confidence as to the difficulty of presenting a calm and plausible picture of South Africa to the non-South African:

> One could go on, of course, recounting the morbid aspects of apartheid, but it all sounds so hopelessly melodramatic that the total effect is to undermine people's credulity.

But by his anecdotal method he avoids any hint of pretentiousness or self-importance, for all the solemnity and, at the same time, the over-familiarity of his subject. This achievement is compounded at every turn by his tough, witty manoeuvrability and deftness of touch. In deploring the ponderousness of the American South, Nkosi asserts 'For wit to exist there has to be an urbane and self-deprecating attitude'; he himself adopts just such an attitude in writing of his homeland. The unobtrusively but carefully selected dramatic incidents provide the proper scale and setting for him to be self-deprecating, and allow an urbanity which would be virtually impossible in any more formally constructed treatise on the South African environment. His dry understatements let facts strike us forcibly without his having to be horrific: 'Every Sunday in Johannesburg, someone was murdered, someone was arrested, someone robbed; friends got married, got divorced, committed adultery. . . .' Such reserve is acidly ironic: there is only 'one community which can be counted on to produce a Helen Suzman. It is not much, I admit, but in South Africa it staggers the imagination.' So Nkosi can balance against the looming seriousness of the social situation a degree of self-mockery which momentarily defuses all explosive emotions and allows us to contemplate the scene with some degree of detachment:[4]

> By this time we were so accustomed to chaperoning visitors around the townships that we knew exactly where to take them, through which appalling slums to drive, in order to wring the last drop of pity out of them.

And the irony leads into the calm statement of unanswerable questions, based on the lively, and indeed wickedly entertaining scenes that he has brought to life for us: 'They know every time a policeman encounters a black man in the street he assumes a crime has been committed; so why bother to live a legal life?' Any connected, logical argument leading up to this same conclusion would have been unbearably oppressive.

The wry, leavening humour is apparent in the imagery, perhaps even more noticeably when the setting is outside South Africa:

> American intellectuals are carrying on an extraordinary love affair with
> pipes. They are always stuffing them with tobacco the same way they
> stuff their minds with facts;

or,

> One falls in love [with New York] – at least I did – in much the same way
> as one falls in love with an incurably and hopelessly bitchy woman.

This open-eyed candour provides the basis for the unflinchingly honest
statement of disturbing convictions which might simply be unacceptable
if we had not already come to terms – willingly – with Nkosi's mordant
wit:

> black people are frequently beaten over the head by marauding gangs of
> white men . . . simply because powerless people invite contempt and de-
> serve being beaten over the head . . . in all fairness it seems to me quite
> wicked for black people to have tempted the powerful with so much
> powerlessness for so long.

Lewis Nkosi's account of South Africa is more than just a general restatement of the conditions which apartheid had by then produced; it is
an attempt to define his own generation's position in relation to these
circumstances. With the same, sometimes ruthless, honesty that we have
already noted, he is prepared to say what may be unpopular with his peers;
but he creates the same disarming impression in his argument of trying
to express useful if unpalatable, truth:

> Perhaps very unkindly but with tough, judging coolness of the young,
> we concluded that for their naïveté and enthusiasm to participate in such
> a war our elders deserved the shabby treatment they received.

He also brings out into the open another lurking misgiving, that the very
resilience of the black population could make people too submissive: if one
is flexible, one may bend; if one is inflexible one may stand firm:[5]

> That the blacks have been able to endure under apartheid is a measure of
> human ingenuity almost difficult to describe or understand. It seems that
> the blacks do have the required humour and wit – almost too much of it!

This reaction lies behind the suspicion of Paton's too accommodating hero,
Stephen Kumalo:

> an embodiment of all the pieties, trepidations and humilities we the young
> had begun to despise with such a consuming passion.

224

For all the insouciance with which he defiantly describes the life he led in South Africa, Nkosi leaves us in no doubt at all that this was an attempt to carry on in the face of a supreme negative force, and he justly uses Paton's own vision in a short story to define this:

> an unsentimentalised encounter with the dark and iron reality of the life of the urban African, to witness, finally, Paton's earnest confrontation of the central issue of Evil and the meagreness of the liberal vision before so challenging a reality.

A new attitude has arisen as young South Africa perceives the smallness, the meanness of the white South African ideal:

> It became a matter of the greatest surprise to us to realise that some of these people were leading appallingly empty lives, even in the midst of plenty.

And Nkosi therefore fully takes us with him when he proceeds: 'I think we began about this time subtly to despise white South Africans.'

An essential way of perceiving and of presenting the South African scene so that horror is justly intensified but melodrama is avoided is through a vision of what in the seventies we would automatically refer to as 'the absurd', a term with which Nkosi is already familiar. As a method of persuasion this would seem to be at once very effective and essentially truthful. A need to retain a sense of balance through humour in becoming finally aware of this phantasmagoria of evil is splendidly stated at the opening of the second section:

> For a black man to live in South Africa in the second half of the twentieth century and at the same time preserve his sanity, he requires an enormous sense of humour and a surrealistic kind of brutal wit, for without a suicidal attack on Dr. Verwoerd's armed forces, these qualities seem to provide the only means of defence against a spiritual chaos and confusion which would rob any man of his mental health.

The section is indeed entitled 'Apartheid: A Daily Exercise in the Absurd', a description which is vindicated even by a single sentence alone:[6] 'the total effect of the apartheid laws in South Africa is to make it almost illegal to live.' A pointedly simple statement of fact can immediately justify Nkosi's comparison of South Africa with Kafka's world of nightmare logic:

Present were Africans, whites, mixed-bloods and Indians, and because of the free admixture of races the party assumed again the proportions of a vast conspiracy against the state.

Here is a calm and lucid, matter-of-fact statement of the absurd come to life. 'In South Africa,' asserts Nkosi tellingly, 'there was often a very thin margin between fantasy and reality.'

Time after time appropriate facts, ably related with a dead-pan expression, are more than enough. Nkosi and his friends are arrested: the police officer rings the local state prosecutor:

'What can I charge them with?' he casually enquired. My first reaction was to giggle. Even Kafka couldn't have bettered that one.

But a pretext is found and Nkosi adds grimly, 'The whole thing was no longer funny.' Yet it is unquestionably still absurd. With a sure sense of selection, Nkosi records the court case against Regina Brooks in which the sympathetic Social Welfare officers find that their case will be best supported by calling absurdity to their aid: 'giving evidence in support of the appeal [they] testified to the effect that for all practical purposes Miss Brooks was a Zulu'; or again when it is sardonically proposed that there is a need to legis-late with regard to kissing.

For all his anecdotal, casual manner, Nkosi has a full awareness of tradi-tional essay structure and style in English. He achieves a classic opening, at once provocative and interesting in its graceful generalisation:[7]

It is the indescribable vanity of every generation to believe that its young men and women are somewhat more beautiful, more plausible, certainly more perceptive and courageous than their elders.

This is made to lead naturally and immediately into the heart of the open-ing discussion:

In South Africa this mutual antipathy and the mutual denigration between the generations are made more painful by the greatly varied nature of the challenges presented by each era. . . .

The next stage in the argument is built, relaxedly but all the same very economically, round the discussion of Alan Paton, the admired moral leader, whose fictional hero is seen nevertheless to run counter to the pattern of his own most significant moral testimony. And so literature becomes the medium of the discussion well before *Drum* is mentioned. In its turn, *Drum* is cleverly used as a narrative centre, one conveniently bristling with personalities, and readily related to the key ideas which are to be developed.

Nkosi uses exact, flexible, concentrated wording and phrasing which skims deliberately close to cliché without being tarnished by it, thereby appearing expansively conversational without becoming dull: 'there were racially mixed parties enjoyed with the gusto of a drowning people'. The white actress insists on shopping with Lewis Nkosi, 'thereby imperilling both our lives and the precarious sanity of white South Africans'. The following short paragraph from page 19 illustrates most of the salient features of Nkosi's style of higher journalism (a phrase in which 'journalism' becomes what one could wish it might more often be: a praise-word):

> This was the city then conquered by big business and by Boer philistines, run by a gun-crazy police force and knife-happy African thugs, a city immune to all the graces of African tribal life and to the contemplative pleasures of European cultural life; finally it had to depend upon this Jewish community, upon its dogged sense of identity and the Jewish nostalgia for things of the heart and spirit.

The challenging generalisation which opens the book is not unique. Such assertions are carefully placed throughout to focus various topics and re-assert full control over the reader's attention:[8]

> they had to get drunk, sleep with one another's wives, go to the movies, and like sensible citizens of a big city, resist all attempts to humanize them through art and literature.
>
> Too much subjectivity is dangerous but none at all is even more dangerous.
>
> It is always dangerous to distort human character in order to serve a political idea.

The reader is willing enough to be dazzled and drawn in by these pyro-technic displays; but will certainly expect such easily memorable statements to be supported and built intelligently into a whole pattern of argument, and in this Nkosi does not disappoint us. Further he carefully retains a sense of balance in putting a point across: 'No doubt a case can be made here against our judgement [of Stephen Kumalo] as being intemperate and biased; but this reasonableness serves in the long run to lend force to his own convictions:

Nevertheless, Stephen Kumalo seems to me quite incredible and I would say he is quite easy to repudiate, for as a character he is no more than a figment of a white's liberal's imagination.

Such are the elements and techniques which Nkosi deploys in developing his basic mode in the two sections of *Home and Exile* which give the book its name, a mode which, as we have seen, allows statement to grow out of incident. This is in contrast to the principal method adopted in *Facing Mount Kenya*, wherein the calm, scholarly, analytical description erupts from time to time into passionate assertion, following naturally from the assembled facts. *Facing Mount Kenya* is apprising one section of its readership that it has, at best, been previously getting its facts all wrong, and another section that it should take pride in those things which have been wrongly allowed to pass underrated. In *Home and Exile* we are concerned with facts which are basically presumed to be familiar to anyone who is likely to read the book; and the author is deliberately and publicly cooling down his passionate reactions so as to avoid appearing to overstate matters or to be extorting emotion by sensationalism.

Characteristic of this method is the passage in which Nkosi expresses definitively, in altogether calm tones, our indictment of the fascist regime in South Africa. To do this he draws a contrast between the situation there and that for the black American in Southern USA. Without defending the American position or minimising its seriousness, he is able to show that in every respect, however bad things may be in the American South, in South Africa they are worse not only in degree but also in kind, a demonstration which quietly but firmly imprints once for all on our minds the enormity of the regime in his home country:

> I am mindful of the fact that some of these things could happen to an American Negro in Georgia. He can be charged with all sorts of trumped-up breaches of the law. In South Africa, however, these are not trumped-up charges. They are written into the law of the country, so that on the surface there is always an appearance of a fair trial. What is at issue is the fundamental concept of apartheid which proclaims the inequality of peoples. Whether the judges are impartial or not is beside the point because they are enforcing laws that are fundamentally unjust.

While the three parts of the book, 'Hone', 'Exile' and 'Literary' are in many ways disparate, Nkosi's passion for literature can be seen as binding them together. By the same count, *Home and Exile* is linked to other aspects of the present volume through its keen awareness of the vital place that books occupy in a society. Nkosi sees works of fiction as subtly persuasive forces just as I am considering works openly intended to influence our opinions as part and parcel of literature. For Nkosi literature provides some kind of yardstick of values; and, even more importantly, in the midst of social incoherence he finds that literature can put one in contact with universal norms and points of reference. He has a passionate sense, as has Ngugi, of the potential importance of literature in helping people to find themselves and know themselves – a function which has previously been fulfilled by oral literature in traditional society. While the present must be different from the past, it can be seen as flowing continuously from it without any traumatic rupture which would make earlier values totally irrelevant today – a sense of concurrent change and continuity which is deeply implicit in *Things Fall Apart*.

The role of literature is a major theme throughout Nkosi's work. He deplores as a harmful gap in South African experience the lack of true literary heroes with whom he and his contemporaries could identify themselves:[9]

> In the moral chaos through which we were living we longed to find a work of literature, a drama or film, home-grown and about us, which would contain a significant amount of our experience and in which we could find our own attitudes and feelings.

Twentieth-century European and American literature naturally offered no substitute, and only by ranging through time as well as space could some kind of vicarious reflection of their own life-style be discovered:

> Ultimately, it was the cacophonous, swaggering world of Elizabethan England which gave us the closest parallel to our own mode of existence.

We have already noticed the important place in Nkosi's argument of his penetrating commentary on *Cry, the Beloved Country*, and how he keeps his criticism paradoxically balanced by his sincere admiration for Alan Paton as a spokesman in South Africa and a short-story writer. Frequent references to specific writers illuminate Nkosi's work. These are never dragged in nor are they at all awkward. They are a natural part of his own reaction to life and are self-explanatory in their contexts, so they will not irritate nor disturb anyone who does not know the authors in question – Jacobson, Shakespeare, James Joyce, Oscar Wilde, Omar Khayyam and Kafka among them, a catholic list.

Literature, then, occupies an important place in the life of a society. This motif is viewed from many aspects:

> I know that for those who do not believe in the power of literature to mould life and manners, the need for literary heroes must seem not only silly but self-indulgent; nevertheless it seems to me that as a generation we longed desperately for literary heroes we could respect and with whom we could identify.

> Unless literature is assumed to be important in itself, for its own sake, unless it is assumed to be its own justification, there was no reason whatever why anyone in our generation should have wanted to write.

And he talks affectionately of his own love-affair with words in a manner which must particularly interest all would-be writers:

> I walked about the streets of the bustling noisy city with new English words clinking like coins in the pockets of my mind; I tried them out on each passing scene, relishing their power to describe and apprehend experience.

One of Nkosi's lines of argument has not perhaps received the attention it deserves in societies where oral literature is regaining status and is regarded as available for serious comparison with written literature. Nkosi thoughtfully diagnoses the different roles of verbal arts in traditional and urbanised societies. In the one it celebrated an integrated and generally accepted communal structure; in the other it criticises a more impersonal and in some ways less coherent administrative schema:

> I mean by this that the Negro approach to singing is not basically to entertain, though people *do* get entertained, but to *celebrate*.

He regrets that a certain black jazz singer sidesteps this function of her art and thus impoverishes both it and her message by treating her songs simply as vehicles for protest:

> she attenuates [jazz's] tragic undertones by making it merely a 'protest music' rather than a means of *celebrating* the troubling complexity of human existence, or that *total* human experience which will necessarily include the protest against the injustice and the suffering of her people.

I have argued elsewhere[10] that Okot p'Bitek's *Song of Lawino* is often put into false perspective by overemphasising it as a comparative analysis of two social modes, and largely overlooking its more important urge to celebrate in their own right the positive qualities of a threatened tradition.

Thus, Nkosi reminds us, the village singer, while he might challenge individuals, was never opposed to the corporate ideals of his group:[11]

> There was no recognised or readily ascertainable conflict between the poet and his community in traditional Africa. The poet's ideals and his social goals were not seen to be necessarily separable from and in conflict with those of the rest of the community.

> In this community the poet or the artist in general is there to *celebrate* his own or his society's sense of being . . . and not there to subvert its social values or moral order.

'The artist in Africa is a man alienated neither from his community nor the world of nature which sustains him.' And yet Nkosi partly attributes literary aridity in modern town-life to the active pressures of communal activity:[12] 'there was no privacy in which to reflect'. It seems that in such a society, where so much is unacceptable to the artist, art inevitably grows personalised; and in becoming more of an individual, the writer at the same time comes to find himself isolated. And so the South African author is faced with the very dilemma which we analysed in the first chapter of this book, and experiences in an extreme form the same kind of social estrangement that troubles the protagonists of many contemporary African novels:

> there has been a change in the social organisation which has resulted in more emphasis being placed on the individual rather than the communal. Hence the art of communal celebration is being replaced by lonely artistic creation – by an individual vision, so to speak. For the first time the African artist is confronting the community as an individual (even an alienated individual) whose vision may not conform to that of the statesman, the political or the religious leader.

Amid these pressures, literature has a critical, constructive, pioneering role to play. Nkosi insists that the artist has a crucial task to undertake in helping to rethink society. It is thus that he argues against, and at length specifically opposes, Sartre's idea that literature is an irrelevant luxury at a time of revolution:

> Unless he is variously talented the best way a writer can contribute anything of worth toward the development of his society is simply by writing – and writing as well as he knows how.

. . . the situation in Africa, if objectively analysed, seems to need even more critically poets and artists, who will remain sufficiently detached from the faiths and pieties of the moment in order to offer a valid critique of the societies of which they are members.

Indeed Nkosi takes a fearless stand on this controversial point. Just as Fanon outlines the positive contribution that the new-style rural story-teller makes in a revolutionary situation, so Nkosi argues with equal confidence the place of the writer:

if we assume that any competent artist who retains a minimum of objectivity in using his materials should and must reflect his society, then writers are even more important in countries undergoing revolutionary changes, where the temptations are greater to suppress any but the desirable truths.

If the novelist or poet is recognised as heir to the heritage of the village narrator, then the usefulness of his (or her) vocation is beyond question:

In the traditional African society . . . the Sartre thesis would not only seem irrelevant . . . but foolish and not worthy of rebuttal.

And so Nkosi briefly raises the very issues with which I was concerned in my second chapter. In the melting pot of contemporary poetry, what – if anything – has survived of the African inheritance? And what more could still be recaptured?

. . . when we consider the role of the poet in the African society of today – a society undergoing enormous social changes – we ought to ask ourselves how far these innate African values have endured the highly assertive thrust of European culture in which modern African writers and artists are schooled.

It is to be hoped that as this schooling itself is transfigured, so also will be its outcome. 'In poetry,' T. S. Eliot has asserted, 'there is no such thing as complete originality, owing nothing to the past.'[13] Need there be a confrontation between the traditions that have fed the modern creative urge in Africa, or can there be – in a manner more familiar to art – a fusion between indigenous modes and the wayfaring English language? Nkosi is optimistic about the developing perspective of the new writing in Africa. Indeed, if Achebe and Ngugi have deliberately structured their works so that they shall be relevant to immediate realities, Nkosi seems to argue that this was natural and inevitable if they were to minister to their own talents:

What social problems in under-developed countries do is force a writer to strike a balance between life as it is lived and life as it is intellectually and metaphysically ordered into a formalised artistic expression. In short the pressing social problems order the writer to be relevant.

Nkosi attaches the greatest importance to the modern literary artist in Africa. Everything is demanded of an author; but everything is possible. So, in being forced to adopt the standpoint of an exile from the South African scene (a standpoint which has proved to be very hard to recapture in the principal genres), Nkosi overrides conventional critical categories and asserts the significance of literature as a whole as a means of grasping and moulding human experience in any and every context:

Rather than making his job hopeless, the situation in a developing country makes the function of a writer more exciting, if somewhat complex. Good literature has always performed the task of educating the people about the external world as well as forcing them to come to terms with that singular loneliness in which all life is lived: the moment of love, the moment of death; and the moment of man's confrontation with the existence or non-existence of God.

NOTES

1 *H. &. E.*, p. 35; the next quotation is from p. 22 ('I have often thought...')
2 *H. &. E.*, p. 11; the following five quotations are from pp. 35, 11, 14–15, 26, and 16.
3 *H. &. E.*, p. 12; the following five quotations are from pp. 38 ('I have to be wary...'), 39, 67 ('For wit to exist...'), 12 ('Every Sunday...'), and 19 ('one community which...').
4 *H. &. E.*, p. 30; the following five quotations are from pp. 40 ('They know every time...'), 56, 59, 95–6, and 4.
5 *H. &. E.*, p. 35; the following five quotations are from pp. 5, 6, 32, 33 ('I think we began...'), and 35.
6 *H. &. E.*, p. 35; the following four quotations are from pp. 25, 22 ('In South Africa...'), 36, and 27 ('giving evidence...').
7 *H. &. E.*, p. 3; the following four quotations are from pp. 3, 8 ('there were racially mixed parties...'), 31 ('thereby imperilling...'), and 19.
8 *H. &. E.*, pp. 17, 47, 106; the following three quotations are from pp. 6 ('No doubt a case...'), 7, and 37–8.
9 *H. &. E.*, p. 8; the following six quotations are from pp. 18, 7, 17, 10, 73, and 75.
10 David Cook, 'Song of Lawino: A Celebration', to appear in a symposium in preparation for E.A.P.H. to mark the tenth anniversary of the publication of this, the first of Okot's 'songs'. I now realise that the title for

this paper very possibly reflected unconscious (and therefore unacknowledged) memories of Lewis Nkosi's discussion in *Home and Exile*.

11 *H. & E.*, p. 102; the following two quotations are also from p. 102.

12 *H. & E.*, pp. 17–18; the following six quotations are from pp. 104, 101, 101–2, 102 and 104 (two).

13 *Notes Towards the Definition of Culture*, Faber, London, 1948, p. 114.

14 *H. & E.*; the final two quotations are both from p. 105.

Index

Authors and individual works are listed separately in alphabetical order. Titles beginning with 'A' or 'The' are arranged according to the first letter of the next word.

235

Index